The Journals of Caroline Fox

The Journals of

CAROLINE FOX

1835-71

A selection edited by
Wendy Monk

Elek London

Published 1972 by Elek Books Ltd
54-58 Caledonian Road London N1 9RN

This edition is selected from *Memories of Old Friends, being Extracts from the Journals and Letters of Caroline Fox, from 1835 to 1871,* edited by Horace N. Pym, London, 1882. The present edition and Editor's introduction and notes copyright © 1972 by Elek Books Ltd

ISBN 0 236 15447 8

Printed in Great Britain by
Weatherby Woolnough Ltd.
Wellingborough, Northants.

Contents

Acknowledgements

I would like to thank my husband, J. C. Trewin, for his encouragement and tolerance; also Malcolm Thomas, of the Friends' House Library, London, and Nancy Kendall, of the Falmouth Reference Library, for their help; Jeremy Hellens and Ion Trewin for their knowledge of coach and railway timetables of the day; and Antony Wood, of Paul Elek Ltd, for being so sympathetic an editor. I should add that, thanks to his charming book, *Caroline Fox* (Constable, 1944), the late Wilson Harris unknowingly made my work easier.

W.M.

Publisher's Note

Some whole entries are omitted from the original edition of these Journals. Omissions within entries are indicated by three dots.

Illustrations

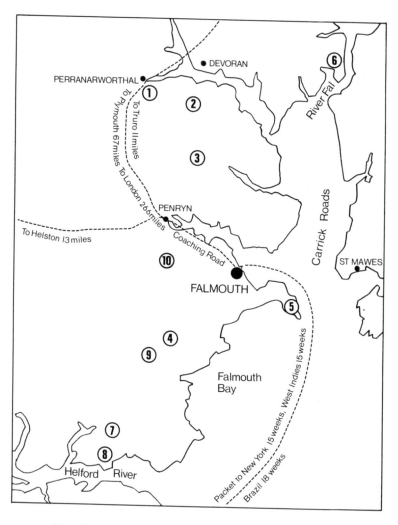

The Falmouth area in Caroline Fox's life-time

Communications between Falmouth and London during the period covered by the *Journals*

Until 1835 the only alternative to the thirty-hour coach journey from London to Falmouth was to go by boat. In 1835, the first year of the *Journals,* the Great Western Railway reached Bristol which meant that it was then possible to get from London to Falmouth within twenty-four hours (by rail to Bath, four hours; then, by coach, eighteen hours). Travelling in the 1840s, my great-grandparents took three days: by rail to Bridgwater, one day; by coach to Devonport on the second day; and by mail coach—on top and they got very wet—through Cornwall on the third day.

The time taken from London was further reduced in 1849 when the railway reached Plymouth (from London to Plymouth, via Bristol, at least seven and a half hours; from Plymouth to Falmouth by Royal Mail coach, eight hours). With the opening in 1859 of the Royal Albert Bridge across the Tamar at Plymouth, Cornwall was linked with the rest of the country by rail, and in that year the railway reached Truro (from London to Truro, via Bristol, ten hours; by coach to Falmouth, one hour). From 1863 the entire journey from London to Falmouth could be done by rail, via Bristol, in ten hours.

W.M.

Key to Map

1 Perran Wharf ironworks, belonging to the Fox family
2 Carcew, Sir Charles Lemon's estate
3 Enys estate
4 Penjerrick, where most of the *Journals* were written
5 Pendennis Castle, to which Caroline went on an expedition with Henry de la Beche in 1837
6 Trelissick, home of Davies Gilbert
7 Glendurgan, home of Uncle Alfred Fox
8 Trebah, home of Uncle Charles Fox
9 Tregedna, home of Uncle Joshua Fox
10 Friends' Burial Ground

INTRODUCTION

Caroline Fox lived 266 miles from London. Though she travelled in England and abroad, most of her *Journals* were written in a country-house three miles from Falmouth, and until her last decade Cornwall was not connected with the rest of the country by rail. If she had lived in a fashionable part of a capital city, she could hardly have led a more social life. From the first entries as a girl of seventeen, she seems to have been determined to write about the people she met (what a novelist she would have made!); that is why, originally, the book was called *Memories of Old Friends*, though it is usually quoted— and it has been quoted liberally—as *The Journals of Caroline Fox*, which is the title of this edition.

Of the main characters in the *Journals* the diarist is the least completely drawn. I have left undisturbed as far as possible such fragments of Caroline herself as the first editor allowed to slip through. My general method of cutting has been to sacrifice the least durable conversations—monologues, usually—of Caroline's more long-winded friends: John Sterling on forgotten German philosophers; Derwent Coleridge on practically anything. Because people—and especially their ideas—interested her so deeply, she was apt to be unselective. Indulgent introspection appears only towards the end when there is much exchange of opinion, chiefly on religious matters, with her friend Elizabeth Carne.

If we ask what kind of woman she was, her *Journals* provide an imperfect answer. She remains in the shadows; her 'lions' spring from the pages, floodlit. Through her we see clearly John Stuart Mill in his thirties (as Richard Garnett put it in the *Dictionary of National Biography*, 'Mill has not elsewhere found a Boswell'); both the Carlyles in astringent and benign moods; and Wordsworth as an old man at his most predictable.

The facts of her life offer a background; they put her in perspective; gossip passed down by members of the vast Fox clan fills the gaps without bringing us face to face with their remarkable Cousin Caroline. Born on May 24, 1819, the same day as another diarist, Queen Victoria, she was the younger daughter of Robert Were Fox, practical scientist and inventor, of Falmouth in Cornwall. Her mother Maria was a member of the Barclay family of Bury Hill, Dorking, Surrey, and a first cousin of Elizabeth Fry, the prison-reformer. Though her name is given on the title page of *Memories of Old Friends* as Caroline Fox of Penjerrick, the home from which most of the diary was written, she was born at another of the series of Fox houses in and around Falmouth: Rosehill, in which the family spent their winters.

Caroline was delicate—though, unlike Jane Welsh Carlyle, she scarcely mentions her health—and towards the end of her life she suffered increasingly from bronchitis which caused her death at fifty-one, on January 12, 1871. From the age of seventeen she recorded her impressions of an astonishing number of thinkers, writers, artists, scientists, inventors, explorers, preachers, politicians. They crowd the pages; modesty, and her Quaker upbringing, one supposes, made her decide very early that they were far more important than she was herself. In a sense they were; but our knowledge of them would be thinner if she had not maintained her habit of putting them down on paper with such wit, clarity, and—with one or two exceptions—judgment. Through her, we see them physically, and in character. Thus Hartley Coleridge: 'A little round, high-shouldered man, shrunk into a little black coat, the features of his face moulded by habit into an expression of pleasantry and an appreciation of the exquisitely ludicrous.' Then Tennyson: 'He wears a beard and moustache, which one begrudges as hiding so much of that firm, powerful, but finely chiselled mouth.' Not least of the qualities of the diary is its freshness. Perhaps because Caroline was a daughter of so progressive a man as Robert Were Fox, she was always, if unconsciously, ahead of her time. Her language is sometimes surprisingly modern, as when she describes Henry de la Beche, the geologist, as 'a regular fun-engine', and her phrase 'swing of London society' seems to belong to a century later.

II

A selection from Caroline Fox's *Journals* published in 1882 —eleven years after her death—was made by Horace N.

Pym, a London solicitor, at the request of the only surviving child of Robert Were and Maria Fox—Anna Maria, Caroline's elder sister, to whom she left her *Journals,* and to whom the published version is dedicated. After such ruthless selection there could be no rounding of the diarist's personality. This was not solely the editor's fault; his task was to carry out Anna Maria's instructions; and Anna Maria, like Jane Austen's sister Cassandra, proved to be a discreet guardian of her sister's reputation. With his legal mind Horace Pym must have been aware of the dangers of rushing into print; many of Caroline's 'old friends' were either still alive or well within living memory. Certainly this explains, in part, why the picture of Caroline is fragmentary; probably it also explains why there are so many gaps between the later entries.

Anna Maria, we must assume, turned to Mr Pym for his professional qualifications, and for his connection with the Foxes. Though not himself a Quaker, he married twice into the family; first to Juliet Backhouse—a niece by marriage of Barclay Fox, Caroline and Anna Maria's only brother—and, secondly, to Barclay's only daughter, Jane, who on the death of her mother was brought up by the Edmund Backhouses. Anna Maria, I feel, would have stood over her editor; family matters, she must have laid down firmly, were to be kept to a minimum. So it is useless to wonder why there are certain omissions. There is no mention of either her mother's death, or of Barclay's marriage. (Anna Maria would not have allowed the public appearance of such an emotional outburst as Dorothy Wordsworth's in the same situation.)

Caroline, obviously, had no thought of publication; she bequeathed her *Journals* to her sister, but wished them to be destroyed on Anna Maria's death. Why did she persist steadfastly until at the end she had filled twelve volumes? Journals were in the Quaker tradition; it had been so since George Fox's day. It was natural then that Robert Were Fox should offer his young daughters a guinea if they would keep a diary regularly; Caroline, with typical thoroughness, earned her guinea; Anna Maria may have done so, but we have no knowledge of hers. Barclay Fox's diary was never published, but it is quoted in Wilson Harris's biography of Caroline, and gives some clues to her relationship with John Sterling.

Ella Coltman, a friend of the Hodgkins—connections of

the Foxes—was shown the manuscript. She told Henry
Newbolt (whose wife's cousin she was): 'Mr Pym's red
editorial pencil had hardly left a page untouched and it
seemed to me he had squeezed out so much of the life's blood
that only a very bare skeleton was left to the public.'

The skeleton appeared before the public in 1882; it was
published by Smith, Elder and Company. There were various
editions including a quarto volume of 350 pages at 21
shillings, and a handier two-volume second edition published
a year later to which was added a batch of letters from John
Stuart Mill to Barclay Fox. *Memories of Old Friends* received a
long review in *The Spectator*. The writer, Julia Wedgwood
(author of a life of Wesley) had met Caroline. It is plain that
she had views on Mr Pym's red pencil when she wrote:

> Many of those who only knew Caroline Fox here would have
> been glad of more unreserve as to her own feelings, and some of
> those who knew her otherwise will feel perhaps that the latent
> fire of an impassioned and enthusiastic nature is too much
> hidden here by shrewd remark, lively recollection and humorous
> anecdote.

The Athenaeum, a year later, contained a paragraph about the
reprint of 'Mr Pym's charming work ... the popularity of
this book is a good sign of the taste of the reading public.'

The *Journals* reached appreciative readers throughout the
world, as well as some unlikely ones: none more so, I think,
than Cardinal Newman. He had a copy from G.T.Edwards,
an Evangelical Friend who was hoping perhaps to convert
him. Edwards received a letter of thanks:

> I had not heard of the book, nor of the lady who is the
> subject of it. It is full of matter, and to those who have a
> curiosity about stars in literature, interesting matter. She has a
> talent for description of character, and a great sense of
> humour. What is most remarkable is her union of taste for
> society with a deep religious sense. And what is most per-
> plexing to me is her boast and glorying in a Quaker's
> truthfulness and her insensibility to truth in matters of faith.

The correspondence continued with further letters from
Newman. In one, he said:

> I have a natural dislike of literary and scientific society *as such*
> ... and for this reason I am perhaps not quite fair to the remark-
> able and beautiful Life which you sent me. ... It is something
> of a wonder that a mind so religious as Miss Fox's should feel

pleasure in meeting men who either disbelieved the Divine
mission or had no love for the person of One she calls her 'Lord
and her Saviour' . . . Our Lord tells us that no man can serve
two masters—how can this religious lady be friends at once with
Him and with Carlyle, Mill and the like?

Returning the book to Edwards Newman said:

I am very much struck and won as to C.F.'s inner mind by this
private record of her thoughts and feelings. Don't think me
flippant when I say that she was too good for a Quaker, and that
she ought to have been a Catholic . . . No, C.Fox never understood what we hold. She might have been a Catholic if she
had.

When Anna Maria saw these letters, she responded with an
attempted explanation of Caroline's attitude to Catholicism.
To which Newman conceded graciously: 'Pray thank C.Fox's
sister for the kind interest she has taken in removing my
criticism, which sincerely troubled me as made in the case of
so excellent and remarkable a person.'

The sisters, both unmarried, were very close; Anna Maria,
though anxious to preserve a proper privacy, could not let a
question of faith go unchallenged. We can be grateful that
she allowed even a trimmed version of the *Journals* to appear;
her concern and Horace Pym's timidity shaped the book, and
distorted the author, but what remains is richly rewarding.
Caroline began writing before the accession of Victoria yet a
substantial proportion of the entries have an immediacy and
meaning for us today.

III

Long out of print, the *Journals* have been a treasure-trove
for biographers of the Carlyles, Mill, Tennyson, and many
others; and no wonder. But paragraphs, quoted again and
again, of Caroline's first-hand reporting of what this man said
or how the other looked, are all that most modern readers
have known of her work. We have seen all that remains; there
is no possibility of anyone finding unpublished pages in an
attic. One of the innumerable Fox cousins remembered how
as a girl of twelve, she helped to burn the twelve red-bound
volumes on the terrace at Penjerrick.

Down the years Caroline has gathered praise from men

whose opinion she would have valued. John Bright, who stayed at Penjerrick in 1868, and whom she once described unexpectedly as 'great fun,' wrote in his own journal soon after the book appeared: 'Much interested in reading "Memorials," etc. of Caroline Fox of Falmouth. Charming book, records of a mind intelligent, and good.' John Morley, the critic, wrote in his diary for 1891:

> In the evening read again Caroline Fox's Journal—especially the part about Mill. It was like visiting the scenes of one's childhood, and friends of whom one has long lost sight. Interesting, exciting, and at the same time soothing, to find myself once more in this luminous atmosphere of abstract questions and disinterested answer, of curiosity about deep problems and detachment as to solutions and persons. Yet abundant sociability, affection and genial friendliness. Well might Voltaire in his memorable visit to England (1726) fix upon the Quakers for our admiration and even reverence, not a common mood with him.

When Lord Rosebery, former Liberal Prime Minister, was speaking at Falmouth in 1905 he said that Caroline's was one of the most delightful books he had ever read, one 'which leads you into the atmosphere of pure, intellectual and devout life.'

For all her intelligence and literary qualities, Caroline is not infallible; sometimes, she gets proper names and titles wrong; her personal pronouns are confusing; and family relationships can defeat her (as with the Calverts and the Bonapartes). But she is a superb journalist in the best sense. How she managed to reproduce so much without shorthand is inexplicable. Her notes on Carlyle's lectures may show certain variations from the printed text, but the text is probably Carlyle's own editing for publication. Caroline's version is so close to his book that in the present edition of the *Journals* it is one of the more reasonable deletions. She speaks of her notes. Did she make them visibly, I wonder, in the drawing-room at Penjerrick, or at Cheyne Row? When she was out walking or riding a pony, with Sterling, how did she manage? Note-taking was another Quaker tradition; John Stuart Mill, in a letter to Barclay, marvelled greatly at the accurate memory that had enabled Mrs Charles Fox (Caroline's aunt) to write from recollection, and evidently almost word for word, a report of a sermon. He added: 'I know that Friends cultivate that kind of talent, but I should think few attain so high a degree of it.' So perhaps her friends were not put off at the appearance of Caroline's note-book and pencil—they took it for granted.

IV

Hers is an important contribution to the records of mid-nineteenth-century England. The continuity made it so. She kept the diary for over thirty-five years, which made it possible for her to observe her characters at different stages; again, they would talk to her about each other, so we get their views as well as hers.

Though she lived in a remote corner of the country a curious set of circumstances gave her a chance to meet many 'names' of the period. First, her family. The Foxes' position in Falmouth, as shipping agents, meant that they knew who would be arriving at this then busy port, and when. The railway did not reach Falmouth until the 1860s; travellers came by sea. The shipping firm of G.C. Fox and Company, which has involved so many generations of Foxes, began in 1759 when George Croker Fox, Caroline's great-grandfather, came west from Fowey where he had conducted a similar business. He saw that Falmouth held greater opportunities; for more than a hundred years the port flourished; the Post Office Packets coming and going, laden with mail, added to the bustle in the harbour.

Today the firm carries on in a Georgian office opposite the sturdy Customs House. During the regime of the founder's son Robert Were Fox Senior, it enjoyed a burst of prosperity when merchantmen were glad to unload in Falmouth and to avoid the risks of venturing further up-Channel during the French wars. (Ironically, the peace-loving Quakers made their fortunes out of war.) In 1794 this Robert became American Consul at Falmouth; George Washington signed the patent of appointment. Robert and his wife—formerly Elizabeth Tregelles—and their large family lived in a solid home known variously as Bank House, The Bank, or 7 Grove Place, in Arwenack Street next door to the Sailors' Home which Caroline visited. (Bank House is now a hostel.) Her father, another Robert Were Fox (1789-1877), whose own consul's patent of appointment bore the signature of President Madison, was the eldest of seven sons.

He was a hospitable man; new arrivals would find themselves invited to breakfast—a favourite meal for entertaining—at Rosehill, or at Penjerrick, three miles out of the town. Botanists and horticulturists came to see the Penjerrick gardens where Chinese palms, bamboos, Californian redwood trees, and much else, thrived in sheltered grounds. Some of Caroline's uncles also had country houses—the names Trebah, Tregedna, Glendurgan recur in the *Journals*—where semi-tropical plants survived in the mild Cornish winters. Gardening was another Quaker tradition. Note how Caroline seized the chance of helping Sterling with his garden when he moved into a house in Falmouth.

Robert Were Fox gathered around him men of various departments of science, among them geologists who pottered about the rocks at Maenporth just below Penjerrick or on one of the Falmouth beaches. Among eminent geologists was Henry de la Beche, who was inclined to be dubious about Mr Fox's theory that mineral veins could be formed in clay by the long-continued passage of an electric current (a process which Caroline, in the *Journals,* calls 'galvanism').

Not all the guests came down merely to admire the natural beauty of the Fox homes, and the Cornish coast. Some were drawn by the tin and copper mines which at this time were prospering. A few miles from the green lawns that dipped to the sea between rhododendron and acacia, there lay the industrial landscape around Camborne, Redruth and Gwennap. By repeated experiment and observation Robert Were Fox had proved that the increase of temperature in Cornish mines was in a constantly diminishing ratio with the increase of depth. Even on his wedding trip to the Continent, he had sought a former antagonist, von Humboldt, the Prussian scientist, whom eventually he converted. He was essentially a practical man, and the purpose behind these experiments was to solve the problems of mine-ventilation.

At Perran Foundry, another family concern, on a creek of the River Fal, machinery was manufactured at first for mines in Cornwall, and later for South Wales and abroad. One of the most important ironworks of its kind in the country, it attracted more guests for the Foxes. Perran, too, brought

about indirectly the foundation of the Royal Cornwall Polytechnic Society. The foundrymen were popular with the family,
and when Anna Maria admired the models they made, and
wondered where such work could be shown, the idea of the
Polytechnic was born, and medals were awarded for prize
exhibits. Caroline, only fourteen at the time, was the legendary
inventor of the word polytechnic (poached five years later by
the London Polytechnic in Regent Street); but this is doubtful.
The Fox family, through succeeding generations, has had much
to do with the Society, long established in the building with its
Doric pillars that stands in narrow Church Street. Today it
encloses the Falmouth Arts Theatre. Invariably, in Caroline's
time, lecturers were entertained at Rosehill or Penjerrick, and
invariably they are mentioned in the *Journals*. Another widening of the circle.

Even more widening was Robert Were Fox's membership
of the British Association. He was often accompanied by his
daughters when he attended their meetings; Caroline went
with him to Bristol, Plymouth, Dublin, Liverpool and Belfast. Here she met distinguished scientists many of whom
received invitations to stay at Falmouth. More geological
picnics, more table-talk about magnetism, meteorology,
mathematics, metaphysics, or merely the anecdotes
—Professor Humphrey Lloyd, provost of Trinity College,
Dublin, was a splendid raconteur—which Caroline obviously loved. Did she smile to herself as she re-told them in
her diary? I think she did.

Robert Were Fox's most important contribution to science
was his Dipping Needle Deflector (first constructed at Perran)
which made possible the correct use and adjustments of the
compass at sea. Other deflectors were made in Falmouth, and
the Cornish town of St Day; the Admiralty took up the instrument and three, as well as Robert Fox's magnetic balance,
were shown in 1851 at the Great Exhibition in Hyde Park.
Earlier the inventor, with his brother Charles and Caroline,
had taken the Deflector to Paris where he demonstrated it to the
French Academy.

Most exciting of all for his daughters was the fame he gained
among explorers—and these were great years for Polar
exploration. Edward Belcher and James Clark Ross both told
good stories of Eskimos, icebergs and miraculous deliverance,

which Caroline reported at great length; and when Ross sent a message to her father, saying that without the Deflector he would not have been able to discover the South Magnetic Pole, it was very gratifying. Both Belcher and Ross were knighted, and both took part in searches for Sir John Franklin, a long-drawn-out drama which Caroline followed much as today one follows astronauts' moon-flights.

When the *Beagle* docked at Falmouth after a five-year voyage of scientific investigation, Robert Fitzroy, commander of Darwin's 'good little vessel', came ashore, took tea with the Foxes, and stayed until eleven. He wanted to see the Deflector for himself, and was delighted with it. Nothing he could have said or done would have given Caroline more pleasure—unless, perhaps, he had brought Darwin with him; but Darwin was one of the lions who escaped her.

When in 1848 Robert Were Fox was made a Fellow of the Royal Society his wife must have recalled such scenes as this one described by a relation of hers, Mary Anne Schimmelpenninck, who visited Falmouth in the 1820s.

> Imagine the back drawing-room strewed with reflectors, and magnets, and specimens of iron, and borax, cobalt, copper ore, blow-pipes, platina, etc., etc., deflagrations, fusions, and detonations, on every side; whilst we were deeply interested in watching the fusions of the ores, or their assaying; only that now and then I, having a house of my own, had a fellow feeling with Maria, at seeing a certain beautiful zebra-wood table splashed with melted lead or silver, and the chased Bury Hill candlestick deluged with acids.

The almost simultaneous discovery of the planet Neptune, in 1847, by John Couch Adams and by Urbain Jean Joseph Leverrier, was dramatic, if heartbreaking—for both. Having met Adams at Sir Charles Lemon's house, Caroline tells the story in detail. She had been much taken with this young Cornishman; when she saw him again years later in Cambridge, his 'boyish zest' delighted her. Nevill Northey Burnard, the Cornish sculptor, told her that when Adams returned to the small farm where he was born on the Bodmin Moors, his father sent him to sell sheep at a fair. Wilson Harris records that in a copy of the *Journals* he saw at Penjerrick, someone had written in the margin beside this story: 'Adams says he *never* would have been entrusted with such transactions.' If, as is likely, Adams read the *Journals* as an old man, he could hardly have read a more pleasing tribute to himself when young.

Plant life, the stones and minerals of the earth, the earth itself, the sea (storms troubled her: 'it is a doubtful luxury to live on the coast'), and the unexplored sky—Caroline was conscious of them all. Though her intellectual curiosity was insatiable—the *Journals*, by their selectiveness, tend to exaggerate this aspect—she was also a countrywoman who rode or walked along the Cornish cliffs, or in the soft hinterland, for no other reason than that she loved them.

V

To Caroline's mother (formerly Maria Barclay, 1788-1858), references are sparse. From Clapham, her birthplace, the Barclays moved to Bury Hill in Surrey. Maria's sister, Lucy, married George Croker Fox, first cousin of Robert; and four years before Maria's marriage to him in 1814 she wintered in Cornwall. From a brief account of her early life— written for her children—we know that though not brought up in 'the strictest of Quaker principles', on her return from Cornwall on First Day (Sunday) morning, she appeared before her family in Quaker dress. She wore it always, and was 'recorded as a Quaker minister' in 1823.

There were varying degrees of strictness, or plainness; how rigidly Caroline kept to the dress we do not know; I suspect not so much as her sister-in-law, Jane. Anna Maria and Caroline admitted that they treated their bonnets 'hardy' by throwing them under the carriage seat. At Pennance, near Penjerrick, two chimneys, relics of a worked-out mine, were known locally as Anna Maria and Caroline because they were tall and straight like the sisters in their narrow-skirted Quaker dress—in contrast to the billowing crinolines worn by other mid-Victorian women. Caroline never speaks of her clothes except to say, as a joke, that after reading Kingsley's *Alton Locke* she bought a more expensive pair of boots.

Mrs Schimmelpenninck found that in Falmouth in 1824 'Friends' dresses, orthodox bonnets, brown gowns, caps white as driven snow, meet your eye in every direction,' but in 1892 Beatrix Potter wrote in her Journal: 'Their family names abound in the town and they appear influential and respected. They do not wear their distinctive dress.' She and her father attended the little Quaker Meeting House in Gylling Street—to which the Foxes went on First Days—and a sermon by Mr Hodg[e]kin of Darlington deeply impressed her: 'I wish I could give any adequate description of this remarkable discourse, but it is quite impossible, and even shorthand could never give an idea of the excited almost painful earnestness of the speaker.'

From her mother Caroline must have gained, or inherited, her spirituality. Mrs Schimmelpenninck, while staying with the Foxes, wrote to a friend:

> It was pleasant to me, as I was dressing, to watch them coming back, winding along the cliffs; and as they drew near, Maria, seated on her mule, with little Carry in her arms, Anna Maria by her side, and the others surrounding her, repeating their hymns and psalms, they used to look just like Raffaelle's picture of the Holy Family in Flight to Egypt. Maria's holy and maternal countenance on these occasions I shall never forget; nor the sweet and tender emotion of her children. Little Carry, especially, used to enjoy the ride. 'O Mamma,' said she, one day, 'do let me say my hymn louder, for the poor mule is listening, and cannot hear me.' Their return I used soon to know by Carry or Barclay besetting me, the moment I opened my door, to tell them stories of wild beasts.
>
> At half-past eight the loud stroke of a Chinese gong called the whole household to assemble for reading.

Maria Fox's first cousins, the Gurneys of Earlham, were as large and flourishing a clan as the Foxes of Falmouth; best known among them was Elizabeth, who married Joseph Fry, a London merchant, had eleven children, and devoted her life to prison reform. She never went to Cornwall during the period covered by the *Journals*; the Foxes visited her when they were in London, and received news of her meetings with royalty with natural family pride.

Caroline's Quakerism, though less strict than her mother's or Mrs Fry's, comes out here and there in the *Journals*; in her letters she uses 'thees' and 'thous'; and the causes she supports are, historically, Quaker causes: the abolition of slavery, and of capital punishment (which explains her interest in murderers and executions). Her Quaker conscience is troubled by the slaughter of animals. Though she hardly ever mentions food, I suspect that she could easily have gone over to a vegetarian diet. But as a cause, peace came first. Naïve politically, she is ready to believe in peace missions and peace speeches in the House. Her hopes are invariably dashed.

The Fox children were educated at home; in 1832, when Anna Maria was fifteen, Barclay fourteen, and Caroline twelve, a young tutor was installed at Rosehill. There was also a visiting French teacher, and a drawing master—Anna Maria was the artist of the family—and there must have been others. Caroline contemplated translating a book into German, and the sisters translated tracts into Italian. But the breadth of their education derived certainly from sitting at table listening. They learnt early to be sociable. Thomas Hodgkin, the historian, remembered how 'we children, brought up in the calm, sedate atmosphere of Tottenham Quakerism, were astonished at the vivacious, sparkling talk of these Cornish cousins.'

For all Maria Fox's piety, she does not appear to have attempted to restrict her children's social life to Quakers. In Cornwall, the Foxes were on visiting terms with such Church of England land-owning neighbours as the Lemons of Carclew, and the Enyses of E-shaped Enys; and they were friendly with the Rev. John Stevenson, rector of Cury, near the Lizard. When Caroline was so alarmingly attacked by a bull its owner, Sir Richard Vyvyan, of Trelowarren, wrote 'in great concern . . . Had the humblest pauper been exposed to the hazard which you have undergone I should have been deeply grieved. Judge then of my mortification and horror that you should have been in peril of your life on this occasion . . .'

Caroline's circle, taking in the family, newly arrived travellers, scientists, and the 'county', was extended by visits, about every other year, to London for the Friends' Yearly Meeting held during the Fifth Month (May).

VI

The friendships that were to mean most to her began at home, and began because the Falmouth climate was considered beneficial to sufferers from the highly prevalent tuberculosis. In 1840 two such men, John Sterling (1806-44) and

Dr John Calvert, arrived hoping to embark for Madeira for the winter. They got no further than Falmouth, and on February 8, 1840, Caroline noted: 'Barclay has been much pleased with a Mr Sterling, a very literary man, now at Falmouth.' Within a few days Sterling was an almost daily visitor; they walked, he talked—how he talked—and Caroline spared him far more space in her diary than anyone else. For her the next three years were the happiest; she replaced her usually crisp and controlled style by something more girlish, sometimes effusive. She even permitted herself a rare exclamation mark on April 26, 1841. 'At about one o'clock J. Sterling entered and announced that he had bought Dr Donnelly's house!' One is reminded irresistibly of that other diarist, Caroline's 'twin,' and her Albert. The difference was that Sterling was married; he brought his wife and children, and remained in Falmouth until, soon after the deaths, within forty-eight hours of each other of his wife and mother, he left for the Isle of Wight. Much of Sterling's table talk (which Caroline thought would make as profitable reading as Coleridge's) has been sacrificed here. It is difficult for us at this remove to understand why so many people should have found him attractive; why John Stuart Mill was 'more attached to him than I have ever been to anyone'; and why Carlyle, feeling strongly that Hare's biography misrepresented Sterling, took the trouble of writing another. This gave Sterling, who wrote one novel, a tale, and some essays, all of them long forgotten, undeserved posthumous fame. As Richard Garnett puts it: 'Johnson for once wrote on Boswell . . . Sterling was a remarkable instance of a literary man of no ordinary talent and desert, who nevertheless owed his reputation to a genius, not for literature, but for friendship.'

It has always been assumed that Caroline was in love with him; certainly, even long after his death, she behaves as if she were. In Barclay's diary there is some evidence, written in a transparent code, that she and Sterling may have been engaged. Such an entry as 'Letter from S!' is followed by 'Poor C! She bears up nobly but not without praying and struggling,' and 'S's final letter to C.'

In the *Friends' Quarterly Examiner* (1945), hardly a scandal-sheet, an article, *Cousin Caroline*, by Mrs L.V. Holdsworth, confirms the engagement theory. Mrs Holdsworth was the daughter of Mrs Thomas Hodgkin, formerly Lucy Fox, a daughter of Caroline's Uncle Alfred, of Glendurgan. She wrote:

> Of course there is much . . . that could never be told, and we shall never know. The only fact I know is that she was engaged to John Sterling very soon after his wife's death, and gave him up at the entreaty of her parents who disapproved of his views.

Her mother, Lucy, said: 'Yes, he and she did love each other; but he was not sound in his beliefs so they could not marry.' Sterling had been Julius Hare's curate at Hurstmonceaux for a brief period; by the time he reached Falmouth he had forsaken the Church. Like Mill, though fascinated by Quaker beliefs, he never held them.

Caroline's portrait of Sterling's friend Dr John Calvert is one of her most charming; his death is touchingly described. For the same reason, the mild air brought another family to Falmouth: The Mills. James Mill had died; his widow and her daughters, Clara and Harriet, had come to nurse young Henry Mill who was dying of tuberculosis. The Foxes did all they could for the boy and his family. When the elder brother, John Stuart Mill, arrived, he was able to renew a friendship with Sterling begun in the Debating Society at Cambridge. Mill, now, was thirty-three, doing well at India House and known already as a philosopher and economist. At a vital stage in his development as a thinker, he found that Caroline would listen sympathetically. He was at his best with her; he also wrote long, self-justifying letters to Barclay. Carlyle described Mill's conversation as 'rather wintry and sawdusty'; Caroline was less critical.

They met in London; the friendship blossomed, and then mysteriously withered. Caroline called *On Liberty* 'a terrible book'; all the same, she wrote regretfully to Elizabeth Carne: 'We knew him well at one time, and owe him very much; I fear his remorseless logic has led him far since then. This book is dedicated to his wife's memory in a few most touching words. He is in many senses isolated, and must sometimes shiver with cold.'

There was a similar fading of a close relationship between Mill and the Carlyles. It seems possible that the Carlyles and other friends in London were more embarrassed than shocked by Mill's association with Mrs Harriet Taylor, whom he married on the death of her husband. Even before the burning of the *French Revolution* manuscript (by Mrs Taylor's servant), an unfortunate incident which understandably might have caused a rift, Jane Carlyle remarked with a customary dash of acid: 'A young Mrs Taylor, tho' encumbered with a husband and children, has ogled John Mill successfully so that he was desperately in love.' Though anxious to make friends with Mrs Taylor, Jane shied away from 'a dangerous-looking woman, and engrossed with a dangerous passion.' The alliance caused a break between Mill and his family; his exaggerated terms of adoration continued long after her death, and are on record even on her tombstone.

In May 1840 Caroline attended—and wrote memorably of—Thomas Carlyle's lectures. The text became available, but Caroline added a bonus: a description of his platform manner. Clara Mill introduced her to Mrs Carlyle, and she was invited to Cheyne Row—the first of a series of absorbing calls. She had heard about the Carlyles from Sterling and Mill; she read his books as soon as they came out; now she could talk to him about the next one, and hear from him and from Jane how devastatingly he suffered during their creation. She catches perfectly the pair's verbal mannerisms; if she had any doubts about their marriage, Mr Pym's red pencil removed them from the original manuscript.

Carlyle liked the Foxes, 'bright, cheery young creatures'; indeed, he so enjoyed their company that when they left his house one day, he got into the fly and rode with them to Sloane Square 'talking with energetic melancholy to the last.' When the sisters saw him at Lady Ashburton's villa in the south of France he was over seventy, and missing Jane who had died a year before. The melancholy remained; the energy was dwindling.

He was at his most likeable in his correspondence with Caroline about Michael Verran, the Cornish miner, whose heroism had so impressed him. Verran and his mate were preparing a hole for blasting at South Caradon mine; accidentally they ignited the fuse; an immediate explosion was inevitable, but only one man could be hauled up the shaft at a time. 'Escape for thy life,' Verran told his mate, 'I shall be with Jesus in a few minutes.' Left alone in the mine, Verran miraculously survived. Carlyle loved this story; the letters he wrote on the subject are full of his own heavy brand of humour, and he ends subscribing himself cordially once more 'Caroline's friend, T. Carlyle.'

VII

Apart from her circle, her *Journals*, her books, Caroline's life was full: travels abroad; good works; teaching infants; hammering out her spiritual beliefs; visiting the Sailors' Home down by the harbour. During 1864 and 1865, she took down in pencil in copybooks the adventures of an inmate. The outcome, *A Sailor's Story*, was published anonymously by Samuel Harris and Company, London. The subject added a paragraph: 'Since this narrative has been written, one of the ladies of whom I am especially indebted has been called away to Heaven.'

After the death of Barclay's widow, his four young sons came to live with the family, a great joy to the aunts. Their own mother, Maria, died in 1858; Robert Were Fox outlived Caroline by six years. Anna Maria, who lived on until 1897, occupied herself with travel, her pet animals (including a marmoset), her convalescent home, the Friends' Meeting of which she was an elder, and her garden. Descendants of Barclay have lived at Penjerrick until recently; the house has been rebuilt; its gardens have been opened to the public. Rosehill has become Falmouth School of Art, and the gardens, now called Fox-Rosehill, were given to the town.

Caroline and Anna Maria and their parents lie in the walled Quaker Burial Ground on the hill at Budock; plainly inscribed, the small blue slate headstones are surrounded by snowdrops in the early spring. Nearby there is a factory in which iron lungs are made; Caroline would have been fascinated.

Wendy Monk

1835

Falmouth, March 19.—Davies Gilbert* and others dined here. He was full of anecdote and interest, as usual. One on the definition of 'treade' was good. It is really derived from 'trad' (Saxon), a thing. When he was on the bench a man was brought before one of the judges on some poisoning charge, and the examination of a witness proceeded thus: *Q.* 'Did you see anything in the loaf?' *A.* 'Yes; when I cut it open, I found it full of traed.' *Q.* 'Traed; why, what is that?' *A.* 'Oh, it's rope-ends, dead mice, and other combustibles.'

March 30.—Heard at breakfast that the famous Joseph Wolff, the missionary, had arrived at Falmouth. He gave an interesting lecture on the subject of his travels in Persia, &c. . . . Lady Georgina Wolff is at Malta, as she does not like the sea.

March 31.—At four o'clock Joseph Wolff came to dinner, and told us more about the various persons and places he has visited. Of Lady Hester Stanhope† he gave a very amusing account. When at Mount Lebanon he sent a message with which he was charged to a lady staying with her. On which Lady Hester sent him a most extraordinary but clever letter, beginning, 'How can you, a vile apostate, presume to hold any intercourse with my family? Light travels faster than sound, therefore how can you think that your cracked voice can precede the glorious light of the Gospel, which is eventually to shine naturally in these parts?' He returned an appropriate answer, but he noticed the servant he had sent with it came back limping, having been actually kicked and beaten by her ladyship *in propria persona.* Many passages in the Bible he cleared up by observation of the places mentioned . . . He sang us some beautiful Hebrew melodies.

October 3.—At breakfast we were pleasantly surprised to see Joseph Wolff walk in, without being announced. He was full of affection, and wanted to kiss Papa, who, retreating, left only his shoulder within reach, which accordingly received a salute. He joined us at breakfast, and described his late

---

* MP successively for Helston and Bodmin; President of the Royal Society.
† Niece of William Pitt. In 1810 she settled on Mount Lebanon, and adopted the dress of an Arab chieftain.

intercourse and correspondence with [Henry] Drummond*
and many of the Irvingite party. Their want of Christian love
speaks strongly against them, and their arrogating to
themselves the titles of angels, prophets, and apostles shows a
want of Christian humility. He embarked soon afterwards on
his way to Timbuctoo, and perhaps we shall never see him
again.

October 15.—Papa and I spent the evening at the Derwent
Coleridges'† at Helston. It left a beautiful impression on us,
and we visited the lovely little sleepers, Derwent and Lily,
saw the library, and the silver salver presented by his boys,
and, best of all, listened to his reading of passages from
'Christabel' and other of his father's poems, with his own rare
felicity. . . . Mary Coleridge was in all her beauty, and
ministered to a bevy of schoolboys at supper with
characteristic energy.

1836

Falmouth, April 7.—Sir Charles Lemon, John Enys, and
Henry de la Beche‡ came to luncheon. The last named is a
very entertaining person, his manners rather French, his
conversation spirited and full of illustrative anecdote. He
looks about forty, a handsome but care-worn face, brown eyes
and hair, and gold spectacles. . . .

Papa read his new theory of 'Veins'; De la Beche
thoroughly seconds his ideas of galvanic agency, but will not
yield the point of the fissures being in constant progression; he
says they were all antediluvian. They stayed several hours,
and were particularly charmed with some experiments about
tin and galvanism.*

* Joint founder, with Edward Irving, of the Catholic Apostolic Church, or Irvingites
  (see note, February 18, 1840).
† Derwent was the son of S.T. Coleridge; biographer of his brother Hartley;
  Headmaster of Helston School.
‡ Eminent geologist who in 1831 put forward a plan for a geological map of
  England—starting with Cornwall—which resulted in the official Geological
  Survey.
* See Introduction, section IV.

Bristol, August 22.—The gentlemen returned from their sections of the British Association Meeting this morning very much gratified, and after dinner we five started by the coach, and in the course of time arrived at the large British Babylon. It was a work of time to get into it most assuredly . . . By most extraordinary muscular exertions, we succeeded in gaining admittance. We got fairish seats, but all the time the people made such a provoking noise, talking, coming in, and going out, opening and shutting boxes, that very little could we hear. But we saw Tom Moore* in all his glory, looking 'like a little Cupid with a quizzing-glass in constant motion.' He seemed as gay and happy as a lark, and it was pleasant to spend a whole evening in his immediate presence. There was a beautiful girl just before us, who was most obliging in putting herself into the most charming attitudes for our diversion.

August 31.—We were returning from the British Association Meeting, and Dr. [William] Buckland [Professor of Mineralogy at Oxford] was an outside *compagnon de voyage,* but often came at stopping places for a chat. He was much struck by the dearth of trees in Cornwall, and told of a friend of his who had made the off-hand remark that there was not a tree in the parish, when a parishioner remonstrated with him on belying the parish, and truly asserted that there were seven . . .

Dr. Buckland says he feels very nervous in addressing large assemblies till he has once made them laugh, and then he is entirely at ease. He came on to the Polytechnic and stayed with us. One wet day he took his turn with three others in lecturing to an attentive audience in our drawing-room; we listened with great and gaping interest to a description of his geological map, the frontispiece to his forthcoming Bridgewater Treatise. He gave very clear details of the gradual formation of our earth, which, he is thoroughly convinced, took its rise ages before the Mosaic record. He says that Luther must have taken a similar view, as in his translation of the Bible he puts '1st' at the third verse of the first chapter of Genesis, which showed his belief that the two first verses relate to something anterior . . .   He   gave   amusing

---

* Irish poet; author of *Lalla Rookh* (1817). Friend of Byron, whose memoirs he destroyed.

descriptions of antediluvian animals, plants, and skulls. They have even discovered a large fossil fish with its food only partially digested . . .

September 12.—Professor [Charles] Wheatstone,* the Davies Gilberts, and Professor Powell were ushered in, and joined our party. Wheatstone was most interesting at dinner; he knows John Martin† intimately, and says he is exactly like his pictures—all enthusiasm and sublimity, amazingly self-opinionated, and has lately taken a mechanical turn. He thinks him a man of great but misdirected genius. He gave some instances of monomania, and mentioned one extraordinary trance case of a man who was chopping down trees in a wood, and laid down and slept much longer than usual; when he awoke life was a blank; he was not in a state of idiotcy, but all his acquired knowledge was obliterated. He learned to read again quickly, but all that had passed previously to his trance was entirely swept away from his memory. At the age of fifty he slept again an unusual time; on awaking, his first act was to go to the tree which he had been felling on the former occasion to look for his hatchet; the medium life was now forgotten, and the former returned in its distinct reality. This is well authenticated.

September 23.—Just after tea 'a gentleman' was announced, who proved to be nothing less than Professor [Adam] Sedgwick! He had unluckily unpacked at the inn, and so preferred keeping to those quarters. He goes to-morrow with Barclay to Pendour Bay in search of organic remains, which he fully expects to find there, and does not think the Cornish have any cause to boast of their primitive rocks, as he has discovered limestone with plenty of organic remains, and even some coal in the east of the county.

September 30.—'Mrs. Corgie,' the rightful Lady George Murray, arrived. She is a delightful woman, and told us many anecdotes of the late Queen Charlotte, whom she knew intimately. Many of the autograph letters of the Royal Family she gave me are addressed to herself. The Queen (Charlotte) japanned three little tables; one she gave to the King, another to the Prince of Wales, and the third to Lady George, which she has filled with the letters she has received

* Suggested the stereoscope and improved submarine telegraphy.
† Landscape and Biblical artist. *Belshazzar's Feast* (1821) is his best known work.

from the Royal Family. She told us that about four years ago the Princess Victoria was made acquainted with her probable dignity by her mother's desiring that when in reading the history of England she came to the death of the Princess Charlotte, she should bring the book and read to her, and on coming to that period she made a dead halt, and asked the Duchess if it were possible she would ever be queen. Her mother replied, 'As this is a very possible circumstance, I am anxious to bring you up as a good woman, then you will be a good queen also.' The care observed in the Princess's education is exemplary, and everything is indeed done to bring about this result. She is a good linguist, an acute foreign politician, and possesses very sound common sense.

October 3.—Captain [Robert] Fitz-Roy came to tea. He returned yesterday from a five years' voyage, in H.M.S. *Beagle,* of scientific research round the world, and is going to write a book. He came to see papa's dipping needle deflector, with which he was highly delighted. He has one of *Gamby's* on board, but this beats it in accuracy. He stayed till after eleven, and is a most agreeable, gentlemanlike young man. He has had a delightful voyage, and made many discoveries, as there were several scientific men on board. Darwin, the 'fly-catcher' and 'stone-pounder,' has decided that the coral insects do not work up from the bottom of the sea against wind and tide, but that the reef is first thrown up by a volcano, and they then surmount it, after which it gradually sinks. This is proved by their never finding coral insects alive beyond the depth of ten feet. He is astonished at the wonderful strides everything has made during the five years afore-passed.

October 27.—Lady George Murray gave me an interesting account of Lady Byron, whom she challenges anybody to know without loving. The first present she made to Ada* was a splendid likeness of Lord Byron, an edition of whose works is in her library, to which Ada has free access. She has done nothing to prejudice her against her father. The celebrated 'Fare-thee-well' was presented in such a manner as rather to take off from the sentiment of the thing. He wrapt up in it a number of unpaid bills, and threw it into the room where she

---

* Daughter of Byron and his wife Annabella.

was sitting, and then rushed out of the house. Ada is very fond of mathematics, astronomy, and music, but possesses no soul for poetry.

November 24.—Large dinner-party. Captain [Edward] Belcher, an admirable observer of many things, was very amusing. In 1827, when among the Esquimaux with Captain James [Clark] Ross, they were treated in a very unfriendly manner; he and five men were wrecked and their boat sunk, and they were obliged to betake themselves to the land of their enemies, twenty-four of whom, well armed with clubs, came down to dispute their proceedings. They had only one brace of percussion pistols amongst them and one load of powder and ball. The natives were aware of the terrible effect of these instruments but not of their scarcity, so Captain Belcher went out of his tent just before their faces, as if looking for something, put his hand in his pocket, and drew out a pistol as if by accident and hurried it back again. The other sailors, by slightly varying the *ruse,* led the natives to imagine the presence of six pair of pistols, and so they did not venture on an attack. Shortly after this, having been repeatedly harassed, they were thankful to see their ship approaching; the Esquimaux now prepared for a final assault, and came in great numbers demanding their flag. Seeing the helplessness of his party, Captain Belcher said, 'Well, you shall have the flag, but you must immediately erect it on the top of that hill.' They gladly consented, and Captain Belcher fastened it for them on a flagstaff, but put it Union downwards. The consequence was that the ship's boats immediately put off and pulled with all their might, the natives scampered off, the flag was rescued, and the little party safely restored to their beloved ship. I should like to hear the Esquimaux's history of the same period. Captain Belcher has invented a very ingenious instrument for measuring the temperature of the water down to 'bottom soundings.' He is a great disciplinarian, and certainly not popular in the navy, but very clever and intensely methodical.

December 2.—We called at Pearce's Hotel on the Begum of Oude, who is leaving England (where her husband is ambassador), on a pilgrimage to Mecca. Her bright little Hindustani maid told us she was 'gone down cappin's'; so to

Captain Clavel's we followed her and spent a most amusing half-hour in her society. She was seated in great state in the midst of the family circle, talking English with great self-possession spite of her charming blunders. Her dress was an immense pair of trousers of striped Indian silk, a Cashmere shawl laid over her head, over a close covering of blue and yellow silk, two pairs of remarkable slippers, numbers of anklets and leglets, a great deal of jewellery, and a large blue cloak over all. She was very conversable, showed us her ornaments, wrote her name and title in English and Arabic in my book, and offered to make an egg curry. At the top of the page where she wrote her name she inscribed in Arabic sign 'Allah,' saying, 'That name God you take great care of.' She sat by Mrs. Clavel, and after petting and stroking her for a while, declared, 'Love I you.' She promised her and Leonora a Cashmere shawl apiece, adding, 'I get them very cheap, five shillings, seven shillings, ten shillings, very good, for I daughter king, duty take I, tell merchants my, make shawls, and I send you and miss.' She has spent a year in London, her name is Miriam and her husband's Molvè Mohammed Ishmael. Her face is one of quick sagacity but extreme ugliness.

December 3.—The next day we found her squatting on her bed on the floor, an idiot servant of the Prophet in a little heap in one corner, her black-eyed handmaiden grinning us a welcome, and a sacred kitten frolicking over the trappings of Eastern state. We were most graciously received with a shriek of pleasure. Her observations on English life were very entertaining. She told us of going to 'the Court of the King of London.—He very good man, but he no power.—Parliament all power.—King no give half-penny but call Parliament, make council, council give leave, King give half-penny.—For public charity King give one sovereign, poor little shopman, baker-man, fish-man, barter-man also give one sovereign. Poor King!—King Oude he give one thousand rupees, palanquin mans with gold stick, elephants, camels: no ask Parliament.' She and Papa talked a little theology, she of course began it. 'I believe but one God, very bad not to think so; you believe Jesus Christ was prophet?' Papa said, 'Not a prophet, but the Son of God.' 'How you think so, God Almighty never marry! In London every one go to ball, theatre, dance, sing, walk, read; no go Mecca. I mind not that, I go Mecca, I very good woman.' She took a great fancy to Barclay, declaring him very like her son. She offered him a commission in the King of Oude's army and £1200 a year if he would come over and be her son; she gave him a rupee, probably as bounty money. There are 200 English in her King's service, two doctors, and three aides-de-camp. She showed us some magnificent jewellery, immense pearls, diamonds, and emeralds, tied up so carelessly in a dirty handkerchief. Her armlets were very curious, and she had a silver ring on her great toe which lay in no obscurity before her. Then a number of her superb dresses were displayed, gold and silver tissues, satins, cashmeres, muslins of an almost impossible thinness, which she is going to give away at Mecca. She is aunt to the present, sister of the late, and daughter of the former, King of Oude. She has a stone house in which she keeps fifteen Persian cats. It is a great virtue to keep cats, and a virtue with infinite reward attached, to keep an idiot; the one with her here she discovered in London, and was very glad to appropriate the little Eastern mystery. Aunt Charles's bonnet amused her, she wanted to know if it was a new fashion; she talked of the Quakers, and said they were honest and never told lies.

December 5.—To-day the Begum began almost at once on theology, asking mamma if 'she were a *religieuse,*' and then began to expound her own creed. She took the Koran and read some passages, then an English psalm containing similar sentiments, then she chanted a Mahometan collect beautifully in Arabic and Hindustani. She made mamma write all our names that she might send us a letter, and then desired Aunt Lucy to write something, the purport of which it was not easy to divine. At last she explained herself, 'Say what you think of Marriam Begum, say she religious, or she bad woman, or whatever you think.' Poor Aunt Lucy could not refuse, and accordingly looked sapient, bit her pen-stump, and behold the precipitate from this strong acid, 'We have been much interested in seeing Marriam Begum, and think her a religious lady.' I think a moral chemist would pronounce this to be the result of more alkali than acid, but it was an awkward corner to be driven into. She was coming to visit us to-day, but had to embark instead, after expressing her hopes that we should meet again in Oude!

December 15.—John Murray arrived, and was very amusing, describing all manner of things. He knows George Combe intimately, and says that at the B.A. Meeting at Edinburgh, he got in among the *savants,* and took phrenological sketches of many of them. He describes him as a most acute original person. With Glengarry* he was also well acquainted; he kept up the ancient Scotch habits most carefully, wore the dress and cultivated the feuds of an old laird, and if a Macleod tartan chanced to be seen, woe betide him! Glengarry went to George IV.'s coronation in his Scotch dress, and during the ceremony a very female marchioness, subject to vapours, observed his hand on one of his pistols. Imagining a projected assassination of his new Majesty, she screamed, and the Highland laird was arrested; he showed, however, that it was purely accidental, the pistols being unloaded and himself not disaffected, so they liberated him; but the affair produced a strong sensation at the time. He died a year or two since in saving his daughters whom he was taking to a boarding school near London; the ship was wrecked, and he being an excellent swimmer took one of them safe to shore, but just before landing the second, he struck against a rock, and died an hour after. With him died ancient Scotland.

December 18.—Amusing details from Cowley Powles of Southey's visit at Helston. He has been delighting them all, rather with his wit than anything political in his conversation. He is very tall, about sixty-five years old, and likes mealy potatoes. He gives the following recipes for turning an Englishman into a Welshman or Irishman: For the former—he must be born in snow and ice from their own mountains, baptized in water from their own river, and suckled by one of their own goats. For an Irishman—born in a bog, baptized in whisky, and suckled by a bull. What a concatenation of absurdities! The other day he took a book from one of the shelves, when Derwent Coleridge, who must have been in a deliciously dreamy state, murmured apologetically, 'I got that book cheap—it is one of Southey's.' It was quietly replaced by the poet; Mary Coleridge

---

* Alexander Ranaldson Macdonnell, fifteenth chief; friend of Scott who called him 'a kind of Quixote of our time'

exclaimed, 'Derwent!' and all enjoyed the joke except the immediate sufferers. William Coope tells us that he used often to see S. T. Coleridge till within a month of his death. . . . He has met Charles Lamb at his house. On one occasion Coleridge was holding forth on the effects produced by his preaching, and appealed to Lamb, 'You have heard me preach, I think?' 'I have never heard you do anything else,' was the urbane reply.

December 28.—On coming home this morning, found Molvè Mohammed, the Begum's husband, and his secretary, in the drawing-room. He has a sensible face, not totally unlike his wife's and was dressed in the English costume. On showing him the Begum's writing in my book, he was much pleased at her having inserted his name as an introduction to her own. 'Ha! she no forget, I very glad see that.' He added some writing of his own in Persian, the sense of which was, 'When I was young I used to hunt tigers and lions, but my intercourse with the ladies of England has driven all that out of my head.' He is said to be by no means satisfied with bigamy, and it is added that one of the motives of the Begum's English visit was to collect wives for the King of Oude . . .

1837

Falmouth, January 7.—Henry de la Beche gave us an amusing account of his late visit to Trelowarren. Sir Richard Vyvyan [MP for Helston] was always beating about the bush, and never liked openly to face an adverse opinion, but was for ever giving a little slap here and a little slap there to try the ground, till De la Beche brought him regularly up to the point at issue, and they could fight comfortably with mutual apprehension. . . . On looking at some of the bad handwritings in my autograph book, De la Beche observed how much we read by inference, and how curious writing is altogether, it is purely thought communicating with thought.

February 2.—Called on some of the old women. One of them said, 'It was quite a frolic my coming to read to them.' What different views some people have of frolics!

February 7.—De la Beche came in at breakfast time and was

a regular fun-engine, and about two we all went off to Gillanvase on a geological expedition. . . . We examined the Castle [Pendennis] and heard somewhat of the principles of fortification, De la Beche having been educated at a military school. The wall round a castle, to be effective, should not let any of the castle's masonry be visible. He dined with us, and we heard many strange stories of the scientific dons of the day, who if fairly sketched must be a shockingly ill-tempered set . . .

February 8.—De la Beche wandered in at breakfast to give Papa the two first fossil remains that have been found near a lode, which he drew forth from their hiding with his own authentic hands. One is the vertebra, the other the body of an encrinite. He read us some of a report he is now drawing up for Government, in which he does Papa all manner of honour. He made some admirable observations on the one-ness of human nature everywhere in all ranks and all countries, with only some little differences of 'localisation.' He says that all the beautiful Greek vases are formed of a series of ellipses, and he has sent for patterns from Mr. Phillips of the Woods and Forests, to give the Cornish better ideas of forms for their serpentine and porphyry vases.

February 21.—John Enys told us that Henry de la Beche had spent some time in the West Indies, and tried to ameliorate the condition of his slaves, and abolished the practice of flogging, though the power was still vested in the overseer; he established a system of education and did much good . . .

April 27.—The De la Beches dined with us, and were peculiarly agreeable. A great deal of conversation went forward, on Ireland, the West Indies, the Roman Catholic and Protestant Churches, education, and phrenology . . .

May 15.—About one o'clock Derwent Coleridge was announced, quickly succeeded by George Wightwick, who blundered into the room on his own ground plan. Took them all over the Grove Hill gardens. Wightwick made a profound bow to the indiarubber tree as having often befriended him in his unguarded moments. He told us several anecdotes of the charming impudence of [William] Snow Harris.* Once when

---

* Electrician. Knighted for his improved lightning conductor.

he (Wightwick) had been lecturing at the [Plymouth] Athenaeum on the superiority of the Horizontal to the Pyramidical style of architecture, he thus illustrated the theory: 'When the French army under Napoleon came to the Pyramids they passed on without emotion, but when they reached the Temple of Karnak, which is a horizontal elevation, they with one accord stood perfectly still.' 'Rather tired, I suppose', murmured Harris.

June 22.—Henry de la Beche was particularly amusing in his black coat, put on in consequence of the King's death, complaining of tomfoolery in thus affecting to mourn when there was little real feeling. After the late Geological meeting they took supper with Lord Cole, and instituted a forfeit in case any science should be talked. Most of the party had to pay the penalty, which was, drinking salt and water and singing a song. Two hammers were put on the table in case of any insurmountable differences of opinion, that the parties might retire into another room and settle their dispute. Spite of fair inferences, he declares they were not tipsy, but simply making good a pet axiom of his, 'toujours philosophe—is a fool.'

July 29.—The Coleridges dined with us; the poet's son expounded and expanded Toryism after a fashion of his own, which was very fascinating. Papa spoke of never influencing votes at an election; to this Derwent Coleridge objected. maintaining that people of superior education and talent should feel the responsibility of these possessions, as a call to direct the judgments of those less gifted. A bright argument ensued between the poet and the man of sense . . .

August 24.—J. Pease gave us a curious enough account of a shelf in the Oxford library, which is the receptacle of all works opposed to the Church of England, which are placed there to be answered as way may open. Barclay's Apology,* and Barclay's Apology alone, remains unanswered and unanswerable, though many a time has it been taken from the shelf-controversial, yet has always quietly slunk back to its old abode. Hurrah for Quakerism!

Grasmere, September 8.—We sent Aunt Charles's letter of

---

* First published in 1676. The author, Robert Barclay, was an ancestor of Maria, née Barclay, Caroline's mother.

introduction to Hartley Coleridge,* and as we were sitting after tea in the twilight, a little being was observed at the door, standing hat in hand, bowing to the earth round and round, and round again, with eyes intensely twinkling—it was Hartley Coleridge . . .

September 9.—A glorious morning with Hartley Coleridge, who gradually unfolded on many things in a tone well worthy of a poet's son. In person and dress he was much brushed up; his vivid face sparkled in the shadow of a large straw hat. He took us to the Wishing Gate which Wordsworth apostrophises, and set us wishing. Barclay accordingly wished for the repetition of some of Hartley Coleridge's poetry, on which he begged us to believe that the Gate's powers were by this time exhausted. He says he never can recollect his poetry so as to repeat it. He took us to the outside of his rosy cottage, also to that which had been occupied by Wordsworth and De Quincey [Dove Cottage] . . . [Wordsworth, he says] is a most unpleasant companion in a tour, from his terrible fear of being cheated; neither is he very popular as a neighbour. He calls him more a man of genius than talent, for whilst the fit of inspiration lasts he is every inch a poet; when he tries to write without it he is very dragging. Hartley Coleridge is very exquisite in his choice of language. I wish I had preserved some of this . . . We idly talked and idly listened, and drank in meanwhile a sense of the perfect beauty and loveliness of the nature around us. We walked up to Rydal Mount, but Wordsworth is in Herefordshire, on his return from Italy. Mrs. Wordsworth was very kind, took us over their exquisite grounds, which gave many openings for the loveliest views, congratulated us in an undertone on our rare good fortune in having Hartley Coleridge as a guide, and gave us ginger-wine and ginger-bread. We saw the last, and as Hartley Coleridge considers, the best portrait taken of Wordsworth in Italy, also a very fine cast from Chantrey's bust. In the garden at the end of a walk is a picturesque moss-covered stone with a brass tablet, on which Wordsworth has inscribed some lines saying that the mercy of the bard had rescued this stone from the rude hand of the builders, and that he trusted when he was gone it might still be regarded for his sake.

* 1796-1849. Eldest son of S.T. Coleridge; poet.

Hartley Coleridge then took us to the Rydal waterfalls and told us stories of the proprietors, the Fleming family. One of the falls, or forces as they call them here, was the most perfect I had ever seen. Our poet's recognition of the perpetual poetry in Nature was very inspiring and inspiriting. He drove with us to Ambleside; I gave him 'Elia' to read, and he read 'Detached Thoughts on Books and Reading' with a tone and emphasis and intense appreciation which Lamb would have loved to mark. At dinner he had a sad choking fit, so queerly conducted as to try our propriety sadly. Then when he had anything especially pointed to say, he would stand up or even walk round the dining-table . . . We asked about Wordsworth's daughter—had she inherited any of her father's genius? 'Would you have the disease of genius to descend like scrofula?' was his answer, and added that he did consider it a disease which amazingly interfered with the enjoyment of things as they are, and unfitted the possessor for communion with common minds. At the close of dinner he presented and read the following lines, which he had written whilst we were on Windermere, Aunt Charles being the inspirant:—

> 'Full late it was last night when first we met,
> And soon, too soon, must part this blessed day;
> But these brief hours shall be like jewels set
> In memory's coronet
> For the dear sake of one that's far away.
> Strangers we are, and strangers may remain,
> And yet the thought of her we all have loved,
> Methinks by some unseen mysterious chain
> Will long detain.
> This one half-day when we together moved,
> Together moved beneath the self-same hills,
> And heard the murmur of the same sweet waters
> Which she, light-footed comrade of the rills
> And "dancing daffodils,"
> Has loved, the blithest of all nature's daughters.'

Then he took us each by the hand, said good-bye, and was gone, just bequeathing to Aunt Charles the finishing sentence, 'to see *her*, I would go a great way.'

I can only aim at a shadow portrait. Conjure up unto thyself, O Caroline, a little, round, high-shouldered man, shrunk into a little black coat, the features of his face moulded by habit into an expression of pleasantry and an appreciation of the exquisitely ludicrous. Such as one could fancy Charles Lamb's. Little black eyes twinkling intensely, as if every sense were called on to taste every idea. He is very anxious to establish an Ugly Club and to be its chairman; but really he is quite unworthy of the station, for odd enough he is, but never ugly, there is such a radiant light of genius over all . . .

Liverpool, September 14.—Papa took us to the meeting of the British Scientific Association. Wheatstone came up to us in the gallery and was most agreeable and cordial; he told us of his electric conversations which are conducted by subterranean wires between here and London in a second or two . . .

September 16.—Went to breakfast with S[haron] Turner and his nieces. Sir William Hamilton [Astronomer Royal of Ireland], Lord Northampton [later President of the Royal Society], Lord Compton, and Lady Marion were there. Lord Northampton sat by me, and we had a thorough set-to on phrenology; Lord Compton was on the other side, and rather disposed to take my part. Lord Northampton bringing up the old arguments of varying thicknesses of skull, and the foolish instances of bad men having large veneration, &c., he acknowledged the force of my arguments . . . After breakfast went to the closing meeting, and heard various papers read and discussed. Then came forward our glorious chairman, Sedgwick: who, after saying many soft things to the soft sex, gave the moral of the science, that if he found it interfere in any of its tenets with the representations or doctrines of Scripture, he would dash it to the ground, gave the whys and the wherefores in his own most admirable method, and sat down; the Synod was dissolved, and Sedgwick had disappeared.

Falmouth, October 5.—Went to Enys . . . Drove on to Carclew; found Sir Charles Lemon and Lady de Dunstanville. Sir Charles told us that Professor [George] Airy [Astronomer Royal] (whom he has invited to Carclew) was so shy that he never looked a person in the face. A friend remarked to him, 'Have you ever observed Miss —'s eyes? They have the principle of double refraction.' 'Dear me, that is very odd,' said the philosopher. 'I should like to see that; do you think I might call?' He did so, and at the end of the visit begged permission to call again to see her eyes in a better light. He, however, found it a problem which would take a lifetime to study, and he married her. Lady de Dunstanville was in the House of Peers when the Queen first appeared. It was a most imposing sight. Her voice was full, clear, and sweet, and distinctly heard. We drove home to a quiet afternoon. W. E. Forster* has come to stay a little, and looks taller than ever.

October 9.—Snow Harris gave us an account of Charles Kemble† going to see Niagara, where he stood lost in the sublime and vast extent of this majestic vision, when he heard a Yankee voice over his shoulder, 'I say, sir, what an omnipotent row! I calculate this is a pretty considerable water privilege, enough to suckle that ocean considera-bly!'

Time this evening was very gracious, for it developed its dear impersonate Davies Gilbert. He had been holding his court and dining with his tenants. Soon after his arrival all the other gentlemen had to go off to a committee, so we had him all to ourselves. He repeated the admirable song of Trelawny with true Cornish energy, and gave us interesting accounts of his interviews with George IV., William IV., and the Queen; the two former he visited in right of his Royal Society's Presidentship to get their signatures. To George IV. he went and requested that he would confirm the patent as his royal predecessors had done, and pointed out to him several of their signatures. 'Would you show me Evelyn's?' said the King; 'I have lately been reading his Memoirs with great interest.' Davies Gilbert found and showed it, when the King remarked, 'He was the founder of the Royal Society.' Gilbert said it was His Majesty Charles II, who gave the first charter. 'Very true,' replied the King; 'but that was only *ex officio,* any man who had happened to be in his situation would have done that; but Evelyn was the real founder, you may depend upon it.' On leaving him Davies Gilbert remarked to his friend, Sir Everard Home, 'if that had not been the King I should have remarked what an agreeable, intelligent man I have been conversing with,' which delighted the King exceedingly on being told of it.

October 11.—Davies Gilbert very amusing on the subject of

* Liberal statesman; later Chief Secretary of State for Ireland.
† Actor; brother of Sarah Siddons.

bringing up children. 'Oh, indulge all their little innocent wishes, indulge them to the uttermost; 'twill give them fine tempers and give yourself much greater pleasure!' Once when in the House of Commons, a bill was brought forward by Fox to forbid the use of porter pots in Westminster! Davies Gilbert opposed the bill as too absurd, and said he did not think it could be one that Mr. Fox himself approved, but that he was only bringing it forward in compliance with the wishes of some of his constituents. Fox was not in the House, but Sheridan immediately rose and declared that as a friend of Fox's he must entirely deny a charge so injurious to the reputation of the honourable member. It was Fox's bill and worthy of its high origin. Davies Gilbert could only say that of course he bowed to conviction, and must therefore bear the weight of the responsibility of differing from Fox. The next day he met Sheridan, who accosted him. 'It was all perfectly true what you said yesterday, but I thought I must say what I did to keep up Fox's credit.'

October 18.—Derwent Coleridge gave Barclay his own idea about Christabel. He thinks the poem all hinges on the lines—

> 'And she in the midnight wood will pray
> For the weal of her lover that's far away,'

and that this is a Catholic idea of expiation, that the lover had fallen into some great sin, and Christabel was thus permitted to do penance for him by her own great suffering.

November 18.—Captain Ross dined with us, a very agreeable well-disposed man. His North-west stories were most interesting. He has been in every one of the Northern voyages, six in number, and fully intends and hopes to go again. The climate he thinks particularly healthy, for in all ordinary expeditions the common average of deaths would be thirty-seven, but on these was but twenty-five. He described the first appearance of the *Isabella*. After an absence of five years, throughout which they managed to keep up hope, Captain Ross said to the look-out man, 'What's that dark object in the distance?' 'Oh, sir, 'tis an iceberg; I've seen it ever since I've been on watch.' Captain Ross thought so too, but he could not be satisfied about it, and sent for his glass; he had no sooner viewed it than his best hopes were confirmed, and at the top of his voice cried, 'A ship! a ship!' Not one of the crew would believe him until they had seen it with their own eyes. They were soon in the boat, but a little tantalising breeze would come and drive the ship on two or three miles and then cease, and this frequently repeated. In spite of all their signals they were too insignificant to be seen, until Captain Ross fired off his musket half-a-dozen times, and at last it was heard and a boat was lowered. As soon as the ship's boat met these forlorn objects, twenty in number, unshaven skin-clad sinners, they said, 'You've lost your ship, gentlemen?' 'Yes, we have,' replied Captain Ross; 'but what ship is this?' 'The *Isabella,* formerly commanded by Captain Ross,' was the reply. 'Why, I am Captain Ross.' 'Oh no, sir, that's impossible; Captain Ross has been dead these five years!' Dead or alive, however, they brought them to Hull, where they felt the most miserable anxiety as to what changes might have taken place in their absence; and Captain Ross added, that in the following week he was the only one of the party not in mourning . . . Captain Ross had an experimental evening with Papa, and left us at ten.

November 19.—Uncle Charles dined with us. He was delighted and dazzled by the display on the Queen's day, and mentioned a right merry quibble perpetrated by my Lord Albemarle, who on Her Majesty saying, 'I wonder if my good people of London are as glad to see me as I am to see them,' pointed out as their immediate Cockney answer to the query, 'V.R.!'

1838

Paris, April 2.—Papa enjoyed his morning at the Academy, of which [Antoine César] Becquerel is President. Our fellow-traveller, the Magnetic Deflector, excited strong interest; even Gamby admitted, though unwillingly, the superiority of Papa's method of suspension. There was a brilliant and very kindly assemblage of *savants.* Becquerel called the next day, and was delighted by a further examination of the instrument; and when Papa showed him the clay with a vein in it galvanically inserted, he not only did not doubt the originality of the experiment (which H— has accused Papa of borrowing from Becquerel), but it was not until after a full discussion and a thorough cross-examination of the Fact, that he could even admit it. He then made Papa draw in his pocket-book the precise manner in which his 'experiences' had been pursued, the relative position of wires, pots, and pans, with the intention of repeating it all himself. Nothing could be more satisfactory than the interview and conversation between these supposed rivals.

April 4.—Papa and Uncle Charles spent the morning most pleasantly at [François] Arago's [astronomer and physicist]. During their merry breakfast the 'toujours philosophe—is a fool' was the accepted motto. Arago pleaded guilty to the definition of Tories imputed to him in England, which originated, he said, in a conversation between Lord Brougham* and himself on the doctrine of final causes. A noted Tory was referred to, and the question started as to his final cause. Arago thus solved the problem, 'That as astronomers like to have some point from which to make their calculations, so the Tory was to be a fixed point whence to mark the progress of civilisation and the development of the human mind.' Speaking of Dr. [John] Dalton,† he said he could not take a joke at all. Once when he had taken a glass of wine, Arago, who does not drink any, remarked, 'Why, you are quite a debauchee compared to me.' The philosopher took it very ill, and did not recover for the evening. He was delighted with the specimens of artificial mineral veins which Papa showed him, and asked, 'Is there not some one who disputed your theory—I forget his name?' Papa suggested H—, who proved to be the worthy referred to. Uncle Charles mentioned some of the circumstances of the case, on which Arago remarked, 'That reminds me of the man who told his friend that some person hated him. "That's strange," he replied, "for I don't recollect ever having done him a kindness." ' So our gentlemen greatly enjoyed their morning with Arago. On begging for an autograph for me, he wrote a very kind note, and sent me interesting specimens of Humboldt's and Odilon Barrot's writing.

* Lord Chancellor; defended Queen Caroline.
† Chemist and natural philosopher; he kept a Quaker school.

London, May 25.—Went to Exeter Hall,* and thanks to my dear brother's platform ticket and the good-nature of the police, we got a place on the platform close to the speakers. Lord Brougham was in the chair, and the subject of the meeting was Anti-Slavery. We came in near the conclusion of Lord Brougham's speech, which was received with immense applause, so much so that very little could we hear, but I mean to get a printed paper. Sir G. Strickland succeeded him, then G[eorge] Thompson,† who was followed by a Lincolnshire M.P., a Mr. [Culling] Eardley, who entreated the meeting's attention for a few minutes whilst he avowed himself a warm supporter of the anti-slavery cause, but opposed Lord Brougham's speech, which was evidently against Ministers, particularly Lord John Russell, and was dictated by private pique and disappointed ambition. Here he was burst upon by a thunder of abuse: 'Hiss, hiss, hiss!' 'Down with him!' 'Take him off!' 'Stop him!' 'Hiss, 'iss, 'iss!' he standing calm and erect till Thompson rose and begged for a little peace and quietness, assuring them that they need not be anxious about their chairman, as he was perfectly able to defend himself. This caused great clapping, and at Thompson's request the speaker was permitted to proceed. He went on to say that he had expected opposition, but not that the avalanche would so quickly descend and overwhelm the expression of his sentiments. He believed that he rose with a conscientious motive (hear! hear!), it was to vindicate in some degree the character of a really upright man (hear!) who had fallen under the Brougham-stick, Lord John Russell (agonies of abusive manifestations!), with whose vote he could by no means agree (hear! hear!), but he viewed him as one on whom the Light had not yet shined, but who would embrace it as soon as he was fortunate enough to perceive it. Lord Brougham arose to declare, from what he could gather of the honourable gentleman—'Mr. What is the gentleman's name? really it is one with which I am quite unacquainted'—he supposed that he wished to supplant him in the chair, which he thought a little unfair, as he had come in at the eleventh hour, whereas his (Lord Brougham's) opinions and efforts had

---

* Built in 1831 where the Strand Palace Hotel now stands.
† Organised an anti-slavery movement in America and was obliged to leave the country.

been acknowledged ever since the first agitation of the subject. He dwelt eloquently for some time upon this point, and seated himself amidst deafening applause. Mr. Eardley arose and replied in the teeth of the multitude, and then Lord Brougham, with his usual nasal contortions, was very witty for some time, and proposed the election of another chairman that he might legitimately engage in self-defence. This was seconded and loudly applauded, till some one assured them that a personal quarrel between Lord Brougham and Mr. Eardley was not at all relevant to the business of the meeting. The cheerful auditory cheered still louder, and hissed the idea of Lord Brougham quitting his imperial seat for an instant. After much more discussion, Lord Brougham just rose to declare that so personal a dispute should trespass no longer on the time of the meeting, and therefore he would sum up and give a verdict in favour of the 'counsel for the attack,' and the people laughed very heartily. Sir George Murray [former Colonial Secretary] then spoke in an agreeable, sensible, modest manner, his statements of the supineness of the legislature being very striking. But I must get a paper, particularly for a report of the speech of the 'Member for Ireland' ([Daniel] O'Connell), which we could not distinctly hear from his turning his head the other way and emphatically dropping his voice. He began with a burst—'I was one of the ninety-six who voted for the Motion the other night, and this I desire may be set forth on my tombstone!' He spoke with energy, pathos, and eloquence. His mouth is beautifully chiselled and his nose *retroussé*; he is an uncommonly strong looking, stout-built man, who looks as if he could easily bear the weight of the whole House upon his shoulders. He gave a grievous account of the Coolie importation—but I absolutely must have a paper.

June 1.—A breakfast party of the Backhouses* and William Edward Forster, after which we sallied forth to Deville's (the phrenologist). A gentleman and lady were there when we entered, and he was explaining several of the casts with which his room was lined, notably a very interesting series of American boys; another of a man who put himself under Deville's care for reformation, who told him that there was a

* Quaker family. Forster wooed their daughter Jane whom Barclay Fox later married.

lady whose development he had taken, and it would precisely suit him, so he married her! upon which one of our gentleman said, 'Oh, that's what makes your science so popular.' Inquiries were made about large heads, and they proved to be generally lymphatic, small heads more energetic. W. E. Forster asked for the casts of Richard Carlile,* having seen them there on a former occasion, but Deville said they had departed, which W. E. Forster believed to be a mistake. He asked twice for them and communicated his suspicions to us. At last, the gentleman and lady leaving the room, Deville said, 'That was Mr. and Mrs. Carlile!' a singularly awkward coincidence. He is now, Deville says, going mad on religion; the lady he has married, a very lovely one, having had a wonderful effect upon him, and he is preparing a new version of the Bible.

June 2.—At Davies Gilbert's invitation we went to his 'habitat' and were hailed at the door by the venerable philosopher. After a little visit to his sister, he got with us into our fly, and we drove to the Royal Society's Rooms at Somerset House. He is very busy establishing the standard of weights and measures, which was lost on the recent burning of the Royal Exchange. They are measured to a thousandth part of a grain. Duplicates are to be kept in all our colonies and the different European capitals, so that a similar loss need not be feared. He is going to-day to put the stars in order at Greenwich with Airy . . .

June 5.—Found yesterday Professor Wheatstone's card, with a note requesting a call to-day at King's College. Therefore, after a quiet morning, went there and found Uncle Charles with the Professor inspecting his electric telegraph. This is really being brought into active service, as last week they began laying it down between London and Bristol, to cost £250 a mile. He then showed us his 'Baby,' constructed in imitation of the human organs of speech; it can beautifully pronounce some words and cry most pathetically. He treated it in a most fatherly manner. His 'Syren' is an extraordinary little instrument, so called because it will act under water; its object is to measure the intensity of sound. He then played the Chinese reed, one of the earliest instruments constructed, exhibited the

---

* Freethinker, disciple of Thomas Paine.

harp, or rather sounding-board, with additaments, which communicates with a piano two stories higher, and received the sound from it quite perfectly through a conductive wire . . .

June 11.—Breakfasted with [Joseph] Lister. He is a great authority on optics. Showed us varieties of fossil sections through his powerful chromatic—or something—microscope.

June 12.—Dined at the Frys', and had the pleasure of meeting the Buxton family. [Thomas] Fowell Buxton [Abolitionist] described his non-election at Weymouth as a most pathetic time. When he made his parting speech he began in a jocose fashion, but soon saw that that would not do, as one old man after another turned aside to cry. On the Sunday he went to church and listened to a most violent sermon against himself, person and principle. He spoke afterwards to one of his party on the bad taste and impropriety of introducing politics into the pulpit; in this he quite agreed, but added, 'You had better say nothing on the subject, as at all the Dissenting chapels they are telling the people that they are sure to go to a very uncomfortable place if they don't vote for you.' He mentioned as a well-authenticated fact in statistics that two-thirds of all the matrimonial separations were of those who had been united by the runaway method.

June 28.—Met Sir Henry de la Beche at the Athenaeum amongst the crowd who came to see all they could of the Coronation. The De la Beche West Indian property is in a very flourishing state, thanks to the beautiful changes there. He has long used free labour, and found it answer well, though he was mightily persecuted for carrying out this system. . . Whilst the Royal party were in the Abbey, we wandered across the Park to see the ambassadors' carriages which were ranged there. They were very magnificent, the top of one being covered with what De la Beche called crowns and half-crowns; Soult's, one of the old Bourbon carriages, richly ornamented with silver; the Belgian very grand, but part of the harness tied together with string! The servants had thrown off their dignity, and were sitting and standing about, cocked hats and big wigs off, smoking their pipes. It was an odd scene.

Helston, August 14.—Derwent Coleridge was luminous on architectural subjects; he cannot bear a contrast being drawn between our own and foreign cathedrals in favour of the foreigner . . .

Falmouth, December 1.—An American gentleman breakfasted with us, a very intelligent young man. I find all Americans are great readers, principally political; each family also takes in two or three daily papers. He thinks the hot Abolitionists have done a great deal of harm to both master and slave . . .

December 8.—Captain and Mrs. Ingram and others dined with us. S. T. Coleridge spent his last nineteen years in their immediate neighbourhood with the [James] Gillmans, who have appeared quite different since the departure of the bard—their spirits broken, and everything testifying that Coleridge is dead. Captain Ingram used frequently to meet him there [at Highgate], and though as a rule not appreciating such things, spoke with rapture of the evenings with him, when he would walk up and down in the glories of a swelling monologue, the whole room hushed to deepest silence, that not one note might be lost as they listened to the strains of the inspired poet.

December 28.—Whilst paying a visit at Carclew, in came the butler stifling a giggle and announcing 'Dr. [John] Bowring* and his foreign friend,' who accordingly marched in. This egregious individual is Edhem Bey, Egyptian Minister of Instruction, and Generalissimo of the Forces. He was dressed in a large blue pelisse with loose sleeves, and full blue trousers, with scarlet gaiters and slippers, a gold waistband a foot and a half in width, and on his right breast his decoration of the crescent in uncommonly large diamonds, said to be worth £50,000! He is a tall man and very stout, with a rich complexion and black rolling eyes, aged about thirty-four. He is married to a beautiful Circassian, and only one, whom he bought at twelve years of age and wedded at fourteen . . . These good people are come into Cornwall to inspect the mines . . .

Dr. Bowring is a very striking-looking personage with a most poetical, ardent, imaginative forehead, and a temperament all in keeping, as evidenced by his whole look and manner. He declared Papa's name as much connected with Falmouth as the Eddystone lighthouse with Navigation. Dr.

* Disciple of Jeremy Bentham; editor of the *Westminster Review*.

Bowring knows Dickens and Cruikshank well; the former a brilliant creature with a piercing eye, the other a very good fellow with excessive keenness of perception . . .

The Bey talked about the Queen, whom he thinks a very interesting and dignified girl, but he laughs at her title as belonging far more properly to her ministers . . . His long pipe was brought into the library by his servant Hassan, and we had a puff all round; it has an amber mouthpiece set with diamonds. Opium and aromatic herbs are his tobacco, wine and lemonade his little by-play. Dr. Bowring seemed rather surprised at my ignorance of his 'Matins and Vespers.' He spoke a good deal of Joseph Wolff, who, he says, has by his injudicious proceedings retarded the progress of Christianity in the East by about a century and a half; sending a letter, for instance, to the Bey of Alexandria denouncing Mahomet as an impostor, instead of commencing on common ground. Lady Georgina Wolff said to Sir Charles Lemon, 'You don't believe all my husband's stories, I hope, do you?' Dr. Bowring could not obtain an interview with Lady Hester Stanhope; everybody in her neighbourhood laughs at her, except her numerous creditors, who look grave enough. All consider her mad. One of her last delusions was, that under a certain stone guarded by a black dragon, governed by a sable magician under her control, all the treasures of the earth were concealed; the query naturally being, why she did not give the necessary orders and pay her debts. Dr. Bowring knew Shelley and Byron intimately . . . In company Shelley was a diffident, retiring creature, but most beautiful, with an interpenetrating eye of intense feeling; he had a fascinating influence over those who were much with him, over Byron especially. His unhappy views on religion were much strengthened, if not originated, by the constant persecution he endured, but these views had very little effect on his conduct . . .

[Giuseppe] Mezzofanti* he knows well; they have just made him a cardinal; he is not a clever man, but has a knack of imbibing the sound of language independently of its principles and its application to reading foreign authors.

On going to the Holy Land, the first voices Dr. Bowring

---

* Celebrated linguist whom Byron called 'a walking polyglot, a monster of languages'.

heard were engaged in singing his hymn, 'Watchman, watch-man, what of the night?' which had been imported and translated by the American missionaries. His 'Matins and Vespers' were the means of converting a poor Syrian, who on being shipwrecked possessed that and that only, which copy is now in the possession of the Bishop of Stockholm . . .

1839

Falmouth, January 22.—T. Sheepshanks paid his respects to us. He told us that some years ago a Miss James, an eccentric lady, was walking from Falmouth to Truro, and fell in with a very intelligent man in a miner's dress. She entered into conversation, and concluded by giving him a shilling. In the evening she dined out to meet Professor Sedgwick, and was not a little astonished to recognise in the Professor her morning's friend of the pickaxe.

February 11.—Rode with Lady Elizabeth Wathen to Flushing. She described Washington Irving,* whom she met at Newstead Abbey, as a quiet, retiring, matter-of-fact, agreeable person. He is unmarried but time was when he was engaged to an American damsel, who caught a bad cold at a ball of which she at last died, but every night during her illness he would take his mattress outside her door and watch there.

April 3.—Found Mr. [Thomas] Sopwith at home, writing a letter and waiting for Papa and Sir Charles Lemon. He is the great isometrical perspective man, and by degrees developed himself as a very agreeable and amusing one. He is come to help Sir Charles in organising his School of Mines. Sir Charles soon joined him there and paid a very nice visit. When Edhem Bey dined with him the other day, he had Sydney Smith† to meet him. Sir Charles told his Excellency that he was 'un ecclésiastique très distingué'; so he was looked upon with the utmost reverence and devotion, until his stories and funnyisms of all descriptions entirely displaced the Bey from his assumed centre of gravity.

---

* Author of *Rip Van Winkle.*
† Wit; Canon of St Paul's.

We were pleased to hear of the exile of the Chartists from Devizes by the public spirit of its inhabitants. Talked about their principles and the infidelity they have been preaching everywhere, our mines included. Sir Charles Lemon said they have been declaring that the difference between the rich and poor abundantly proved the non-existence of a God. Some one remarked that it is the rich, not the poor, who become infidels; only those renounce a Providence who do not feel the want of one.

April 6.—Whilst sitting quietly writing, George Wightwick most unexpectedly burst upon us . . . His conversation was most interesting, comprising various details of the last days of Charles Mathews [Comedian]. He was quite aware of his nearness to death, saying to Snow Harris, who thought him a little better, 'Yes, I shall soon be very much better.' The day before his death they were anticipating his birthday which would follow, when he would enter his sixtieth year. He said, 'You may keep it, I don't expect to.' He lived half-an-hour into it, when his wife, hearing him in pain from the next room, ran in to help, but by the time she reached the bed he was dead. During his illness he liked to have his friends about him, and was sometimes so irresistibly funny, that even when he was in an agony they were obliged to laugh at his very singular expressions. Once they thought he was asleep and were talking around him, and one related how he had been in a fever and was so overcome with thirst that he seized a bottle by his side and swallowed its contents, which proved to be ink: Wightwick remarked, 'Why, that was enough to kill him.' The supposed sleeper yawned out, 'Why no, he'd nothing to do but swallow a sheet of blotting-paper!' As he was once sitting by the window they saw him manifesting considerable and increasing impatience. 'Why, what's the matter, Mathews?' 'There, look at that boy, he's got a cloak on, little wretch! a boy in a cloak! I was a boy once, I never had a cloak, but see that little ruffian in a cloak! Faugh!' Once Wightwick brought a modest friend of his to see him, who gave up his chair successively to every person who entered the room; at last Mathews, growing irritable, called to Wightwick, 'Do you know, your friend has given up his chair to every person who has entered the room and has never received a word of thanks from any of them. Do go and sit by him and hold him on it. I am quite fatigued by seeing him pop up and down.' He was much tried at his son Charles's want of success as an architect, saying, 'It is all very well his getting good dinners and good beds at the Duke of Bedford's, but they don't give him houses to build.' He is now on the stage and acts in vaudevilles and those French things. When in Dublin Mathews expressed a great desire to get an invitation to meet Curran; Curran heard of it, and unlike most men, on meeting Mathews accidentally in the street, addressed him as follows: 'Mr. Mathews, I understand you have a desire to take my portrait; all I have to request is that you will do it to the life. I am quite willing to trust myself in your hands, persuaded that you will do me justice; may I offer you a ticket to a public dinner where I am to-day going to speak on the slave trade?' He went, was thoroughly inoculated with the great orator's *savoir faire*, studied the report of the speech, and gave it soon after in Dublin, Curran being present *incog*. He afterwards electrified London with the same speech, and infinitely increased its effect, his audience kicking each other's shins with excitement and crying 'hear, hear' as if it was a genuine harangue . . .

Wightwick remarked that Sir John Soane, the architect [of the Bank of England], was a highly nervous and, I should think, rather affected person; he could not abide truisms or commonplaces, and if any one made the common English challenge to conversation of 'a fine day,' he would either deny it flatly or remark, 'Evidently the sun is shining and the sky is blue, there cannot be a question on the subject.' When Wightwick first went there he sent up his card, and soon followed it in person. Feeling nervous at being in the real presence of so great a man, he knew not how to begin, so said, 'My name is Wightwick, sir,' to be rebuffed by the reply, 'Sir, I have your card; I see perfectly what your name is.'

August 9.—Went to Trebah, heard an interesting and consecutive account of the P— family of G—, who in the heyday of Irvingism* were led into such wild vagaries by a lying spirit in the mouths of their twin-children of seven years old. These little beings gave tongue most awfully, declaimed against Babylon and things appertaining. Their parents

* See note on Edward Irving, February 18, 1840.

placed themselves entirely under the direction of these chits, who trotted about the house, and everything they touched was immediately to be destroyed or given away as Babylonish! Thus this poor deluded man's house was dismantled, his valuable library dissipated, and himself and family thoroughly befooled. At last the younglings pointed out Jerusalem as the proper place for immediate family emigration, and everything was packed up, and off they set. The grandfather of the sprites was infinitely distressed at all these goings-on and goings-off, and with a pretty strong power intercepted his son at the commencement of his pilgrimage, and confined him to the house, inducing him to write to Irving to inquire how they were to find out whether they were influenced by a true or a false spirit. Just before this letter reached him, a Miss B—, under whose care these children first became possessed, had an interview with Irving, and instead of being received by him with open arms, heard the terrible sentence, 'Thou hast a lying spirit!' She flew into a vehement rage, and such a 'spirituelle' scene took place between them as is quite indescribable. His remark was perhaps deduced from the fact that he had been informed of the failure of many of her prophecies. So he was prepared to write Mr. P— a sketch of an infallible ordeal for his young prophets. He was to read them the text 'Try the spirits' and several others, and see how they acted. The letter was received by Mr. P— in his library, Lord R—, Mr. W—, and some other Irvingites being assembled to receive it with due honour. The children, quite ignorant of the test preparing for them, were playing about the nursery. No sooner had the library party opened and read the letter, than little master in the nursery flew into a most violent rage, tore downstairs on his hands and feet like a little demon, uttering in an unearthly voice, 'Try not the spirits, try not the spirits,' and in this style he burst in upon his fond relatives, and found them engaged in conning the test act. This opened their eyes at last pretty wide, and the papa said, 'You're a bad boy, go up into your nursery and you shall be punished!' By a judicious discipline these two children were rescued from what is considered, with some show of reason, to have been a demoniacal possession. The father, however, became insane ultimately from what he had passed through, and died in that state.

September 3.—Mr. Gregory told us that, going the other day by steamer from Liverpool to London, he sat by an old gentleman who would not talk, but only answered his inquiries by nods or shakes of the head. When they went down to dinner, he determined to make him speak if possible, so he proceeded, 'You're going to London, I suppose?' A nod. 'I shall be happy to meet you there; where are your quarters?' There was no repelling this, so his friend with the energy of despair broke out. 'I-I-I-I-I'm g-g-g-going to D-D-D-Doctor Br-Br-Br-Brewster to be c-c-c-cured of this sl-sl-sl-slight im-impediment in my sp-sp-sp-sp-speech.' At this instant a little white face which had not appeared before popped out from one of the berths and struck in, 'Th-th-th-that's the m-m-m-man wh-wh-who c-c-c-c-c-cured me!'

Letter from E. Crouch, dated, like the negro when asked where he was born, 'All along de coast.'

October 4.—Though the weather was abundantly unfavourable, we started at eight for Penzance. At Helston found Sir Charles Lemon, who had got wet through, and after drying himself was glad to accept a place in our carriage instead of his gig, and we had an exceedingly pleasant drive to the Geological Meeting . . .

Of Dr. Lardner he mentioned that, having quarrelled with his wife and got a divorce, and his name being Dionysius and hers Cecilia, has gained for him the august title of—Dionysius, tyrant of Sicily!

October 8.—The Bucklands dined with us, after a Polytechnic morning. Mrs. Buckland is a most amusing, animated woman, full of strong sense and keen perception. She spoke of the style in which they go on at home, the dust and rubbish held sacred to geology, which she once ventured to have cleared, but found it so disturbed the Doctor, that she determined never again to risk her matrimonial felicity in such a cause. She is much delighted at the idea of sitting in St. Michael's chair,* that she may learn how managing feels. Davies Gilbert tells us that Dr. Buckland was once travelling somewhere in Dorsetshire, and reading a new and weighty book of Cuvier's which he had just received from the

* On St Michael's Mount, Cornwall, a stone seat, difficult to reach. There is a legend that whichever—man or wife—sits in it first shall rule the roost.

publisher; a lady was also in the coach, and amongst her books
was this identical one, which Cuvier had sent her. They got
into conversation, the drift of which was so peculiar that Dr.
Buckland at last exclaimed, 'You must be Miss [Morland] to
whom I am about to deliver a letter of introduction.' He was
right, and she soon became Mrs. Buckland. She is an
admirable fossil geologist, and makes models in leather of
some of the rare discoveries. Dr. Buckland gave a capital
lecture at the Polytechnic this evening — a general, historic,
and scientific view of the science of geology, beautifully
illustrated by De la Beche's map. Sir H. Vivian was chuck-
ling over the admirable Ordnance map. 'I got that map for
you; I was determined he should do my county first, and so I
sent him down direct.' . . . Speaking of the modern tendency to fancy danger to religion in the investigations of
physical science, he remarked, 'Shall we who are endowed by
a gracious Creator with power and intelligence, and a
capacity to use them—shall we sit lazily down and say, Our
God has indeed given us eyes, but we will not see with them;
reason and intelligence, but we will exert neither? . . . ' He
made some good allusions to Sir Charles Lemon's mining
school, and mentioned the frequent evidence of the fact that
barbarians of all nations (no allusion to Sir C. L. or Cornish
miners) have hit on similar expedients for supplying their
necessities; the old Celtic arms, for instance, are of precisely
the same form as the axes and hatchets contrived by the New
Zealanders. Speaking of the immense real value of iron, he
remarked, 'What a fortune for a man, cast into a country
where iron was unknown, would the bent nail from the
broken shoe of a lame donkey be!' and altogether the lecture
was much more agreeable and less coarse than when he treats
of the footsteps of animals and birds on the Old Red
Sandstone. Davies Gilbert walked home with us, and was
very bright after all the labours of the day. Gave us instances
of his mediation with papas in favour of runaway daughters,
and mentioned as a good converse to his system the manner
in which old Thurlow* received the news of his dear daughter,
who had taken her fate into her own hands. 'Burn her picture!
Break up her piano! Shoot her horse!'

October 9.—Snow Harris lunched with us; much pleasant

* Lord Chancellor; presided at Warren Hastings' trial.

conversation on different modes of puffing. He mentioned that Day & Martin used to drive about in a gig in their early days all over the country, one as servant to the other, and at every inn the servant would insist on having his master's shoes cleaned with Day & Martin's blacking, 'as nothing else was used by people of fashion', and so induced large orders.

October 25.—G. Wightwick and others dined with us. He talked agreeably about capital punishments, greatly doubting their having any effect in preventing crime. Soon after Fauntleroy [fraudulent banker] was hanged, an advertisement appeared, 'To all good Christians! Pray for the soul of Fauntleroy.' This created a good deal of speculation as to whether he was a Catholic, and at one of Coleridge's soirées it was discussed for a considerable time; at length Coleridge, turning to Lamb, asked, 'Do you know anything about this affair?' 'I should think I d-d-d-did,' said Elia, 'for I paid s-s-s-seven and sixpence for it!'

October 26.—Poor J— B— in distressing delirium, having taken in ten hours the morphia intended for forty-eight. He was tearing off his clothes, crying out, 'I'm a glorified spirit! I'm a glorified spirit! Take away these filthy rags! What should a glorified spirit do with these filthy rags?' On this E— said coaxingly, 'Why, my dear, you wouldn't go to heaven stark naked!' on which the attendants who were holding him were mightily set off.

November 5.—A pleasant visit to Carclew. E. Lemon told us much of the Wolffs: he is now Doctor, and has a parish near Huddersfield. She was Lady Georgina's bridesmaid, and the wedding was an odd affair indeed. It was to her that Lady Georgina made the remark, after first seeing her future husband, 'We had a very pleasant party at Lady Olivia Sparrow's, where I met the most interesting, agreeable, enthusiastic, ugly man I ever saw!' She is a clever, intellectual woman, but as enthusiastic, wandering, and desultory in her habits as himself. E. Lemon has been not long since at Venice. She told us that poor Malibran* when she was there did not like the sombre regulation causing the gondolas to be painted black, and had hers coloured green; this, she was informed officially, would never do. 'Then I won't sing!' was

---

* Mezzo-soprano famous in London and Paris who died in 1836 at the age of twenty-eight.

the prompt and efficacious reply, and the syren lulled to slumber the sumptuary law of Venice.

December 8.—Barclay brought home a capital answer which a Cornish miner made to Captain Head (when travelling with him), who, looking at the Allegheny Mountains, asked him, 'Can anything be compared to this?' 'Yes; them things at home that wear caps and aprons!' said the faithful husband.

December 13.—Papa and I were busy writing when, to our surprise, in walked Dr. Bowring. He is come to stand for this place, an enterprise in which Papa said what he could to discourage him. He promises to incur no illegitimate expenses, and therefore has not the least chance of success . . .

December 14.—Dr. Bowring dined with us after addressing the Penryn constituency and being rather disgusted by their appearance. The only thing in his speech that at all touched them was his declaration that he was half a Cornishman, his mother being the daughter of the clergyman and schoolmaster of St. Ives, Mr. Lane, whose memory, he understood, is still held in the odour of sanctity . . . When in the Holy Land he felt himself completely thrown back into Gospel history and Gospel times, so stationary are the customs of the people. Often were passages of Scripture recalled to his mind by events passing around him, as when on the shore of the Lake of Tiberias one of those sudden storms arose so beautifully described in the Bible. He was once at Sychar in Samaria, just at the foot of Mount Gerizim, and had been recommended to the High Priest, with injunctions to show him everything in his church. Amongst other treasures he showed him the oldest MS. extant, namely, the Samaritan version of the Bible, 3500 years of age. In this the High Priest pointed out to him a text, 'On Mount Gerizim is the place where men ought to worship,' which he said the Jews had purposely omitted in their version; he inveighed against them in the very same spirit described 1800 years ago. In accordance with this text all the Samaritans assemble annually on Mount Gerizim and perform their worship there . . . He was very anxious to see Lady Hester Stanhope, and wrote to her physician for leave to do so. Her reply was, 'No, I won't receive any of those rascally English.' She had a notion that the Scotch and Albanians were the only honest people to be found anywhere. She greatly blamed Joseph Wolff for apostatising from so old and respectable a religion as Judaism, and in a celebrated letter to him she says, 'Can you for an instant think anything of Christianity if it requires the aid of such a vagabond as yourself to make it known?' . . . In Phoenicia the people eat cream just like the Cornish folk, which raised the question whether it was imported from Cornwall with the tin.

December 16.—A government messenger has persuaded Dr. Bowring to resign his parliamentary views in favour of another who has a long purse and is willing to use it. He was low and vexed about the business, having had the trouble and expense of coming here to no purpose; however, he does not wish to split the Falmouth Reformers, and accordingly published his farewell address and retired.

1840

Falmouth, January 1.—Entered on another year. Happy experience emboldens us to look forward with joyful anticipations to the voyage of life; we have been hitherto in calm water indeed, and for this how thankful should we be, but we must expect some gales before we drop our anchor. May we be prepared to meet them!

Alexander Christey left us after dinner for Nice *via* London. He told us about Robert Owen (the Socialist), an old friend of his father's. He is making numberless converts amongst the manufacturing districts. He and his family dwell in New Harmony in the United States. William Fenwick spoke of his grandfather having fished out Sir John Barrow from behind a linen-draper's counter, discovered his latent talents, had him taught mathematics, and finally introduced him to the world, in which he has made such good way.*

January 5.—After dinner Nadir Shah was announced, and in waddled this interesting *soi-disant* son of the late Sultan. He does not look nearly so distinguished as in native costume. He talks English beautifully, having been here three times, and

---

* Mrs Charles Fox, of Trebah, claimed that it was her great-grandfather, Dr John Fell, of Ulveston, who discovered Barrow. Barrow became Secretary to the Admiralty.

described the manner in which he learned it in five months:
took an English professor, made himself master of the alpha-
bet, but resolutely resisted the idea of spelling, told his
master, 'I'll pay you ten times as much if you will teach me in
my own way. I understand that Milton and Shakespeare are
the finest writers in English, so you must now teach me in
them.' The plan succeeded, to the astonishment of the
professor . . .

January 10.—Received my last frank to-day from Sir
Charles Lemon. What a happiness for the M.P.'s, that daily
nuisance being superseded.*

January 23.—Went to Perran to breakfast, and found we
had been preceded about five minutes by Derwent Coleridge
and his friend John Moultrie.† The first half-hour was spent
in petting the cats; but I should begin by describing the Leo
Novo. Moultrie is not a prepossessing-looking personage,—a
large, broad-shouldered, athletic man, if he had but energy
enough to develop his power . . . but his countenance
grows on you amazingly; you discover in the upper part a
delicacy and refinement of feeling before unrecognised, and
in the whole a magnanimity which would inspire confidence.
But certainly his face is no directing-post for wayfaring men
and women: 'Take notice, a Poet lives here!' He talks as if it
were too much trouble to arrange his words, but out they
tumble, and you gladly pick them up and pocket them for
better or for worse; though, truth to tell, his conversation
would not suggest the author of the 'Three Sons.' Derwent
Coleridge was bright and genial—his mobile, refined, even
fastidious countenance, so truly heralding the mind and heart
within. Breakfast was fully appreciated by our hungry poets:
something was said about the number of seals lately seen
sporting off Portreath, and the idea was mooted that the
mermaids were nothing but seals, and their yellow locks the
long whiskers of the fish. 'Oh don't say so,' pleaded Moultrie.
Then came some anecdotes of the mild old (Quaker) banker
[Charles] Lloyd, father to the poet, and himself a translator.
Derwent Coleridge asked him why he had never translated
the Iliad. 'Why,' answered the old Friend of seventy-four, 'I

---

* Before the introduction of the Penny Post MPs could frank their own and their
friends' mail.
† Poet; rector of Rugby during Arnold's Headmastership.

have sometimes thought of the work, but I feared the martial spirit' . . . J. Moultrie wrote a sonnet for me, illustrating the difference between the sister arts of Poetry and Painting, and read it; his voice and reading a painful contrast to the almost too dulcet strains of his beloved friend. But there is such honesty in his tones! He quarrelled with certain gilt scissors of Anna Maria's because they were a deceit in wishing to appear gold, and an unreasonable deceit, because gold is not the metal best adapted for cutting, and doubly unsuitable for Anna Maria, considering her religious principles, which bound her over to abhor alike gilding and deceit. He very properly lectured us for saying 'thee,' promised to *tutoyer* us as long as we liked, but not to answer to *thee*. Coleridge had mentioned to him as one of the attractions of the place that *thou* was spoken here. The mutual affection of these two men is very lovely. Never does Moultrie know of Derwent Coleridge being in troubles or anxieties but down he posts to share them . . .

February 8.—Barclay has been much pleased with a Mr. Sterling, a very literary man, now at Falmouth, who was an intimate friend of S. T. Coleridge during the latter part of his life . . .

Mrs. Mill* with her daughters, Clara and Harriet, have been some weeks nursing Henry Mill, who is dying of consumption in lodgings on the Terrace. Mamma and Barclay have both seen him, and speak of him as a most beautiful young creature, almost ethereal in the exquisite delicacy of his outline and colouring, and with a most musical voice.

February 10.—The Queen's wedding-day. Neck ribands arrived, with Victoria and Albert and loves and doves daintily woven in. Falmouth very gay with flags. Mr. Sterling called—a very agreeable man, with a most Lamb-liking for town life. He went with Papa to Penjerrick.

February 13.—To Perran Foundry under Aunt Charles's guidance; met there Derwent Coleridge, and Barclay brought John Sterling to see them cast fourteen tons of iron for the beam of a steam-engine. This was indeed a magnificent spectacle, and induced sundry allusions to Vulcan's forge and other classical subjects. The absolute agony of excitement

* Widow of James Mill, philosopher, and mother of John Stuart Mill.

Robert Were Fox, FRS, Caroline's father

John Sterling: engraving after a painting by
B. de la Cour, 1830

displayed by R. Cloke, the foreman, was quite beautiful . . . This beam was the largest they had ever cast, and its fame had attracted almost the whole population of Perran, who looked highly picturesque by the light of the liquid iron. My regretting that we had not chestnuts to employ so much heat which was now running to waste induced a very interesting discourse from Sterling, first, on the difference between utilitarianism and utility, then on the sympathy of great minds with each other, however different may be the tracks they select . . . Sterling exceedingly admires our Hostess's face, fancying himself in company with a Grecian statue, and in reference to the mind evolved in her countenance, quoted beautiful lines from the opening of 'Comus'—

> 'Bright aerial spirits live insphered
> Above the smoke and stir of this dim spot,
> Which men call Earth!'

Surveyed the Foundry, almost everything eliciting something worth hearing from one of our genii. After luncheon we went to Barclay's cottage, looked over engravings, and listened to Sterling's masterly criticisms which kept almost every one silent. Sitting over the fire, a glorious discussion arose between Coleridge and Sterling, on the effect of the Roman Catholic religion . . . Spent a most happy morning.

February 16.—Saw Dr. Calvert* for the first time. John Sterling brought him in; a nervous suffering invalid, with an interesting and most mobile expression of countenance. They joined Mamma and Anna Maria in a pony ride, and left them perfectly enchanted with their new acquaintances. He is staying at Falmouth on account of ill-health. We afterwards had a delightful walk to Budock. Dr. Calvert described being brought up as a Friend, and he perfectly remembers riding on a little Shetland pony to be christened. He is very anxious to go to Meeting . . .

February 17.—Took a short walk with Clara Mill. Her eldest brother, John Stuart Mill, we understand from Sterling, is a man of extraordinary power and genius, the founder of a new school in metaphysics, and a most charming companion.

---

* Nephew of Raisley Calvert, Wordsworth's friend and benefactor.

February 18.—Little visit from John Sterling, to the fag-end of which I became a witness. The talk was of Irving,* who came up to town with a magnificent idea of being like one of the angels in the Apocalypse or prophets of old; had he followed out this idea with simplicity, he might have succeeded, for it was a grand one. Chalmers† is a man of very inferior genius, but by working out his more modest ideas and directing his attention to the good of others rather than to his own fame, he has been much more useful. Fine ladies would go and hear Irving just as they would to see Kean or anything good of its class, and his eloquence was singularly impassioned, though, through all, his love of admiration was distinguishable. Sterling holds that a man's besetting sin is the means employed for his punishment; thus vanity acted in the case of Irving. Henry Melvill [canon of St Paul's] is considered the most eloquent clergyman of the present day . . .

[William] Wilberforce was likewise talked over, and the Clarkson controversy. The Wilberforce party quite own themselves defeated. When [Thomas] Clarkson's‡ book on Slavery came out some thirty years since, Coleridge, though quite unknown to the *Edinburgh Review*, wrote to Jeffrey, [editor of the *Review*], described Clarkson as a sincerely good man, writing with a worthy object, and therefore begged that his work, though abounding with literary defects, might not be made ridiculous after the fashion of the *Edinburgh Review*. Jeffrey answered, entirely agreeing with him, and requesting him to undertake the work. This he did, and a most beautiful piece of writing it is, so different from the *jejune* spirit in which the *Edinburgh Review* articles are generally composed . . . Sydney Smith's works then came on the tapis; Sterling considers them mere jest-books . . .

February 19.—Violent snowstorm through the day. In spite of it we walked with John Sterling and Clara Mill round Pennance; talked first of the education of the mind and how to train it to reflection . . .

* Founder of the Catholic Apostolic Church or Irvingites after he had been excommunicated as a minister of the Church of Scotland on account of his approval of the 'tongues' theory (see entry for August 9, 1839).

† Theologian who pioneered a movement which led to the formation of the Free Church in Scotland.

‡ Leading Abolitionist; he presided at the Anti-Slavery Meeting of June 13.

We geologised at the Elvan course and scrambled at Pennance; gave Clara Mill a thorough insight into the practicabilities of Cornish miners, and returned well pleased with our expedition. Discovered many mutual friends.

February 22.—Took Clara Mill a nice blowing walk; joined by John Sterling, who declared himself a hero of romance, having just been robbed of his hat by Aeolus, who forthwith drowned it in Swanpool; he tried to bribe a little boy to go in after it, but he excused himself upon the ground of not having been brought up to the water! Our talk was of Sir Boyle Roche, the bully of the Irish Parliament . . . of which Sterling's grandfather and great-grandfather were clerks. Those were the days of claret and conversation, and he spoke of one of the Speakers who always kept a strawberry at the bottom of his glass, and declared in the invervals between his first and seventh bottle that his physician ordered him to do so to keep the system cool . . .

February 23.—Directly after breakfast, Sterling and Dr. Calvert called to challenge us to a walk. Collected Clara, and Catherine Lyne, and Bobby (the pony), and sallied forth to Budock Rocks, and a great deal of interesting conversation made our time pass like 'Grecian life-fulness,' with very little intervals for the experience of 'Indian life-weariness.' . . .

John Sterling wrote the following impromptu to me by way of autograph—

'What need to write upon your book a name
Which is not written in the book of Fame?
Believe me, she to reason calmly true,
Though far less kind, is far more just than you.'

He dined with us. Thorough good conversation . . . Sterling is taking up geology as a counter-current for his mind to flow in, a subject so far removed from humanity that he considers it one of the least interesting of human sciences. The nearer you approach humanity, the more the subject increases in interest. Papa and he settled down to the artificial veins, which he is very anxious to understand; then he joined us in a capital game of Question and Noun. One of his questions was, 'How can you distinguish between nature and art in the complexion of a negro chimney-sweeper?' He brought me some charming autographs of Hare, Carlyle, Milnes, and others.

February 24.—Sterling, Calvert, Anna Maria, and I took Clara out. She spoke of Sterling having been invaluable to them, and can quite fancy him reading prayers with old women, from what they have lately known of his most feeling nature. Sterling . . . talked about Friends: we are the first he ever encountered; he had formed a very incorrect notion of them, conceiving that they never smiled—a slight mistake. Thinks that the ladies of the Society must very often marry out of the bounds; thinks it a grievous thing for husband and wife to be of different religious sentiments, not however to be compared to the horrors of a union between Catholic and Protestant, the former imagining the latter to be lost irremediably . . . As we neared home Bobby got his bit out of his mouth, and it was delicious to see the ignorance of common things manifested by our Transcendentalists. 'You'd better let him go, he'll find his way home,' said Sterling, with a laudable knowledge of natural history and a confused recollection of the instinct of brutes. We, thinking it would go probably to Kergillack, thought it best to lead him; so Sterling took his forelock and I his tail and marched the little kicking beast homeward. 'Calvert, just put the bit in his mouth, can't you; it's very easy.' 'Oh yes, perfectly easy,' said Calvert; 'do *you* do it, Sterling.'

February 26.—John Sterling and Dr. Calvert strolled in at breakfast; on a something being offered to the latter he said, 'No, I'll do anything with my friends but eat with them. I'll quarrel as much as they like, but never eat with them.' Something or other induced him to say, 'I conceive mankind to be divided into men, women, and doctors—the latter a sort of hybrid.' A spirited argument on capital punishments, ended in John Sterling's hope that if ever he committed murder he should be hanged, and Dr. Calvert's that he should be mad before, rather than after the solitary confinement.

A delightful Pennance and Penrose walk with the two gentlemen, everything looking glorious in the sunshine of reality and imagination . . .

February 27.—A walk and ride to Penjerrick, which looked eminently lovely basking in the sunshine. Sterling was, as usual, our life . . . [We] walked home together. Talked much about Friends; analysed and admired many of their principles; discussed learned ladies. Talked over Bentham's and Coleridge's philosophy, and Mill's admirable review . . .

February 28.—Found Sterling at Perran, where he had spent the last day or two. On hearing the bad account of Henry Mill a struggle between duty and inclination took place, and the former triumphed. Though he felt that he could not be of the least real use, he thought his presence might possibly be some comfort; and we accompanied him some part of the way. We brought him his letters. So he went away, and we had the satisfaction of finding our Uncle and Aunt quite as enthusiastic about him as we could wish . . .

February 29.—Sterling came and walked with us to Pennance Cave on a day as brilliant as his own imagination . . . He is exceedingly delighted with Uncle Charles, and has been writing enthusiastically to his wife about him and Perran and all; he says he never spent happier days in his life . . . He would always trust to the practical judgments of women, and thinks it the greatest mistake and perversion to educate them in the same manner as men; they have a duty equally clear and equally important to perform, but quite distinct. He has been reading [Sir Thomas Noon] Talfourd's Lamb (in consequence of my recommendation—Hem!), and has been perfectly delighted, and has come to the conclusion that his letters are better than Cowper's, and his essays than Addison's. Oh! there was such a vast deal more . . .

March 1.—Sterling and Clara called, and I joined them in a famous walk. Reviewed the poets, with occasional illustrations well painted. Shelley's emotions and sympathies not drawn forth by actual human beings, but by the creations of his own fancy, by his own ideal world, governed by his own unnatural and happily ideal system. This species of egotism very different to Byron's, who recognised and imprinted George Gordon, Lord Byron, on every page. Shelley fragmentary in all his pieces, but has the finest passages in the language. Wordsworth works from reflection to impulse; having wound up to a certain point, he feels that an emotion is necessary and inserts one—the exact converse of the usual and right method. Coleridge had no gift for drawing out the talent of others, which Madame de Staël possessed in an eminent degree. She was by no means pleased with her intercourse with him, saying spitefully and feelingly, 'M. Coleridge a un grand talent pour le monologue.' She would just draw from people the information she required, which her champagne and her wit never failed to do, and then let them return to their dusty garrets for the remainder of their existence, and live on the remembrance of an hour's beatitude. Sterling considers the female authors we have lately had very creditable to this country, though they have produced nothing that the world could not have done very well without. Mrs. Carlyle the most brilliant letter-writer he has met with.

March 2.—Found John Sterling waiting to challenge us to a walk, so with this right pleasant addition we went to Crill, collected money and ideas, the former to the amount of one shilling and fourpence, the latter to an extent irreducible to formulae, so I'll barely glimpse at anything therewith connected. Talked about eloquence, of which he thinks Jeremy Taylor the greatest master; he had enough genius to ennoble a dozen families of the same name. It is very odd that so few of our great men should have left any sons—Taylor, Shakespeare, Milton, &c. Talked over Coleridge—'The Friend,' his best prose work; a terrible plagiarist in writing and conversation. Particularly addicted to Schlegel. Described Dr. Calvert's character beautifully as one of pure sympathy with all his fellows, who delights to trace the outlines of the Divine image in even the least of His creatures. Talked over the mental differences between the sexes, which he considers precisely analogous to their physical diversities, her dependence upon him—he the creative, she the receptive power.

March 3.—Invited Sterling for this evening, preparatory to a visit to Kynance; and he came, and we had a pretty evening of it. Now for my notes . . . Lord Herbert, brother to the poet, a refined Deist, but inconsistent; he wrote a book utterly denying signs and miracles, and then prayed that he might be assured whether or no it was right to publish it by some trifling sign, he thinks it was of a bit of paper blowing in or out of the window . . . [Bertel] Thorwaldsen [Danish sculptor] one of the greatest geniuses and clearest intellects in Europe. When engaged over his Vulcan, one of his friends

said to him, 'Now, you must be satisfied with this production.' 'Alas!' said the artist, 'I am.' 'Why should you regret it?'
asked his friend. 'Because I must be going downhill when I
find my works equal to my aspirations.' Talked enthusiastically about his friend Julius Hare.* Invites us to meet him at
Clifton this summer; spoke of a coach journey with [Walter
Savage] Landor, who was travelling incognito, but made
himself known by the strange paradoxical style of conversation in which he indulged; this wound Sterling gradually up
to the point of certainty, and he said, 'Why! this sounds
amazingly like an Imaginary Conversation.' He just started at
this remark, but covered his retreat. He afterwards met him
at one of Hare's breakfasts, and got into a hot dispute with
him and a Frenchman concerning the Evangelicals, whom
they were running down most unfairly; so he supported their
cause, showing that there was much good in them . . . He
and Papa had a very spirited argument on the progress of
civilisation since the Christian era. Papa contended that there
were intervals when it retrograded; the other that there was a
constant zig-zag progress . . . Papa showed him the Polytechnic medal with Watt's head, when he wrote the following
lines on a slip of paper and handed them to me:—

'I looked upon a steam-engine, and thought,
'Tis strange, that when the engineer is dead,
A copy of his brains, in iron wrought,
Should thus survive the archetypal head.'

March 5.—Dr. Calvert joined us; we did not at first recognise him, as he was mightily muffled up, which he accounted
for by remarking, 'Why, inside I'm Dr. Calvert, but outside
certainly Mr. Sterling,' being enveloped in a cloak of that
gentleman's. He is tenderly watching over Henry Mill from
time to time, who is fast fading from the eyes of those who
love him.

March 15.—Mamma had an interesting little interview
with Henry Mill, and took him a bunch of *Bignonia sempervi-
rens* which he exceedingly admired, and thanked her warmly
for all the little kindnesses that had been shown him. He
peculiarly enjoys looking into the flowers, and wanted them

* Archdeacon of Lewes. He wrote a life of Sterling, who had once been his curate.

explained, so we sent him Lindley. Mamma led the conversation gradually into a rather more serious channel, and Henry Mill told Clara afterwards that her kind manner, her use of the words *thee* and *thou*, and her allusions to religious subjects quite overcame him, and he was on the point of bursting into tears. She gave him a hymn-book, and Clara marked one which she specially recommended—'As thy day, thy strength shall be.' For the last few evenings they have read him a psalm or some other part of Scripture.

March 16.—His eldest brother John is now come, and Clara brought him to see us this morning. He is a very uncommon-looking person—such acuteness and sensibility marked in his exquisitely chiselled countenance, more resembling a portrait of Lavater than any other that I remember. His voice is refinement itself, and his mode of expressing himself tallies with voice and countenance. He squeezed Papa's and Mamma's hands without speaking, and afterwards warmly thanked them for kindnesses received. 'Everything,' he said, 'had been done that the circumstances of the case admitted.' Henry received him with considerable calmness, and has at intervals had deeply interesting and relieving conversation with him. On Dr. Bullmore's coming in he sent the others out of the room, and asked him how long he thought he should last. 'Perhaps till the morning,' he answered. When the morning was past, and he was still in the body, he remarked to the doctor, 'I wish your prophecy had come true.'

March 17.—Saw John Stuart Mill after a morning spent in his brother's room, when they again had very interesting conversation as his strength permitted, particularly in giving many directions about his younger brother and sister, which from his own experience he thinks may prove useful to them. Indeed, his brother says, 'We have all we could desire of comfort in seeing him in this most tranquil, calm, composed, happy state.' He begs me to keep them informed of any autographs I wish to have, as he has great facilities for getting them. To-day he was to have met [François] Guizot* at the Grotes'.

March 20.—J. S. Mill says that Henry has passed another tranquil night; he delights in everything that speaks of life,

---

* French historian and statesman whose government fell in 1848.

watching the boys at play and the men with their telescopes, and sympathising with all. Cunningham is taking a likeness of him and trying to convey some sense of the beauty, refinement, and sentiment of the original. He was a good deal fatigued by the exertion of sitting. John Mill speaks thankfully of the tissue of circumstances which had located them here: amongst others, he said, was the pleasure of making John Sterling and us known to each other; for, said he, it is very delightful to introduce those who will appreciate each other. He talked enthusiastically of him; I remarked on his writing being much more obscure and involved than his conversation even on deep subjects. 'Yes,' he said, 'in talking you address yourself to the particular state of mind of the person with whom you are conversing, but in writing you speak as it were to an ideal object.' 'And then,' said I, 'you can't ask a book questions' which, I was proud to be informed, was what Plato had said before me, and on that ground accounted books of little value, and always recommended discussions. 'Certainly,' he added, 'it is of little use to read if you can form ideas of your own' (I suppose he meant on speculative subjects), 'but there is an exquisite delight in meeting with a something in the ideas of others answering to anything in your own self-consciousness; then you make the idea your own and never lose it.' He is a great botanist, so Anna Maria excited him about the luminous moss found in the cave at Argall; he informed us that the nature of all phosphoric lights is yet unknown, but it is generally believed to be an emission of light borrowed from the sun. We made a walking party to Pendennis Cavern, with which they were all delighted. Sterling . . . thought we had better have the passage in the cavern excavated, 'as you may very likely find the Regalia, for Charles II. was a very careless fellow.'

J. S. Mill proposed leaving the lighted candles there as an offering to the gnomes. He was full of interesting talk. A ship in full sail he declared the only work of man that under all circumstances harmonises with nature, the reason being that it is adapted purely to natural requirements . . .

March 21.—At breakfast Sterling heartily thanked Papa for the discussion of the other night; he had continued thinking on the subject, and had at last discovered a law for it, of which he had long been in search. The highest power of civilisation of any age can only be determined by contemplating the best minds of that age . . .

John Mill joined us at dinner, and Sterling came to tea . . . Oh! how much there was this evening of Poetry, of Truth, of Beauty . . .

March 22.—Took the pony to the Mills for Clara, who is troubled with asthma and a little cough; and joined by her brother, we went to Lake's to get a keepsake which Henry wanted for his little niece, something that would amuse her now but will be valuable afterwards. So we chose two volumes of the Naturalist's Library with coloured plates. He has sat again to-day to Cunningham with admirable result, though he feels it an exertion; he says, 'I think you would like to have it now.' He has been dividing all his things amongst his family, a deeply-affecting employment to them all. They think him growing decidedly weaker, and take it by watches to sit up with him; He'll just make a little remark sometimes, and then sink away into sleep or its semblance; so their nights pass. Clara has been collecting flowers, and they have been together pressing many of them: he says, 'this belongs to us two, and she is going to make it the foundation of a herbarium and the study of botany.' J. S. Mill gave a very interesting sketch of the political history of India . . . Sketched a curious character, the Begum Saumarooz, who, with the idea of taking Heaven by storm, has given large sums to the Protestants, Roman Catholics, and Mahometans. He gave many details of that horrid people the Thugs, 'that black passage of history.' . . . Henry has been sketching a little to-day, and displayed his work to Cunningham. He said afterwards, 'I wonder why I showed my sketch to him. I suppose it was to show the feeling of a fellow-artist.' Good conversation with Papa on the state of things in China, but too complicated for me to chronicle. Sterling described [Alfred] Count D'Orsay* coming to sketch Carlyle: a greater contrast could not possible be imagined; the Scotch girl who opened the door was so astonished at the apparition of this magnificent creature that she ran away in a fright, and he had to insinuate himself the best way he could through the narrow passage. He is the most fascinating person that ever

* Artist, wit and dandy; described by Byron as an ideal Frenchman of the *ancien régime.*

was, can make anything of anybody that he takes in hand; and the grand mistake of Sir 'Robert Peel, when the Lady-question was agitated, was not putting in his hands the business of negotiating it with the Queen!

March 23.—Took Clara a ride. Spoke much of her father and how he had entirely educated John and made him think prematurely, so that he never had the enjoyment of life peculiar to boys. He feels this a great disadvantage. He told us that his hair came off 'when you were quite a little girl and I was two-and-twenty.' He has such a funny habit of nodding when he is interested in any subject.

March 24.—John Mill joined us at dinner. Last night for an hour and a half Henry Mill conversed at intervals, partly about his past life, in which he thought he might have done more and done better; now, however, he hopes that his death may be of some use to others: he feels perfect confidence in looking to the future . . . Asked [John] whether he was going to write a review of Coleridge as a poet (he has lately written a wonderfully lucid article on his philosophical character); he said, 'No, those who would read Coleridge with pleasure seldom mistake his meaning or his character. Words-worth prepared peoples's minds for the higher flights of Coleridge, and now that his fame is recognised by the second generation, the true umpires, it must be permanent.'

March 25.—John Mill drew a parallel, by way of contrast, between his own character and Carlyle's; they are very intimate without much association. 'Mill has singularly little sense of the concrete,' says Sterling, 'and, though possessing deep feeling, has little poetry. He is the most scientific thinker extant—more than Coleridge was, more continuous and severe. Coleridge's silken thread of reasoning was sometimes broken, but then it was for the sake of interpolating a fillet of pure gold.'

March 26.—Dr. Calvert at breakfast in specially good spirits, and saying all sorts of funny things. He brought the portrait that Cunningham has taken of him—a beautiful thing, but, says he, 'not the Dr. Calvert that I shave every morning.' He was at Oriel College when he took his degree, where they were said to drink nothing but tea; nevertheless, they kept up the gentlemanly appearance of good living by rolling about in the quads, as royally as the men of Christchurch . . .

March 27.—Barclay desperately busy winding up affairs
and acquaintance. He did, however, manage to meet us at
Penjerrick, where Sterling, John Mill, Clara Mill, Anna
Maria, and I prepared an elegant luncheon *al fresco.* Walked
back not unpleasantly . . . They all went to Glendurgan;
they were excessively delighted with the drive, and in one
part, where there were a few trees, Sterling said, 'Why, really,
this reminds one of England.' He has heard from the Carlyles;
Mrs. Carlyle's letter was to this effect:—'Do come and see us!
Here are many estimable families.—J. C.' She plays all
manner of tricks on her husband, telling wonderful stories of
him in his presence, founded almost solely on her bright
imagination; he, poor man, panting for an opportunity to stuff
in a negation, but all to no purpose; having cut him up
sufficiently, she would clear the course. They are a very
happy pair. Carlyle and Edward Irving were schoolmasters at
Annan, formed an intimacy there, and Carlyle loved Irving to
the last, with all the ardour of an early affection; he deeply
regretted the weakness which he exhibited, and considered
that vanity was his friend's quicksand . . . They talked on
politics. I asked if they would really wish for a Radical
Government. Sterling explained that under existing circumstances it was impossible such a thing could be. John Mill
sighed out, 'I have long done what I could to prepare them
for it, but in vain; so I have given them up, and in fact they
have given up me.' He spoke of the extreme elation of spirits
he always experienced in the country, and illustrated it, with
an apology, by jumping.

On consumption, and the why it was so connected with
what is beautiful and interesting in nature. The disease itself
brings the mind as well as the constitution into a state of
prematurity, and this reciprocally preys on the body. After an
expressive pause, John Mill quietly said, 'I expect to die of
consumption.' I lectured him about taking a little more care
of himself. 'Why, it does not much signify in what form death
comes to us.' 'But time is important to those who wish to help
their fellow-creatures.' 'Certainly', he replied, 'it is pleasant to
do some little good in the world.' When Barclay joined us the
first question agitated was the influence of business
on literary pursuits. John Mill considers it the duty of life to

endeavour to reconcile the two, the active and the speculative; and from his own experience and observation the former gives vigour and system and effectiveness to the latter. He finds that he can do much more in two hours after a busy day, than when he sits down to write with time at his own command . . .

March 28.—A walk with John and Clara Mill to Pennance and Penrose . . . Talked about Barclay (who left for Wales this morning), and I said how glad I was that they had such open talk together yesterday. 'Why,' said he, 'yesterday's conversation made just the difference between my knowing and not knowing your brother . . . ' The process of unhooking a bramble made him philosophise on the power of turning annoyances into pleasure by undertaking them for your friends—genuine alchemy.

Then we went to Germany, inquired into the reason for the contemplative character of its inhabitants: he lays great stress on the influence of the domestic affections, which are so strong there, and so much called out by circumstances; then they are not continually striving to become rich or to appear so, as the English are, but settle down into quiet, contemplative habits, without an idea of happiness but what is subjective to themselves: this constant habit of carrying in themselves the elements of their happiness increases and gives a tranquil tone to it . . . He therefore likes the plan, now so much followed, of sending young men to German universities. Talked a good deal about Italy: the Italians carry with and in them such a sense of native dignity, the result of associating themselves with remembrances of Rome in its glory . . . Their great sensibility and emotion he ascribes to the general prevalence of music, and to the magnificence of their ceremonies. He wound up with Conversation Sharp's [Richard Sharp, Whig MP] enumeration of the true accomplishments for ladies—a love of reading and a love of walking.

March 29.—John Mill is going to concoct for me an almanack of the odours that scent the air, to be arranged chronologically according to the months, beginning with the laurel and ending with the lime. Speaking of motives, he said it is not well for young people to inquire too much into them, but rather let them judge of actions, lest seeing the wonderful mixture of high and low they should be discouraged: there is besides an egotism in self-depreciation . . .

Perran, April 1.—Dr. Calvert rode over, and spent an hour or two here. He saw Henry Mill yesterday, who asked him how soon Death was likely to appear. 'My dear fellow, I can't pretend to say, but I may tell you that you are not likely to suffer any more pain.' (When Dr. Calvert began to practise, a celebrated physician gave him this valuable piece of advice, 'Never say when you think a patient is going to die; nothing can be more dangerous, and you cannot predict with certainty.') Last night John Mill sat for hours at the foot of Calvert's bed, who had a racking headache, expatiating on the delights of John Woolman (which he is reading) ['A Quaker Journal'] and on spiritual religion, which he feels to be the deepest and truest. In this Dr. Calvert thoroughly delights . . .

April 2.—George Mill has arrived. John sitting for his portrait; fell into a reverie, and then into a doze; nevertheless the artist is hopeful. Today he spoke of Teetotalism; on first thoughts it seems such a ridiculous idea that people should associate and pledge themselves *not* to do a thing, but the rationale of the experiment develops itself afterwards. Glorious collection of autographs from Sterling with a kind note, and an exquisite little autograph poem of Wordsworth's.

April 4.—On returning from Truro, found that Henry Mill had quietly departed this morning at half-past ten; very sudden it was at the last.

April 5.—A great parcel arrived in the evening with John Mill's kind regards, containing all the *London and Westminster Reviews* from their beginning, with notes in his own hand, and the names of the writers attached to the articles—a most valuable and interesting gift.

April 6.—Dr. Calvert, in speaking of the great humility compatible with high metaphysical research, spoke of John Mill standing on one side, and himself on the other, of his brother's deathbed. Dr. Calvert remarked, 'This sort of scene puts an end to Reason, and Faith begins'; the other emphatically answered, 'Yes.' . . .

. . . Then the Friends became our topic; [Dr. Calvert] again extolled their code of laws, partly because they do not dogmatise on any point, do not peremptorily require belief in any articles. As to particular scruples, he would hold that circumstances should have the greatest effect in giving them a direction: in his own case, for instance, when living in a county where hunting is ruinously in vogue, he bore his testimony against it by neither riding nor lending his hunter; here he would not object to do either. So in George Fox's time, dress was probably made a subject of great importance; 'but,' he added, 'Satan probably tempts the Foxes of Falmouth in a very different way to that in which he attacked their spiritual ancestors; he is vastly too clever and fertile in invention to repeat the same experiment twice.'

April 7.—John Mill wanted to know all about the constitution and discipline of our Society (*à propos* of a quarterly meeting which is taking place here, some of our guests having, to our deep disappointment, scared them away, when they crept over last evening), then dilated on the different Friends' books he was reading; on John Woolman he philosophised on the principle that was active in him—that dependence on the immediate teaching of a Superior Being, which gave him clear views of what was essentially consistent or inconsistent with Christianity, independent of and often opposed to all recorded or common opinion, all self-interest. He had read Sewell [a Tractarian] and Rutty [a Quaker diarist] before he was ten years old. His father much admired Friends, thinking they did more for their fellow-creatures than any other Body. He was a warm coadjutor of William Allen's [Quaker Abolitionist] in promoting the Lancastrian Schools. He much admires the part Friends have taken about tithes, and values that testimony against a priesthood as at present organised. In a statistical table he has seen, the longest-lived professions are the Catholic priests, and the Protestants come very near them; the shortest are Kings and beggars.

The *London and Westminster Review* is to be continued by Mr. W. E. Hickson under the title of the *Westminster*: he declares himself a disciple of Mill's—'the first disciple I have ever had,' said John Mill but he believes his opinion to be very different in reality from his own . . .

April 9.—I received from Sterling letters from [Richard Chenevix] Trench,* Carlyle, and Coleridge. That of the latter was as follows:—

'My Dear Sterling,—With grief I tell you that I have been, and now am, worse—far worse than when you left me. God have mercy on me, and not withdraw the influence of His Spirit from me! I can now only thank you for your kind attentions to your most sincere and afflicted friend,

S. T. Coleridge.

'P.S.—Mr. Green is persuaded that it is gout, which I have not strength enough to throw from the nerves of the trunk to the extremities.

'Monday Afternoon.'

The date is March 18, 1833.

Sterling says he would not part with this except to a person he valued and who values S. T. C. All things considered, I thought it too precious a relic for me to keep, and returned it, (a moral conquest!).

Talked with the Mills over their father, and of many of their friends. Bentham was long their next-door neighbour— such a mild, good-natured person, always so kind to children. He and their father were very intimate, and they tried educational experiments on John! Many anecdotes of Carlyle; he has a peculiar horror of lion-hunting ladies. He will talk in a melancholy strain; entering with earnestness into the abuses, grievances, and mistakes into which men fall; deeply commiserating alike the oppressor and the oppressed—the former gaining rather more of his pity, as being further removed from what must constitute happiness.

April 10.—John Mill is summoned to town, and goes to-night; the rest leave to-morrow. They feel leaving Falmouth deeply, and say that no place out of London will be so dear to them. Now for some last glimpses at Truth through those wonderfully keen, quiet eyes. On education: his father's idea was to make children understand one thing thoroughly; this is not only a good exercise for the mind, but it creates in

---

* Archbishop of Dublin; a keen philologist, he suggested the Oxford English Dictionary.

themselves a standard by which to judge of their knowledge of other subjects, whether it is superficial or otherwise. He does not like things to be made too easy or too agreeable to children; the plums should not be picked out for them, or it is very doubtful if they will ever be at the trouble of learning what is less pleasant. For childhood, the art is to apportion the difficulties to the age, but in life there is no such adaptation. Life must be a struggle throughout; so let children, when children, learn to struggle manfully and overcome difficulties. His father made him study Ecclesiastical History before he was ten. This method of early intense application he would not recommend to others; in most cases it would not answer, and where it does, the buoyancy of youth is entirely superseded by the maturity of manhood, and action is very likely to be merged in reflection. 'I never was a boy,' he said; 'never played at cricket: it is better to let Nature have her own way.'

In his essays on French affairs he has infused more of himself than into any of his other writings—the whole subject of that country so deeply interests him . . . A Republic, even if right on the abstract principle of men being trustworthy of the charge of self-government, would never suit them; they must follow a leader, so an Elective Monarchy will be their probable form of government in after-years. The French care most for persons, the English for things . . . Then to America: He is thankful that the experiment of a Republic has been tried there; it has failed, and ever must fail, for want of the two contending powers which are always requisite to keep things in proper order—Government and Public Opinion. America subjects herself to the latter only, and public opinion there having decided in favour of one particular type of character, all aim at a resemblance to it, and a great sameness is the result. There is as much of tyranny in this process as in that more commonly so called. These two counteracting motive powers are essential to the well-being of a State; if either gains supremacy, it becomes, like a self-willed, unsubdued, spoilt being, very troublesome. Its experience in excess changes its nature from good to evil. On capital punishments: to which he entirely objects, and thinks with Carlyle that the worst thing you can do with a man is to hang him. John and Clara had been to visit

Henry's grave; it is just to have his name and age inscribed on the stone, no eulogy or epitaph. *'Henry Mill, aged 19'* is surely expressive enough for any one who will rightly read it. J. S. Mill gave me the calendar of odours, which he has written for the first time:—

A Calendar of Odours, being in imitation of the various calendars of Flora by Linnaeus and others.

The brilliant colouring of Nature is prolonged, with incessant changes, from March till October but the fragrance of her breath is spent before the summer is half ended. From March to July an uninterrupted succession of sweet odours fills the air by day and still more by night, but the gentler perfumes of autumn, like many of the earlier ones here for that reason omitted, must be sought ere they can be found. The Calendar of Odours, therefore, begins with the laurel, and ends with the lime.

March.—Common laurel.
April.—Violets, furze, wall-flower, common broad-leaved willow, apple-blossom.
May.—Lilac, night-flowering stocks and rockets, laburnum, hawthorn, seringa, sweet-briar.
June.—Mignonette, bean-fields, the whole tribe of summer roses, hay, Portugal laurel, various species of pinks.
July.—Common acacia, meadow-sweet, honeysuckle, sweet gale or double myrtle, Spanish broom, lime.

In latest autumn, one stray odour, forgotten by its companions, follows at a modest distance—the creeping clematis which adorns cottage walls but the thread of continuity being broken, this solitary straggler is not included in the Calendar of Odours.

To Miss Caroline Fox, from her grateful friend,

J. S. Mill

Talked of Uncle Charles; something about both his person and manners reminds him of Southey. Dr. Calvert sees it also. Mill was much pleased to come to such a little oasis as Perran, a spot so different to the general character of Cornwall . . .

Cunningham showed us his portrait of J. S. Mill, which is very beautiful; quite an ideal head, so expanded with patient thought, and a face of such exquisite refinement.

April 11.—Dr. Calvert says he prefers Hartley Coleridge's poetry to his father's, because he finds in it more thought and less imagination. Speaking of Dr. [Friedrich] Schleiermacher,* whom he enthusiastically admires, he described his death-hour, of which he was so conscious that he begged for the Sacrament, calling out, 'Quick, quick!' He administered it to himself and his family, and expired. This may be compared with Goethe's dying exclamation, 'Light, more light!'

April 13.—Dr. Calvert described old Lord Spencer† (whose travelling and family physician he was) looking over and burning one after another of the letters his wife had received from the most eminent persons of the day, because he thought it a crying modern sin to make biographies piquant and interesting by personalities not necessary to them; he therefore resolved to leave nothing of which his executors might make this ill use. At length he came to one from Nelson, written just after a great victory, and beginning with a pious ejaculation and recognition of the Arm by which he had conquered. Dr. Calvert snatched it out of his hand—it was on its way to the fire—and put it in his pocket, saying, 'My lord, here is nothing personal, nothing but what everybody knows, and burn it must not.' His lordship was silent. A few hours after, he said, 'Doctor, where is that letter which you put in your pocket?' 'Gone, my lord.' 'Indeed? I was wanting it.' 'I thought you probably would, so I immediately put it in the post-office and sent it to a young lady who is collecting autographs.'

April 17.—In the evening the Rev. T. Pyne was announced, introduced by the Buxtons, who proved to be the tutor and travelling companion of William Quantamissa and John Ansah, Prince of Ashantee, whose father had killed Sir C. MacCarthy‡ (a particular recommendation). They had just arrived at Falmouth and came to consult about plans, so Papa recommended them to go on to-morrow to Penzance and return here to stay next week. They are youths of

---

* German philosopher who attempted to construct a religion in which Kant, Spinoza and Christianity would be reconciled.
† First Lord of the Admiralty under Pitt; he sent Nelson to the Battle of the Nile.
‡ Governor of Sierra Leone; killed in a battle with the Ashantees, and not as Caroline relates.

seventeen and nineteen, tolerably intelligent, quite disposed to be haughty if that spirit is fostered, have been educated in England, and are now travelling with their eyes wide open. But more anon of 'these images of God cut in ebony.'

April 18.—Parcel and note from John Sterling. He encloses the letter from S. T. Coleridge, on which he has written, 'Given to Miss Caroline Fox by John Sterling,' to oblige me to keep it, and other letters of his to read; also his memoranda of his first conversation with S. T. C., which Hare considers the most characteristic he has seen.

April 21.—Met their Royal Highnesses and many others at Consols Mine; they were much delighted with the machinery . . . Yesterday they went sixty fathoms down Huel Vean and were much tired, but their Cornish exploration has charmed them. Each one keeps a journal, and a certain red memorandum-book which occasionally issues out of Mr. Pyne's pocket is a capital check on our little members. The Princes have unhappily imbibed the European fashion of sticking their hands through their hair, which, says Dr. Calvert, they might just as well try to do through velvet. Every one was pleasant and witty according to their measure.

April 22.—Took them up the river to Tregothnan. T. Pyne gave interesting details of a visit to Niagara, and the inquiries he instituted there concerning poor F[rancis] Abbott.* These were very satisfactory. His servant said that he used to sit up very late reading his Bible, and then meditate in silence for a long time. He also spoke of his extremely eccentric habits, hanging by his feet on a branch over the Falls.

April 24.—Our Ashantee friends enjoyed themselves thoroughly at Glendurgan, playing at cricket and leap-frog, and fishing. In the evening many joined our party, and all were amused with galvanism, blow-pipe experiments, and such like scientific pastimes until between eleven and twelve . . .

April 25.—We were a large party at breakfast, after which we had a capital walk to Pendennis. Mrs. Coope was in her chair, which the Princes seized and galloped off with up the steep hill. They mightily enjoyed playing with the cannon-balls . . . They laugh in a knowing manner when slavery is alluded to, and they left us this afternoon after a really

---

* Known as the Recluse of Niagara, who lived a hermit's life at the Falls, and was drowned in them while bathing.

pleasant visit.

April 26.—Barclay forwarded us the following letter from John Stuart Mill:—

India House, 16*th April* 1840.

'My Dear Friend (if you will allow me to adopt this "friendly" mode of address),—Your kind and sympathising letter has given us great pleasure. There is no use in my saying more than has been said already about him who has gone before us, where we must so soon follow; the thought of him is here, and will remain here, and seldom has the memory of one who died so young been such as to leave a deeper or a more beneficial impression on the survivors. Among the many serious feelings which such an event calls forth, there is always some one which impresses us most, some moral which each person extracts from it for his own more especial guidance; with me that moral is, "Work while it is called to-day; the night cometh in which no man can work". One never seems to have adequately *felt* the truth and meaning of all that is tritely said about the shortness and precariousness of life, till one loses some one whom one had hoped not only to carry with one as a companion through life, but to leave as a successor after it. Why he who had all his work to do has been taken, and I left who had done part of mine, and in some measure, as Carlyle would express it, "delivered my message," passes our wisdom to surmise. But if there be a purpose in this, that purpose, it would seem, can only be fulfilled in so far as the remainder of my life can be made even more useful than the remainder of his would have been if it had been spared. At least we know this, that on the day when we shall be as he is, the whole of life will appear but as a day, and the only question of any moment to us then will be, Has that day been wasted? Wasted it has not been by those who have been for however short a time a source of happiness and of moral good, even to the narrowest circle. But there is only one plain rule of life eternally binding, and independent of all variations in creeds, and in the interpretations of creeds, embracing equally the greatest moralities and the smallest; it is this—try thyself unweariedly till thou findest the highest thing thou art capable of doing, faculties and outward circumstances being duly considered, and then DO IT.

'You are very kind to say what you have said about those reviews; the gift of unsold copies of an old periodical could under no circumstances have called for so warm an expression of thanks, and would have deserved an opposite feeling if I could not say, with the utmost sincerity, that I do not expect you to read much of it or any of it unless thereunto moved. My principal feeling in the matter was this, You are likely to hear of some of the writers, and judging of your feelings by what my own would be, I thought it might be sometimes agreeable to you to be able to turn to something they had written and imagine what manner of persons they might be. As far as my own articles are concerned, there was also a more selfish pleasure in thinking that sometimes, however rarely, I might be conversing with my absent friends at three hundred miles' distance.

'We scribblers are apt to put not only our best thoughts, but our best feelings, into our writings, or at least if the things are *in* us they will not *come out of us* so well or so clearly through any other medium and therefore when one really wishes to be *liked* (it is only when one is very young that one cares about being admired), it is often an advantage to us when our writings are better known than ourselves.

'As to these particular writings of mine, all in them that has any pretension to permanent value will, I hope, during the time you are in London, be made into two little volumes, which I shall offer to no one with greater pleasure than to you. The remainder is mostly politics—of little value to any one now—in which, with considerable expenditure of head and heart, an attempt was made to breathe a living soul into the Radical party, but in vain—there was no making those dry bones live. Among a multitude of failures, I had only one instance of brilliant success. It is some satisfaction to me to know that, as far as such things can ever be

said, I saved Lord Durham,*—as he himself, with much
feeling, acknowledged to me, saying that he knew not
to what to ascribe the reception he met with on his
return from Canada, except to an article of mine which
came out immediately before. If you were to read that
article now, you would wonder what there was in it to
bear out such a statement but the *time* at which it
appeared was everything; every one's hand seemed to
be against him, no one dared speak a word for him; the
very men who had been paying court and offering
incense to him for years before (I never had) shrunk
away or ventured only on a few tame and qualified
phrases of excuse—not, I verily believe, from cowardice
so much as because, not being accustomed to think
about *principles* of politics, they were taken by surprise
in a contingency which they had not looked for, and
feared committing themselves to something they could
not maintain; and if this had gone on, opinion would
have decided against him so strongly, that even that
admirable Report of his and [Charles] Buller's† could
hardly have turned the tide and unless some one who
could give evidence of thought and knowledge of the
subject had thrown down the gauntlet at that critical
moment, and determinedly claimed honour and glory
for him instead of mere acquittal, and in doing this
made a diversion in his favour, and encouraged those
who wished him well to speak out, and so kept people's
minds *suspended* on the subject, he was in all probability
a lost man; and if I had not been the man to do this,
nobody else would. And three or four months later the
Report came out, and then everybody said I had been
right, and now it is being acted upon.
    'This is one of only three things, among all I
attempted in my reviewing life, which I can be said to
have succeeded in. The second was to have greatly
accelerated the success of Carlyle's "French Revolution," a book so strange and incomprehensible to the

* MP. On being denounced as high-handed, he resigned as governor-general of
British provinces in North America.
† Liberal politician; Durham's secretary in Canada.

greater part of the public, that whether it should succeed or fail seemed to depend on the turn of a die; but I got the first word,* blew the trumpet before it at its first coming out, and by claiming for it the honours of the highest genius, frightened the small fry of critics from pronouncing a hasty condemnation, got fair-play for it, and then its success was sure.

'My *third* success is that I have dinned into people's ears that Guizot is a great thinker and writer, till they are, though slowly, beginning to read him, which I do not believe they would be doing even yet, in this country, but for me.

'This, I think, is a full account of all the world has got by my editing and reviews.

'Will you pardon the egotism of this letter? I really do not think I have talked so much about myself in the whole year previous as I have done in the few weeks of my intercourse with your family; but it is not a fault of mine generally, for I am considered reserved enough by most people, and I have made a very solemn resolution, when I see you again, to be more *objective* and less *subjective* in my conversation (as Calvert says) than when I saw you last. — Ever yours faithfully, J. S. Mill.

'It seems idle to send remembrances; they saw enough to know I am not likely to forget them.'

May 2.—Dr. Calvert dined with us on the lawn at Penjerrick, amidst a party of schoolboys. He spoke of having made up his mind not to expect anything positive in life, and he has found great comfort in this conclusion . . .

May 7.—[Dr. Calvert] says that at Falmouth he has met with two new and most interesting facts, John Mill and Grandmamma. The satisfaction he derives from finding that the experience of the latter—an aged and earnest Christian— tallies often with his own theories, is extreme.

London, May 19.—We had heard much of Thomas Carlyle from enthusiastic admirers, and his book on Chartism had not lessened the excitement with which I anticipated seeing and hearing him. These anticipations were realised at the lecturing-room in Edward Street [off Cavendish Square]. We

* But he fails to recall that Carlyle's first MS of Volume One was burnt when he lent it to Mrs Taylor (later his wife) whose servant laid the grate with it!

sat by Harriet Mill, who introduced us to her next neighbour, Mrs. Carlyle, who kindly asked us to come to them any evening, as they would both be glad to see us. The audience, amongst whom we discovered Whewell, Samuel Wilberforce and his beautiful wife, was very thoughtful and earnest in appearance; it had come to hear the Hero portrayed in the form of the Man of Letters.* Carlyle soon appeared, and looked as if he felt a well-dressed London crowd scarcely the arena for him to figure in as popular lecturer. He is a tall, robust-looking man; rugged simplicity and indomitable strength are in his face, and such a glow of genius in it—not always smouldering there, but flashing from his beautiful grey eyes, from the remoteness of their deep setting under the massive brow. His manner is very quiet, but he speaks like one tremendously convinced of what he utters, and who had much—very much—in him that was quite unutterable, quite unfit to be uttered to the uninitiated ear; and when the Englishman's sense of beauty or truth exhibited itself in vociferous cheers, he would impatiently, almost contemptuously, wave his hand, as if that were not the sort of homage which Truth demanded. He began in a rather low nervous voice, with a broad Scotch accent, but it soon grew firm, and shrank not abashed from its great task. In this lecture, he told us . . .

Returned with Harriet Mill from Carlyle's lecture to their house in Kensington Square, where we were most lovingly received by all the family. John Mill was quite himself. He had in the middle of dinner to sit still for a little to try and take in that we are really here. A good deal of talk about Carlyle and his lectures: he never can get over the feeling that people have given money to hear him, and are possibly calculating whether what they hear is worth the price they paid for it. Walked in the little garden, and saw the Falmouth plants which Clara cherishes so lovingly, and Henry's cactus and other dear memorials. Visited John Mill's charming library, and saw portions of his immense herbarium; the mother so anxious to show everything, and her son so terribly afraid of boring us. He read us that striking passage in 'Sartor Resartus' on George Fox making to himself a suit of leather.

* A series of lectures published in 1841 as *On Heroes, Hero-Worship, and the Heroic in History*.

How his voice trembled with excitement as he read, 'Stitch away, thou noble Fox,' &c. They spoke of some of the eccentricities of their friend Mrs. Grote, whom Sydney Smith declares to be the origin of the word 'Grotesque.' Several busts of Bentham were shown, and some remark being made about him, John Mill said, 'No one need feel any delicacy in canvassing his opinions in my presence;' this indeed his review sufficiently proves. Mrs Mill gave us Bentham's favourite pudding at dinner!

After a most happy day we walked off, John Mill accompanying us through the Park. He gave his version of John Sterling's history. In early life he had all the beautiful peculiarities and delicacies of a woman's mind. It at length dawned upon him that he had a work of his own to accomplish; and earnestly, and long unsuccessfully, did he strive to ascertain its nature. All this time he was restless and unhappy, under the sense that doing it he was not. This lasted till his returning voyage from the West Indies, where his patience and perseverance, his earnestness and sincerity, received their reward; he saw the use he might be to others, in establishing and propagating sound principles of action, and since that time he has known quietness and satisfaction. Though his writings are such as would do credit to anybody, yet they are inferior to his conversation; he has that rare power of throwing his best thoughts into it and adapting them to the comprehension of others. John Mill wrote him the other day that he would gladly exchange powers of usefulness with him . . .

May 22.—To Carlyle's lecture . . .

Upton, May 24. [Caroline's 21st birthday]—The Buxtons dined here to-day, and after dinner Thomas Fowell Buxton addressed the assembly on the subject of the Anti-Slavery Meeting next month, which he thinks it is the duty of Friends to attend. Prince Albert has become President, the first Society which he has patronised. Afterwards, walking in the garden with Barclay and me, he talked much more about it, regretting the scruples of many as to the armed vessels which are to accompany the Niger Expedition; he thinks their arguments apply equally to mail-coach travelling . . . John Pease* gave us a striking sermon this evening, on which

* Prominent Quaker minister known as 'the silver trumpet of the north'.

Fowell Buxton remarked that he exceeded in true eloquence—that is, in fluency, choice of language, and real
feeling—any man he had ever heard.

May 25.—This afternoon the young Buxton party returned
from Rome; their advent was performed in characteristic
fashion. Fowell Buxton was sauntering in the Park when a
bruit reached him that they were approaching; so he flung his
legs across the back of a coach-horse which crossed his path,
with blinkers and harness on but no saddle, and thus
mounted flew to the house shouting, 'They are come!' so the
family were fairly aroused to give such a welcome as Gurneys
well know how to give.

London, May 28.—Met Dr. Calvert in Finsbury, and had
some quiet talk in the midst of that vast hubbub. He has been
seeing Sir James Clark* about John Sterling, and has written
the latter a letter, which will drive all Italian plans out of his
head. In his case it is the morale rather than the physique
that must always be attacked, and a quiet winter in Cornwall
with his family would be vastly better for him than the
intoxication of Italy. Went with him to meet the Mills at the
India House† . . . Surveyed the Museum, wherein are
divers and great curiosities: the confirmation of the Charter
to the East India Company in Cromwell's own hand . . .
Then to the apartment of our host, where in all comfort he
can arrange the government of the native states, raising some
and putting down others. The political department of the
East India House is divided into six classes, of which this is
one. They have their Horse-guards in another part of the
same immense building, which was built for the accommoda-
tion of four or five thousand, the population of the capital of
Norway, to which number it amounted in its most prosperous
days; now there are but two or three hundred. As we had a
few hours at our disposal, we thought it a pity not to spend
them together, so we travelled off to the Pantheon [in Oxford
Street; used as a bazaar]. John Mill very luminous all the way,
spite of the noise. He considers the differences in national
character one of the most interesting subjects for science and
research. Thus the French are discovered to possess so much
nationality; every great man amongst them is, in the first

---

* Court physician; unpopular for his part in the case of Lady Flora Hastings.
† Correctly, East India House, in which both Lamb and Mill started as clerks.

place, essentially a Frenchman, whatever he may have
appended to that character. The individuality of the English,
on the other hand, makes them little marked by qualities in
common; each takes his own road and succeeds by his own
merits. The French are peculiarly swayed by a leader, and so
he be a man of talent, he can do anything with them. Custom
and public opinion are the rulers in England. Any man of
any pretension is sure to gather some disciples around him in
this country, but can never inspire a universal enthusiasm.
The French take in all that is new and original sooner than
others, but rarely originate anything themselves; and when
they have sufficiently diluted it, they re-introduce it to
Europe . . . The Germans are the most tolerant people
breathing, because they seem to form a community entirely
for the development and advancement of truth; thus they hail
all as brothers who will throw any light on their demi-god,
through however obscure and discountenanced a
medium . . . The macaws and gold-fish of the Pantheon
prevented further settled conversation, but I think I had my
share for one day.

May 29.—The Mills, Mrs. King, and W. E. Forster to
breakfast. We had a snug time till eleven, and took advantage
of it. Talked of the influence of the love of approbation on all
human affairs; Mill derives it from a craving for sympathy.
Discussed the value of good actions done from mixed or bad
motives—such as dread of public opinion: this dread is a very
useful whipper-in, it makes nine-tenths of those affected by it
better than they would otherwise be, the remaining tenth
worse; because the first class dare not act below the standard,
the second dare not act above it . . . John Mill has a
peculiar antipathy to hunting the hare . . . he has never
attended races either. We all went off together, John Mill
going with us to the door of Devonshire House, evolving his
'clear because profound truths (as he calls Guizot's) in a
crystal stream, his spirit's native tongue.' . . .

June 3.—Spent the evening at the Mills', and met the
Carlyles and Uncle and Aunt Charles. Conversation so
flowed in all quarters that I could not gain any continuous
idea of what took place in the most remarkable ones, but
what I did catch was the exposition of Carlyle's argument
about the progressive degeneracy of our lower classes, and its

'Elizabeth Fry entering Newgate': painting by
Henrietta Ward

Top. Anti-Slavery Convention, London, June 1840. Thomas Clarkson, President of the Convention is speaking

Bottom. 'A Chelsea Interior' by Robert Tait, *c.* 1857: Thomas and Jane Carlyle at home

only obvious remedies, education and emigration: about Ireland and its sad state, and how our sins towards it react on ourselves; but it was to the Condition-of-England question that his talk generally tended. He seems to view himself as the apostle of a certain democratic idea, bound over to force it on the world's recognition. He spoke of George Fox's 'Journal': 'That's not a book one can read through very easily, but there are some deep things in it, and well worth your finding.' They had some talk on the teetotal societies, and his laugh at some odd passages was most hilarious. Mrs. Carlyle was meanwhile giving Aunt Charles some brilliant female portraiture, but all in caricature. Speaking of her husband in his lecturing capacity, she said 'It is so dreadful for him to try to unite the characters of the prophet and the mountebank; he has keenly felt it; and also he has been haunted by the wonder whether the people were not considering if they had had enough for their guinea.' At last we were going, but our postillion was fast asleep on the coach-box. Barclay gave him an intimation of our presence, to which he languidly replied, 'All right,' but in a voice that showed clearly that it was all wrong. We asked for a hackney coach, but J. S. Mill was delightfully ignorant as to where such things grew, or where a likely hotel was to be found; and as our culprit was now a little sobered by fright and evening air, and passionately pleaded wife and children, we ventured forward, Barclay and J. Mill walking for a long way beside us.

June 13.—Went with the Mills to the Anti-Slavery Meeting at Exeter Hall, and had capital places assigned us. It was soon immensely crowded, and at eleven we were all ordered to take off our hats, as Prince Albert and an illustrious train appeared on the platform. The acclamations attending his entry were perfectly deafening, and he bore them all with calm, modest dignity, repeatedly bowing with considerable grace. He certainly is a very beautiful young man, a thorough German, and a fine poetical specimen of the race. He uttered his speech in a rather low tone, and with the prettiest foreign accent. As the history of the meeting is in print, I need not go into details of the brilliant set of speakers to whom we listened. Fowell Buxton's was a very fine, manly speech; and the style in which he managed the public feeling on O'Connell's entrance greatly raised my notion of his talent and address. Samuel Wilberforce's was a torrent of eloquence, seeking and finding a fitting vent. The Prince's eyes were riveted upon him. Sir Robert Peel's demeanour was calm, dignified, and statesmanlike; the expression of his face I did not like, it was so very supercilious. He was received with shouts of applause, and truly it is a fine thing to have him enlisted in the enterprise. Lord Northampton was very agreeable, speaking as the representative of British science, which he hoped might have a new field opened in Africa. Sir Thomas Acland was manly and energetic, and would make himself heard and felt. Lord Ashley,* a very handsome young noble, spoke well and worthily. Guizot [now French Ambassador in London] was on the platform; his face is very interesting, illustrating what John Mill said the other day about every great Frenchman being first essentially French, whatever else might be superadded. Guizot's head and face are indisputably French, but 'de première qualité.' He entered with much animation into the spirit of the occasion, nodding and gesticulating in unison with the speakers. O'Connell seemed heartily to enjoy the triumph of his own presence; though not permitted to speak, a large minority of the audience would hardly allow any one else to address them whilst he was silent. The meeting was altogether considered a most triumphant one; the Prince's appearance, the very first as patron of any benevolent enterprise, is likely to tell well on other countries; and the unanimity of so many parties in resolving to try this great commercial experiment in Africa was most encouraging.

Clifton, July 17.—Whilst driving we met a fly, which hailed us right cheerily, and to our no small delight and surprise, John Sterling issued forth and warmly greeted us. So Anna Maria got in with his wife, and he joined us; they had been paying Mamma a visit at Combe, and were now wandering forth in search of us. He looks well, and was very bright. He has been more with the Carlyles than any one else in London, and reports that he is writing his lectures for publication—the first time he has done so.

July 18.—We went off to the Sterlings'. He did the honours of a capital breakfast very completely, during which conver-

---

* Better known as Lord Shaftesbury. He worked ceaselessly for the poor and oppressed. Eros, in Piccadilly Circus, was erected to his memory.

sation, even on high matters, was not suspended. Methinks Sterling's table-talk would be as profitable reading as Coleridge's. . . . On Carlyle; his low view of the world proceeding partly from a bad stomach. The other day he was, as often, pouring out the fulness of his indignation at the quackery and speciosity of the times. He wound up by saying, 'When I look at this, I determine to cast all tolerance to the winds.' Sterling quickly remarked, 'My dear fellow, I had no idea you had any to cast.' . . . Sterling then showed us portfolios of engravings, out of which he gave Anna Maria a beautiful Rubens, and me a drawing of an ideal head by Benedetto, Guercino's master. On my remonstrating against such overpowering generosity, he said, 'As that is the only drawing I have, my collection will be much more complete without it.' His engravings of Michael Angelo's pictures are sublime. He has that wonderful figure of Jeremiah and another hung up in the drawing-room. He was saying something about them one day to Julius Hare, who answered, 'Yes, I should admire those two pictures of him as you do, only they remind me of two passages in the life of W. S. Landor which I have witnessed: the first, Landor scolding his wife; the second, his lamentation over the absence of a favourite dish of oysters!' . . .

Julius Hare was the translator of those tales from Tieck which I have. Hare met Tieck once, and reference being made to his translation, Tieck thought that he would have found some of the rhapsodical parts very difficult to render, but afterwards agreed with Hare that the soft, delicate touches and shades of feeling and opinion with which he abounds must have required the more careful handling. Madame de Staël was regretting to Lord Castlereagh that there was no word in the English language which answered to their *'sentiment.'* 'No,' he said, 'there is no English word, but the Irish have one that corresponds exactly—"blarney".' Considering who the interlocutors were, this was inimitable. It is supposed to be Lord Castlereagh's one good thing. Then he showed a beautiful portrait of Guizot, so like him. The other day Guizot was sitting at dinner next a Madame M—, who has just written a novel, on which she imagines herself to have founded a literary reputation. She wished to extend a little patronage to her next neighbour, so began, 'Et vous,

Monsieur, est-ce que vous avez écrit quelque chose?' 'Oui, Madame, quelques brochures,' was the cool reply . . .

[Sterling] told us a story which Samuel Wilberforce mentioned to him the other day. The Archbishop of Canterbury was examining a Girls' National School, and not being a man of ready speech, he ran through the gamut of suitable openings: 'My dear young friends—My dear girls—My dear young catechumens—My dear Christian friends—My dear young female women:' the gamut goes no higher.

July 21.—John Sterling appeared at breakfast. Last night he was very much exhausted, for, as it was his birthday, his children expected him first to play wolf, and afterwards to tell them stories . . . Asked him concerning his belief in ghosts: 'Of course I believe in them. We are all spectres; the difference between us is that some can see themselves as well as others. We are all shadows in the magic lanthorn of Time.' When S. T. Coleridge was asked the same question, he replied, 'No, ma'am, I've seen too many of them.' Then we gravely discussed the subject: he imagines the number of cases in favour of the common belief in ghosts to bear no proportion to those where ideal ghosts have been seen and no answering reality or coincidence to be found . . .

August 3.—J. Sterling has made up his mind not to go to Italy.

Falmouth, August 7.—Dr. Bowring paid us a charming little visit . . . He spoke of Mill with evident contempt as a renegade from philosophy, Anglicè—renouncer of Bentham's creed and an expounder of Coleridge's. S. T. Coleridge's mysticism Dr. Bowring never could understand, and characterises much of his teaching as a great flow of empty eloquence, to which no meaning was attachable. Mill's newly-developed 'Imagination' puzzles him not a little; he was most emphatically a philosopher, but then he read Wordsworth, and that muddled him, and he has been in a strange confusion ever since, endeavouring to unite poetry and philosophy.

Dr. Bowring has lately had to look over multitudes of James Mill's, Bentham's, and Romilly's* letters, in which there are many allusions to the young prodigy who read Plato at five years old. The elder Mill was stern, harsh, and

* Reformist lawyer, Abolitionist and supporter of Catholic Emancipation.

sceptical. Bentham said of him, 'He rather hated the ruling few than loved the suffering many.' He was formerly a Scotch farmer, patronised for his mental power by Sir John Stuart [of Fettercairn], who had the credit of directing his education. For Carlyle Dr. Bowring professes a respect, in so far as he calls people's attention, with some power, to the sufferings of the many, and points out where sympathy is wanted; but he regards him as ignorant of himself and sometimes of his meaning, for his writings are full of odd, unintelligible entanglements. and all truth is simple. 'The further men wander from simplicity, the further are they from Truth.' This is the last of Dr. Bowring's recorded axioms. He is Bentham's executor, and is bringing out a new edition of his works. He lives in the Queen's Square, where Milton's house still stands, and the garden in which he mused still flourishes, as much as London smoke will let it.

August 18.—At Helston called on the Derwent Coleridges. He is much interested in Carlyle, though of course he does not sympathise with him in many things. He thinks his style has the faultiness peculiar to self-taught men . . .

August 20.—Dined at the Taylors' to meet a very agreeable Prussian family, the Count and Countess Beust . . . The Countess talked about Schlegel . . . He gives a course of lectures every year, sometimes for gentlemen only, with a licence to a few to bring their wives; at others only for ladies, with a similar proviso for some husbands . . .

1841

Falmouth, January 27.—To our great surprise and pleasure, Dr. Calvert suddenly appeared amongst us; though only an hour landed, he declared himself already better for Falmouth air: certainly he looks better.

January 31.—Dr. Calvert has been taking a malicious pleasure in collecting primroses and strawberry flowers to send to his sister as evidences of climate. Talked of Carlyle . . . None but those of great buoyancy and vigour of constitution should. he thinks. subject themselves to his depressing influences. Carlyle takes an anxious forlorn view of his own physical state, and said to him one day, 'Well, I can't wish Satan anything worse than to try to digest for all eternity with my stomach; we shouldn't want fire and brimstone then.'

February 8.—A thaw came on, and Dr. Calvert crept in . . . Papa and he agree in believing that the doings of this world, and the phenomena we call action and reaction, are but manifestations of some great cyclical law, profoundly unknown but not unfelt.

February 18.—Our afternoon visit to Bank House was enlivened by Dr. Calvert's presence and occasional outbreak into words . . . I am exceedingly enjoying Boz's 'Master Humphrey's Clock,' which is still in progress. That man is carrying out Carlyle's work more emphatically than any; he forces the sympathies of all into unwonted channels, and teaches us that Punch and Judy men, beggar children, and daft old men are also of our species, and are not, more than ourselves, removed from the sphere of the heroic. He is doing a world of good in a very healthy way.

March 3.—Dr. Calvert announces the coming of his friend Sterling next week. He talked of their first intercourse in Madeira. John Sterling had heard of him as eccentric and fancied him Calvinistic, and in fact did not fancy him. They met at the house of a very worthy lady, who argued with Sterling on points connected with Calvinism. Dr. Calvert was a silent listener, but at last shoved a German book which he was reading right under John Sterling's nose, the significance of which made him start and see that he had read him wrongly. A warm friendship almost instantly resulted, and they soon took up their abode together.

March 6.—Dr. Calvert told us interesting things of the Jesuits. When he was ill in Rome, one came to him and begged to be made useful in any way. 'Thank you, sir, I have a servant; pray don't trouble yourself.' 'Sir, my profession is to serve.' They are picked men from childhood, and brought up at every stage in the strictest school of unquestioning submission to authority and a fixed idea. The Roman Catholic priests are always better or worse than the Protestant clergy— either intensely devoted to God and their neighbour, or sly, covetous, and sensual.

March 7.—Little Tweedy and Bastian, two beautiful boy-children, to dinner; the theory of the latter concerning his majority is that in twenty months from this time (he being now of the mature age of four) he shall awake and find himself a man. He concludes he shall have to pass three days in bed whilst new clothes are being made.

March 13.—The Doctor at breakfast again; he actually drinks tea like any other Christian. He talks of going to Kynance or somewhere to rusticate for a little, probably as a place of refuge. He described the present Lord Spencer's mode of proceeding when his good-nature has been grossly imposed on. A confidential butler was discovered to have omitted paying the bills for which he had received about £2000; this came to light in an investigation preparatory to settling a life annuity on him. Dr. Calvert asked Lord Spencer, 'Well, what shall you do now?' 'Oh, I shall settle the annuity on his wife: I can't afford to lose £2000 and my temper besides.' . . .

March 16.—A nice long gossiping breakfast visit from Dr. Calvert. He has made up his mind to go to Penzance and see how it suits him. We shall miss him much . . .

March 18.—The Doctor went away this morning, leaving a farewell note. He speaks of half envying a simple friend of ours who told him this morning that she had never been further than Redruth, and on his asking her if she were born here (meaning Falmouth, not his house), she answered, 'Oh no, sir, down below in the town.'

March 29.—Barclay heard from Sterling on his way to Torquay. He writes in the highest terms of Carlyle's volume of lectures; thinks it more popular, and likely to do more good than any of his other books.

April 10.—At about seven o'clock, what was our delight and astonishment to meet John Sterling in the drawing-room, just come per *Sir Francis Drake* steamer, looking well, though anything but vigorous, and going almost directly to Dr. Calvert. We exchanged the warmest, kindliest greetings, and he agreed to lodge here; so we had an evening with plenty of talk. I wish I could preserve something of the form of Sterling's eloquence as well as the subject of it . . .

April 11.—Got up at six o'clock to make coffee for Sterling. As the talk fell on Luther, he sketched a fine imaginary picture of him at the moment of seeing his friend struck by lightning . . .

April 19.—Between the hours of nine and ten, Sterling returned from Penzance. He is come to look at some habitations with an eye to inhabitancy. He told us Dr. Calvert has been depressed and poorly for some time . . . A drawing of Shelley being produced, he remarked, 'What an absence of solidity in the expression of that face!' When at college, Sterling had venerated and defended Shelley as a moralist as well as a poet, 'being rather youthy.' Whenever Shelley attempted to enter into a real human character, it was a monstrous one—the Cenci, for instance. He was only at home and freely breathing in a quite abstract empyrean. Shelley's head was most strangely shaped—quite straight at the back.

April 20.—Sterling asked if we had seen 'Trench on the Parables,' a very interesting work, though he cannot sympathise with the idea that every expression and every feature in the parables is intended to bear a moral significance, but thinks they are often added for the completeness and picturesqueness of the story. Some talk on capital punishment; his views much more worthy of him than last year. Of the many mysteries in Germany and elsewhere: after thoroughly examining the subject, he believes that Kaspar Häuser* was an impostor. The Iron Mask much more fascinating, but unluckily there was no prince in Europe missing at the time . . . Talked about men of science; he does not wish to attend the British Association; such would be the hurry and bustle, that it would only be like intercourse on a treadmill. He called Whewell (with whom he is well acquainted) a great mass of prose, a wonderful collection of facts. Whewell once declared that he could see no difference between mechanic and dynamic theories, and yet the man reads Kant, has domesticated some of his ideas, and thinks himself a German. Sedgwick he owns to be of a different stamp, a little vein of genius running through his granite. He knows the Countess Beust well; she was the woman at Bonn whose manners he thought most calculated to make society agreeable. Schlegel had clear poetic feeling and a fine insight, which enabled him to give those masterly criticisms on Shakespeare, till Madame de Staël came in his way, and by her plaudits of 'société, esprit,' &c., he learnt to think that for such things man was to

---

* A boy who appeared in Nuremberg in 1828 as if from nowhere; he was thought to be Crown Prince of Baden; legal proceedings lasted long after his death in 1833.

live! He has therefore turned his energies all that way, and is now about the vainest man in Europe. Beau Brummel once plaintively remarked, 'The ladies! they ruin all my wigs by begging locks.' When Calvert reads 'Tom Thumb,' he (Sterling) betakes himself to Molière. He thinks 'The Misanthrope' his best, and considers that all the din and stir of French Revolutionism is prefigured in it . . .

April 26.—At about one o'clock J. Sterling entered and announced that he had bought Dr. Donnelly's house! How little did we think of such a climax a month since, and even now I can't realise it. They intend moving early in the summer . . . After a very interesting hour or two, we separated.

April 29.—Very bright note from Sterling with reference to his talk with Mamma about dress. He says, 'I would cut off all my buttons to please her.'

May 5.—J. Sterling arrived last evening. We went all over his comfortable house with him, and were his assistants in choosing papers, positions of store cupboards, and other important arrangements. He spent the evening here. Much pleasant conversation, but little to record . . .

May 6.—Busy gardening at 'Sterling Castle'; after which its Governor joined us in a sauntering ride. He was talking much to-day of his own early life, when he took a step which he has never regretted. His parents designed him for the Bar, and raised their hopes high on this foundation; but when he decided that he could not honestly accept this for his profession, because he knew well how specially dangerous to his temperament would be the snare of it, he had to disappoint them . . .

May 7.—J. Sterling busy gardening with us: talked over many people. Of Buxton's Civilisation Scheme*: he has little faith that the savages of Africa will perceive the principles of political economy, when we remember the fact that the highly educated classes of England oppose the alteration of the Corn Laws . . .

May 8.—To-day Father received a letter from Captain James Ross, informing him that they have discovered the South Magnetic Pole, a result they could not have attained

* In which T. Fowell Buxton (see June 12, 1838) advocated repression of the African slave-trade.

without Papa's Deflector.

On Hartley Coleridge and his beautiful introduction to Massinger: S. T. Coleridge once said to Sterling that Hartley often exhibited a sort of flat-sharpness, which he did not think he derived from him, but probably picked up from Southey. He thinks that about 'Genius not descending like Scrofula' is a signal instance of it . . .

May 10.—Amusing day. J. Sterling has a friend and connection here, a Mr. Lawrence, an Indian judge [later Viceroy of India], and he brought him to call. India the principal topic . . . Lawrence spoke of the stationary kind of progress which Christianity was making amongst them. When a native embraces this new creed he retains his old inveterate prejudices, and superadds only the liberty of the new faith. This Lawrence has repeatedly proved—so much so, that he would on no account take one of these converts into his service; all his hope is in the education of the children, who are bright and intelligent. The Indians will, from politeness, believe all you tell them; if you speak of any of Christ's miracles they make no difficulty, but directly detail one more marvellous, of which Mahomet was the author, and expect your civility of credence to keep pace with theirs. If you try to convince them of any absurdities and inconsistencies in the Koran, they stop you with, 'Do you think that such an one as I should presume to understand it?' Sterling remarked, 'Have you never heard anything like that in England?'

May 13.—Of his friend Julius Hare, and the novelties of spelling which he has ventured on, Sterling remarked that his principle is to keep up the remembrance of the original root of the words; thus, he would retain the *u* in honour, to remind us of its French extraction. Our language wants weeding greatly, and the right meaning of words should be restored by any one able and willing for the task. Voltaire did wonders for French in this way.

May 16.—Pleasant visit from Sterling and Lawrence. Dr. Calvert has had a sad illness, and is coming here: Sterling will stay and nurse him. He has just heard from Carlyle, who says that the problem which of all others puzzles him is whether he is created for a Destroyer or a Prophet. (Is he not both, and must not every great man, if a Destroyer, be also a

Builder?) . . .

May 20.—After a busy morning at Falmouth and Flushing,
Sterling offered to take us back to Penjerrick in his car. He
said, 'You must see many eminent persons; why don't you
make notes of their appearance as well as their conversation?'
The idea being good, I'll try my hand.—John Sterling is a
man of stature, not robust, but well-proportioned; hair brown
and clinging closely round his head; complexion very pale,
eyes grey, nose beautifully chiselled, mouth very expressive.
His face is one expressing remarkable strength, energy, and
refinement of character. In argument he commonly listens to
his antagonist's sentiments with a smile, less of conscious
superiority than of affectionate contempt (if such a combination may be)—I mean what would express, 'Poor dear! she
knows no better!' In argument on deep or serious subjects,
however, he looks earnest enough, and throws his ponderous
strength into reasoning and feeling: small chance then for the
antagonist who ventures to come to blows! He can make him
and his arguments look so small; for, truth to tell, he dearly
loves this indomitable strength of his and I doubt any human
power bringing him to an acknowledgment of mistake with
the consequent conviction that the opposite party was right.
Sterling possesses a quickness and delicacy of perception quite
feminine, and with it a power of originating deep and striking
thoughts, and making them the foundation of a regular and
compact series of consequences and deductions such as only a
man, and a man of extraordinary power of close thinking and
clearness of vision, can attain unto. He is singularly uninfluenced by the opinions of others, preferring, on the whole, to
run counter to them than make any approach to a compro-
mise.—We found no lack of conversation; but really, as he has
become a resident, I dare not pledge myself to continue
noting. He offered to-day to have readings with us sometimes,
in which his wife would join. This will be a fine chance for us.
He spoke of there being but three men in England in whom
he could perceive the true elements of greatness—Wordsworth, Carlyle, and the Duke of Wellington. We took poor
Billy, the goat, a walk with us, when Sterling chose to lead it,
and presented a curious spectacle—his solemn manner with
that volatile kid!

May 24.—Dr. Calvert appeared at our Penjerrick tea-table

to our great surprise, and talked very much as if he meant to remain at Falmouth. He says, 'I know when I come to you I need not talk unless I like it.' Certainly he has rather lost ground during his stay at Penzance, but he has come to the conclusion that he is not to be well in any climate, which he says teaches him to make the best of, and be thankful for, the one he is in. He does not agree with Carlyle and others who think that we all have a message to deliver. 'My creed is, that Man, whilst dwelling on the earth, is to be instructed in patience, submission, humility.' He and H. Molesworth dined with us, with John Lawrence—Dr. Calvert's mild wisdom flowing as usual in its deep and quiet channel.

Joseph Bonaparte, his son and grandson, in the Harbour. Barclay and Lawrence visited them under the shade of the American Consulate. Shook hands and conversed with the old man for some time, and admired exceedingly the little boy, who is the image of Napoleon. His father, the Prince Charles Bonaparte de Canino, a fine-looking man.

May 25.—The Suttons, Macaulays, and J. Sterling dined with us. Sterling quoted the Italian lady who was asked by Napoleon whether all the Italians were thieves—'Non tutti, ma buona parte!'

June 2.—We had a nice talk with Sterling about Frederic II. of Prussia, whom he greatly admires, and thinks the greatest man that was ever born a king . . .

June 6.—Uncle and Aunt Charles paid the Carlyles a delightful little visit when in town, the most interesting point of which was, that Carlyle ran after them and said, 'Give my love to your dear interesting nephew and nieces!' which had better be engraved on our respective tombstones. I walked *tête-exaltée* the rest of the day consequentially! On consulting Sterling on the singular fact of Carlyle remembering our existence, he said, 'Oh! he's interested about you; he likes your healthy mode of Quakerism; it's the sort of thing with which he can sympathise more than any other.' Sterling is deep in Emerson's 'Essays,' and said, 'It would answer your purpose well to devote three months entirely to the study of this one little volume; it has such a depth and originality of thought in it as will require very close and fixed attention to penetrate.'

June 8.—J. Sterling showed me Emerson's book, and drew a parallel between him and Carlyle; he was the Plato, and

Carlyle the Tacitus . . .

June 9.—Anna Maria and I paid Dr. Calvert a snug little visit by special invitation. He is growing sadly weak, and every day more sleepy. 'I used to find it a difficulty,' he says, 'to sleep one hour; now I find it none in the world to sleep twenty-four.' He has formed an intimacy with a cheery-hearted old woman, Nancy Weeks, who busies herself with the eggs of Muscovy ducks; they exchange nosegays, and he sits for much of his evenings with her and her husband. He has stuck a portrait of Papa over a painting to which he has taken a great antipathy, and spite of the incision of four pins, his landlady quite approves of the arrangement. He is still often able to shoot curious little birds, which he brings to Anna Maria to draw and stuff.

June 14.—On leaving the bathing machine, Dr. Calvert joined us; he is extremely weak and tottering, ready to fall off little Z's back (so he has named a recent purchase of his, thinking it the last of ponies both in size and price — £5). However, he brightened up and was quite cheerful.

June 15.—Dr. Calvert joined us at dinner, and we all lounged under our drooping spruce, with Balaam the ape, which I had borrowed for the afternoon, in the foreground, and the kid near by, quite happy in our companion-ship . . . After a good deal [of] talk, he declared, 'Now I'm tired of ladies' society'; but as all the servants were gone out haymaking, he had to submit to it a little longer, whilst I enacted groom and brought out his little pony; in consequence of which, when we met next at Trebah, he gave me a delicious piece of soap, which he thought would surely be useful in my new office. John Sterling's wisdom and Aunt Charles's wit seemed to do him good, but he speaks of himself as physically very miserable. She has given him a Neapolitan pig which is an amusement to him; he has it washed and shampooed every morning.

June 16.—All the Trebahs dined with us. J. Sterling joined us at dessert in famous spirits . . .

June 21.—Called on the Sterlings. Found Dr. Calvert squatting in a corner at the prospect of a call from the Candidate for Falmouth; J. Sterling sitting bolt upright, anxious to give every support to the Liberal Candidate; but, alas! we had not our expected diversion, for a card was the

only candidate for our favour . . . Much fun about Dr.
Calvert's Neapolitan pig, which has shown no marks of
civilisation so far . . .

June 27.—Saw the Sterlings . . . He wishes me to translate some of Schleiermacher's sermons, which I think I shall
attempt.

June 28.—To breakfast with Grandmother. William Ball*
very eloquent on the subject of Wordsworth; they never heard
him praise any poetry but his own, except a piece of Jane
Crewdson's!† To strangers whom he is not likely to see again
he converses in the monologue style as the mood is upon him,
but with his friends he is very willing, and indeed desirous, of
hearing them state their own opinions. He makes no secret of
this view that Poetry stands highest among the arts, and that
he (William Wordsworth) is at the head of it. He expresses
such opinions in the most naïve manner, pleasant to witness.
He so feels the importance of high finish as not to begrudge a
fortnight to a word, so he succeed at last in getting a
competent one.

We wandered down to Dr. Calvert's. He has now given up
all thoughts of being better . . .

July 19.—An interesting evening at the Sterlings'. Time
spent in looking at Raphael's heads from his frescoes in the
Vatican . . . [Sterling] called Cruikshank the Raphael of
Cockneydom. We examined a portrait of him which he has
just given forth. It is not known if it be a genuine likeness or a
capital joke, but it is quite what one might fancy him to be.

Webster, the American, after being three months in town,
was asked what his feeling was about London. 'The same as it
was at first,' he replied. 'Amazement!'

July 27.—The Doctor has brightened up a little since the
arrival of the Stangers [his sister and her husband], and to-
day crept out with us on 'Z' to Penjerrick . . . Rumball, the
Phrenologist, has been examining his head, and he is quite
willing that his character of him should be seen, because he
thinks it an instructive one, just as he would have his body
examined after death for the benefit of medical science.

Plymouth, July 30.—Attended the British Association
Meeting here. Sir Henry de la Beche was President of the

* Quaker minister who had a summer home next to the Wordsworths at Rydal.
† 1808-63; wrote religious verse.

Geological Section . . . This evening, as we were taking tea at Colonel Mudge's, he wandered in, and was forcibly reminded of old times in seeing us all . . .

August 3.—Dined at the W. S. Harris's, and met a very pleasant party. My lot at dinner was cast with Henry de la Beche . . . He was complimented on the way in which he had performed his duties as chairman, and confidentially told me that the secret of pleasing in that department was to bring others forward and keep yourself in the background.

Falmouth, August 7.—Professor [Humphrey] Lloyd [physicist and Provost of Trinity College, Dublin] and his wife appeared after breakfast; we took shipping and went to Trelissick. Talked about [L. A. J.] Quetelet:* he is a sort of universal genius, his present object the investigation of cycles. [Charles] Babbage has been attempting to form statistics of suicides, but remarked, 'We must have many more examples before we can get at an accurate result.' When the Franklins and Sabines† were excursing in Ireland, they went through some difficult pass. Professor Lloyd was with them and vastly amused at Lady Franklin again and again saying, 'John, you had better go back, you are certainly giddy.' At last, poor woman, she could proceed no further. Sir John found it advisable to carry her back, and asked Colonel Sabine to assist him. The Colonel thought it nervous work and hesitated, until encouraged in a grave matter-of-fact way by the excellent husband. 'Don't be afraid, Sabine; she never kicks when she's faint!'

August 8.—Took a calm little walk with Professor Lloyd . . . Charming evening over poetry, ghosts, &c . . . His own belief in ghosts extends thus far—At the moment at which the soul is separated from the body, he thinks the spirit may range for any definite purpose, our comprehension of which is by no means necessary for its reality.

August 10.—Went to Grove Hill . . . Professor [Richard] Owen‡ was of our party . . . He is a very interesting person, his face full of energetic thought and quiet strength. His eye

---

* Belgian statistician and astronomer who employed mathematical ideas in an estimation of man's physical and moral qualities.

† Sir John Franklin, Arctic explorer, was posthumously recognised as discoverer of the North West Passage. Sir Edward Sabine was astronomer to expeditions in search of the North West Passage, 1818-1820.

‡ Naturalist and anatomist who devised models of extinct animals at Crystal Palace.

has in it a fixedness of purpose, and enthusiasm for that
purpose, seldom surpassed.

August 12.—Breakfast made most joyous by Colonel Sabine
announcing that he had got glorious news for us, which he set
us to guess. His wife looked keenly at him, and asked, 'It is
about Captain Ross?' Such is the sympathy between these
married magnetists; for in very truth it was about Captain
Ross—that he had reached 78" South lat., being 11" further
than any one before him. He had discovered snow-capped
mountains. Twenty-two years since (in 1818) Colonel Sabine
and he had stood upon the North Pole Ice, and the former
said, 'Well, Ross, when you become a post-captain and a
great man, you must go through the same work at the South
Pole.' Colonel Sabine's excitement is delightful, and the spirit
of reverent thankfulness with which he receives the tidings
truly instructive. They are so charmed at the coincidence of
the news arriving here, when Lloyd, Sabine, and Fox are
assembled together.

To [Robert] Hunt's* lecture in the evening, on 'The
Influence of Poetry and Painting on Education.' John Sterling in the chair, where he sat with tolerable composure till
the conclusion. He then thanked our Lecturer for the pains he
had taken to instruct us, and added a few impressive words:
'Guard against self-deception of every species. True poetry is
not the plaything of an idle fancy, nor the pursuit of a vacant
moment, but the result of concentrated energy and the
offspring of untiring perseverance.'

August 18.—Breakfasted at the Joseph Carnes' and met
[William Daniel] Conybeare [geologist], who . . . once
attended a Unitarian Chapel, and was much astonished at
their prayer at the end; it was no petition, but a sort of
summary of the perfections of the Deity. He went to one of J.
J. Gurney's† meetings, and listened to a kind of apologetic
discourse for the peculiarities of our Body. He was especially
tickled at his mention of women's preaching. 'Shall we silence
our women? We cannot do it! We dare not do it!' . . .

August 30.—John Sterling is extremely pleased with his visit
to Carclew, and the society there of two men of European

---

* He published the first English treatise on photography; he was later president of
  the Royal Cornwall Polytechnic.
† Quaker philanthropist and writer, brother of Elizabeth Fry.

celebrity. He characterises Lloyd as a highly cultivated and naturally refined abstract thinker, living and dreaming in his abstractions, feeling 'the around him' as nothing, and 'the beyond him' everything; his course, therefore, very naturally takes the direction of pure mathematics. Owen, with his strong perceptions, vigorous energy, and active will, chooses organic matter for his investigations, and dwells rather in what is and what has been, than in what may be . . .

A large party met on Meudon beach to draw a seine for Professor Owen, the result of which was one cuttle-fish, which he bore back in triumph on his stick. We all lounged on the beach most peacefully, John Sterling reading some of Tennyson to us, which displays a poetical fancy and intense sympathy with dreamy romance, and withal a pure pathos, drawn direct from the heart of Nature.

Owen was very delightful; he is such a natural creature, never affecting the stilted 'philosophe,' and never ashamed of the science which he so ardently loves . . .

September 1.—Went to the Sterlings', where he talked of Poetry . . . Wilson, the landscape-painter, when he first looked on Tivoli, exclaimed, 'Well done water—by God!'

September 2.—With Sterling, who professes himself quite happy with society, philosophy, scenery, and Cornish cream. He delights in Owen, with all his enthusiasm for fossil reptiles; and then he so cordially acknowledges Shakespeare as one of the hugest amongst organised fossils! Dora Lloyd asked Sterling what Kant thought. 'He thought fifteen octavo volumes,' was the reply.

September 4.—Mrs. Owen gave us many sketches of her own life and experiences. She has been a great deal with the Cuvier family, and considers Cuvier an infinitely great man—so great, indeed, that you could never approach him without feeling your own inferiority . . . Mrs. Owen told us about her education, which was very much left to herself. She said, 'I determined to get to myself as much knowledge as possible, so I studied languages, even Russian; music, drawing, and comparative anatomy. My father being Curator at the College of Surgeons, I had great facilities for this latter branch. I determined I would never love any but a very superior man, and see how fortunate I have been.' She is a very perfect little Fact in the great history of the world.

September 5.—Professor Owen talked about phrenology, which he considers the most remarkable chimera which has taken possession of rational heads for a long time . . . Talking of Carlyle's message of sympathy with the entire race, Owen dissents, from adopting Johnson's principle, 'I like a good hater.' We battled this, and the result did not weaken my faith in the premises. In the evening Owen gave us the individual adventures of different specimens of heads and a foot of the Dodo now existing in this country, the history of the Oxford one traceable from Elizabeth's time. In [Elias] Ashmole's* time it was a whole bird, but his executors finding it dusty, broke off the head and burnt the rest, and successive naturalists have chanted a loud miserere. He gave a lecture on going to bed early: the two hours before midnight the most important for health.

September 6.—On the Pennance Rocks in a *dolce far niente* state; the Professor perfectly happy. He gave me lesson No. 1 on the primary divisions in Natural History. John Sterling joined us there, and we had some talk over Wordsworth, Carlyle, and collateral subjects. Lady Holland† has established a sort of tyranny over matters of literature and criticism. Henry Taylor [Colonial Office official and dramatic poet], dining one day at Holland House, Lady Holland asked him what he was doing now. 'I am writing a review of Wordsworth for the *Quarterly*.' 'What!' exclaimed her Ladyship, 'absolutely busied about the man who writes of caps and pinafores and that sort of thing!' Taylor replied in the gravest, quietest way, 'That is a mode of criticising Wordsworth which has been obsolete for the last ten years.' And Taylor has not since been asked to Holland House.

Sterling attributes the obscurity often met with in Wordsworth to his unavailing attempt to reconcile philosophical insight with those forms of opinion, religious and political, in which he had been educated, and which the majority around him held. Owen thinks that Coleridge had a bad effect on the young literary men about him, in teaching them to speak, instead of write, their thoughts. His delight in Carlyle is refreshing to witness.

* Seventeenth-century antiquary who bequeathed his collection to Oxford; the Ashmolean Museum is named after him.

† Hostess of a Whig salon; she made many enemies in literary and political circles.

The Owens and Sterlings joined us this evening to listen to a very beautiful lecture on Light which Professor Lloyd was so good as to give us . . .

September 12.—Dr. Calvert so much better as to be again in his garden. His state lately has been distressing from extreme languor, weakness, and depression. If he ever gave way to such expressions as 'I wish I were dead,' he always suffered afterwards most bitterly from self-reproach.

September 14.—John Sterling said this morning that he supposed Schiller was the only person who could bear to have all his words noted down. Of him, Goethe said to a friend of Sterling's, 'I have never heard from him an insignificant word.' . . .

September 23.—John Sterling joined us . . . He thinks Barclay amazingly improved in his poetry, and his admiration is great for one line—'A plant that seeks the sun, yet grasps the soil.' . . .

Uncle Joshua remarked that the majority of fashionable women keep themselves in tolerable health by talking: they would die otherwise for want of exercise.

September 30.—Saw Dr. Calvert again to-day, who was quite his old self, talking on his old subjects in his old way . . .

October 5.—Colonel Sabine forwarded Captain Ross's Journal to Papa . . . full of the spirit of British enterprise, and enthusiasm for his object, and intolerance towards all other nations which attempt discovery, as though it were the indisputable prerogative of England.

Attended Hunt's lecture on Chemistry; very pretty, popular, explosive, and luminous.

October 16.—Interesting visit to John Sterling, who was not well . . .

October 25.—Paid Dr. Calvert and his sister a charming visit. The Doctor quite himself, advocating passive rather than active heroism, yet making vast allowances for his friend's physical mistakes about this, 'for it must be tremendously hard for him who deems himself a teacher to sit down in acquiescing patience in a do-nothing state.' . . .

November 3.—John Sterling read us extracts from a letter from Carlyle received to-day. Much was in reference to a remark of Sterling's whether any one had ever actually loved Goethe. Carlyle thinks that Schiller did, though with a full appreciation of the distance which separated them; but he adds, 'However we may admire the heavens' lightning, we are not apt to love it in the way of caressing.' . . .

November 6.—This morning I began to disbelieve in accidents; does not everything, both in mind and matter, act definitely, every event have a necessary cause? In nature, events are called accidental which are the direct consequences of some pre-established law of being, known or unknown; in mind, the result of a conflux of causes, equally definite and certain, though often mysterious and unfathomed. Thus a carriage is overturned by some infringement of the laws of matter generally discoverable enough. A man is led to adopt a particular line of conduct consequent on his peculiar constitution, modified by his education, association, line of thought, and outward surrounding circumstances. Suppose he were to get drunk and neglect his family. This proves his animal instincts strong, and his social ones weak, a deficient moral sense and an abused understanding, the intensity of all heightened by bad association. Suppose he at length recognises his mistaken mode of life. Self-love, respect for the good opinion of his fellows, brightening intellectual vigour, or the power of religion,—may any of them be a sufficient motive to induce him to change his mode of life; and it is an irrefragable law of mind, that moral efforts become definitely easier by repetition. That which first discovered to him his altogether false position, did so because exactly addressed to his perceptions and consciousness; whilst another might have passed it by, and been roused by quite a different cause. In all cases the cause is sufficient to produce the effect. This consideration might make us more lenient in judging others, that motives or reasons which present themselves to us as irresistible, are not recognised in precisely the same manner by any other existing individual, whilst we might pass by as foolish or insufficient, arguments which our Heavenly Father has disposed His weak and erring prodigal to accept as unanswerable, and of power to regulate the remainder of his existence. Thus in Luther the monstrous imposition of Indulgences was just of sufficient weight to overbalance his devotion to Rome. The passion into which this discovery kindled him, and the mode he took to express it, just availed to stir up the particular sort of opposition by which his antagonists tried to suppress him and his doctrines.

This reacted on him, and he learnt self-confidence and confidence in Him who is the Truth, and continued his opposition with equal vigour and more system. His intrepidity drew to his cause those whose mental constitution could best appreciate that part of his activity: his logical deductions attracted others: his honest devotion to Truth had its disciples: his assertion of freedom of conscience was embraced by others again: and every fresh adherent reacted on Luther in some often unappreciable manner, either cheering him on to vigorous action, or modifying his innovating spirit: every smallest fact in his history had a definite result, and necessitated the Reformation in the form we see it.

November 10.—Took an early dinner with the Sterlings, to draw and talk in peace. One of the last Yankeeisms has greatly amused him, that a child in Kentucky was so exceedingly small as to be obliged to stand upon a footstool to kick the kitten . . .

November 27.—An interesting visit to Sterling: he still keeps the house, but his chest is better even than in the summer . . .

November 30.—Dr. Calvert is increasingly ill, generally extremely depressed, though at times cheerful, and always striving after submission. 'Beg Mr. Patey to pray for my release,' was his pathetic injunction to his sister on her going to church. Dr. Boase paid him a long visit. His sister asked what he had recommended. 'An apple,' answered the Doctor. 'Dear me! that does not seem a matter of great importance.' 'Oh yes,' said her brother; 'an apple drove Adam and Eve out of Paradise, and perhaps this apple may drive me in.' He amused himself afterwards by always calling Dr. Boase 'Eve.'

December 3.—Went to the Sterlings' . . .

Talked of 'Philip van Artevelde' (Taylor), Irving, Coleridge, and Charles Lamb being together; and the conversation turning on Mahomet, Irving reprobated him in his strongest manner as a prince of imposters, without earnestness and without faith. Taylor thinking him not fairly used, defended him with much spirit. On going away, Taylor could not find his hat, and was looking about for it, when Charles Lamb volunteered his assistance, with the query, 'Taylor, did you come in a h-h-hat or a t-t-t-turban?'

December 5.—Sad account of Dr. Calvert to-day. He is very, very low, lying in silence all day and taking interest in nothing. 'Will you see Sterling to-day?' 'Why, yes,' he said; 'he may come and look at the beast, but I can't speak to him. He may just shake hands with me, but nothing more.' He speaks of his mind being through all in great peace.

December 7.—John Sterling has written him a most touchingly beautiful leave-taking letter, which they have not yet ventured to show him.

December 9.—He feels as if the Almighty had hidden His face from him, and yearns for the bright glimpses which have been so often vouchsafed him. A few days since he had a full outpouring to his sister concerning his faith in his Redeemer being the only support for him now.

December 18.—He has taken a fancy to have a series of old nurses to sit by him at night; he is interested in drawing them out on their experience of life.

December 26.—This morning he was supposed to be dying; he had passed twelve hours without food, and then fell asleep in utter exhaustion, from which they thought he could scarcely awake. He was himself surprised at the vigour he showed, and said, 'Perhaps God may see it best for my further purification that I should again be shipwrecked into life!' He said he had had a glorious prospect, a view of such happiness, and ejaculated a little prayer for its realisation . . . The other day J. Stanger gave him some wine, which he liked and asked for another glass; in this a large dose of morphia was insinuated, which the Doctor presently discovered, and insisted on his mild brother-in-law swallowing. He was so peremptory that there was no escape. This is very characteristic of the fun which still lurks in his nature.

December 31.—At twelve o'clock the Old Year went out in obscure darkness, leaving us, I hope, somewhat wiser and better from our intercourse and close friendship with him. He has been a faithful friend to me, and his sunny side has been generally turned towards us. May we use the young Heir well for the sake of its ancestors and its own.

1842

Falmouth, January 1.—What an era is every New Year's Day, if well considered. Another stage in our journey, a shifting of the scene without interrupting the continuity of the piece, but rather essential to its representation as a Whole, a Unity; the winding-up of our watch that it may tell us the time to-morrow; a fresh page in our Book of Existence, on which much may be written; by itself a fragment, but how important to the order of narration and to the train of thought, shaping, colouring, modifying, developing; how much does a quiet year silently affect our condition, character, mode of thought and action; explain mysteries of outward and inward life, and trace some of the sequences in the phenomena of Being.

Our dear friend Dr. Calvert is very low. On hearing that John Sterling inquired after him, he said, 'I shan't see Sterling again, but I love him very much.' He is so earnest that every one should rather rejoice than grieve for him when he is gone, that he wishes, through Barclay, to give dinners at the Workhouse, and make it a time of festivity.

January 6.—Large party of Bullers, Tremaynes, Dykes, and J. A. Froude* to lunch. There were too many to enjoy any thoroughly. Anthony Froude, a very thoughtful man, with a wonderful talent for reading lives in written characters. To John Sterling he spoke of the beautiful purity of the early Christian Church; Sterling answered, 'If any of those early Christians were to appear now, I rather think we should disclaim fellowship.'

Dr. Calvert very restless and wandering. He is often heard saying to himself, 'There is a great Unseen near me.' His old love of incongruities looked out when his sister spoke of his brothers [sic] William and Raisley† being in Heaven. 'Yes,' he said, 'William and Raisley, and Nimrod and Solomon, all in Heaven.'

January 7.—Sterling read us a New Year's letter from Carlyle, thanking him for much kindness, and wishing him increasing steadiness, zeal, and spiritual life . . .

January 8.—Dr. Calvert's longings for death this morning were most touching. 'Oh lead me to the still waters,' was his

---

* Historian and Carlyle's literary executor and biographer.
† Correctly, William was his father and Raisley his uncle.

cry.

January 9.—Our dear friend Dr. Calvert was this morning permitted to put off the life-garment which has so painfully encumbered him, and is, I trust, drinking of those still waters after which he pined. Oh we do rejoice that he is at rest, though his poor sister is overwhelmed by the sense of being the sole survivor of her family. He fell into unconsciousness last evening, and his first awakening was in that Eternity which is so far off and yet so near. We spent a quiet hour with the Sterlings, to whom this event is a great sorrow but John Sterling earnestly congratulates his Friend on having finished his battle well . . .

January 10.—Visit from John Sterling; he was very full of a letter from J. S. Mill on Puseyism: it is written in the same spirit of calm philosophical toleration as Carlyle's Essay on Diderot; he views it as a consistent expression of Church-of-Englandism, very interesting to investigate.

Went to Perran: Sterling came too. Uncle Charles asked if [J. A. W.] Neander was a Neologian. 'Why,' said Sterling, 'just as every German is one—that is, submitting the Bible to the same rules of criticism as are applied to other ancient records.' . . .

January 13.—Our dear Friend was followed to his last resting-place on earth by a heavy-hearted train of mourners. John Sterling wrote this little Epitaph, to be read hereafter over his grave:—

> *'To the memory of John Mitchenson Calvert, M.D.,*
> *who died on the 9th of January 1842, aged 40.*
>
> Pure soul! strong, kind and peaceful, 'mid the pain
> That racked and solemnised thy torch of Love:
> Here in our world below we mourn in vain,
> But would not call thee from thy world above.
> Of varied wisdom, and of heart sincere,
> Through gloomy ways thy feet unfaltering trod:
> Reason thy lamp, and Faith thy star while here;
> Now both one brightness in the Light of God.'

His sister showed me a series of his letters from Germany and Italy when travelling there with John Sterling. They are as much a journal of his inner as of his outer life, telling amongst other things how the impulses from without—those old religious paintings, for instance— affected his inward being . . .

January 19.—Mr. Stanger showed us a letter of condolence from Wordsworth, in which he says that the bequest of Dr. Calvert's uncle, Raisley, was what enabled him to devote himself to literary pursuits, and give his talents, such as they were, opportunity to develop themselves. He also says that the last two lines of Sterling's epitaph are excellent—rare praise from Wordsworth.

January 28.—A long walking ride with John Sterling . . . On Coleridge he was very interesting. Spoke of womanly delicacy of his mind: his misfortune was to appear at a time when there was a man's work to do—and he did it not. He had not sufficient strength of character, but professed doctrines which he had ceased to believe, in order to avoid the trouble of controversy. He and Carlyle met once; the consequence of which was, that Coleridge disliked Carlyle, and Carlyle despised Coleridge . . .

February 2.—Cousin Elizabeth Fry sends a simple and characteristic account of her dinner at the Mansion House, on the occasion of Prince Albert's laying the foundation-stone of the Royal Exchange.—'I think you will be interested to hear that we got through our visit to the Mansion House with much satisfaction. After some little difficulty that I had in arriving, from the crowd which overdid me for the time, I was favoured to revive, and when led into the drawing-room by the Lord Mayor I felt quiet and at ease. Soon my friends flocked around me. I had a very satisfactory conversation with Sir James Graham [Home Secretary], and I think the door is open for further communication on a future day. It appeared most seasonable, my then seeing him. I then spoke to Lord Aberdeen [Foreign Secretary] for his help, if needful, in our foreign affairs. During dinner, when I sat for about two hours between Prince Albert and Sir Robert Peel, we had deeply interesting conversation on the most important subjects. With Prince Albert upon religious principle, its influence on Sovereigns and its importance in the education of children; and upon modes of worship, our views respecting them—why I could not rise at their toasts, not even at the one for the Queen, why I could rise for prayer; also on the management of children generally; on war and peace; on prisons and punishment. I had the same subjects, or many of them, with Sir Robert Peel. The kindness shown me was extraordinary. After dinner I spoke to Lord Stanley [Colonial Secretary and later Prime Minister] about our Colonies, and I think I was enabled to speak to all those in power that I wanted to see. I shook hands very pleasantly with the Duke of Wellington, who spoke beautifully, expressing his desire to promote the arts of peace and not those of war; he said he was not fond of remembering the days that were past, as if the thought of war pained him. Although this dinner, as numbers I have been at, may not in all respects accord with my ideas of Christian simplicity, I have felt and feel now, if on such occasions I seek to keep near to my Guide and in conduct and conversation to maintain my testimony to what I believe right, I am not out of my place in them, when, as it was the other day, I feel it best to go to them.'

February 4.—Bessie Fry sends an account of the King of Prussia's visit to Cousin Elizabeth Fry. They spent the morning at Newgate, where Cousin Fry read with the women, and then prayed for them and for the King, which greatly affected him; he knelt all the time. Bunsen* went with him to Upton, where all the small Fry were introduced to him, and he did them the honour to wash his hands and to eat their luncheon.

April 7.—Letter to Barclay from J. S. Mill, dwelling on Sterling's character and intellectual position, and condoling with us on his absence . . .

April 8.—Barclay took a carriage-full to the Mines. Lieutenant Shadwell, a son of the Vice-Chancellor [Sir Lancelot, last Vice-Chancellor of England], was very interesting about New Zealand and the character of his cousin, the new Bishop, who has gone out to live there in the true spirit of a Christian missionary, with a wife as an able assistant.

April 18.—Gossiping with Lucy Ellice about her literary friends. She is C. J. Fox's cousin, and was almost brought up at Holland House. She spoke of the stool which Lady Holland always kept by her side, to which any one was to be

---

* Christian Charles Josias, Baron de Bunsen, Prussian Ambassador in London from 1841 until his death.

called, whose conversation her ladyship fancied for the time being. Once when Lucy was called there to describe some Paris ghost for the benefit of a large party, she told her hostess that she reminded her of a French lady who was getting up a conversation with some *savants*, and after having gone systematically through a number of subjects, said, 'Et à présent, Monsieur, un peu de religion s'il vous plaît.' Sydney Smith said, 'Lady Holland is not one woman, but a multitude; just read the Riot Act and you'll presently see them disperse!'

May 12.—Barclay had one of John Mill's letters. He writes of his (Barclay's) lecture on Modern British Poets in the warmest terms: had it been the production of a young writer unknown to him, he should have said that he had taken the right road, and was likely to go on far. His 'Logic' comes out at Christmas.

London, May 17.—To the College of Surgeons to meet Professor Owen, who showed us over their Museum, and added infinitely to its interest by his luminous expositions. The things are arranged altogether physiologically on the idea which Hunter first struck out and worked on, that there is a certain analogy of structure running throughout Nature, vegetable as well as animal; a hyacinth, for instance, has its fibres, but no internal stomach, so the earth in which it is embedded acts as one. Owen believes that no animal has sensation unless furnished with a brain, therefore the cuttle-fish is the lowest creature which can be effectively treated with cruelty. Examined a long series of skulls; those of babies so much phrenologically better than grown persons—which Owen thinks quite natural, as they came uncontaminated from the Author of all Goodness, and degenerate after contact with the world.

May 28.—Called at Cheyne Row, where Carlyle and his wife received us with affectionate cordiality. He looks remarkably well and handsome, but she has not at all recovered [from] the shock of her mother's death. He wanted to know what we were doing at the Yearly Meeting, and what were its objects and functions, and remarked on the deepening observable amongst Friends; but when we told of the letter to the Queen recommendatory of peace in Afghanistan, he was terribly amused. 'Poor little Queen! She'd be glad enough to

live in peace and quietness if the Afghans would but submit
to her conditions.' He feels somehow but little interest in the
whole affair, it is such a long way off, and there is plenty of
stirring serious work to be done at home. 'I take a greater
interest in Sir Alexander Burnes* than in any of them, I
suppose just because I have seen him, and can represent him
to myself as a person not very fit for the sharp work they had
for him to do, and so they took the life out of him at last, poor
fellow!' Of himself he says that it is just the old story of
indigestion; dyspepsia is a sort of perennial thing with him
(how much does this explain!); he can do no work before
breakfast, but is just up to viewing Life in general, and his
own Life in particular, on the shady side. Got somehow to
Emerson, who is quietly but deeply influencing a few both in
England and America . . . The Carlyles like his conversation much better than his books, which they think often
obscure and involved both in conception and execution. I
remarked on the democratic way in which he had levelled all
ranks of subjects and holy and unholy personages. 'Why,'
Carlyle answered, 'they are all great Facts, and he treats them
each as a Fact, of value rather with reference to the whole
than to any preconceived theory!' . . . Carlyle gave me a
number of the *Dial*,† which Emerson has marked and sent
him as a good sample of the tone and struggling nature of
earnest American thought; also an American pamphlet on
Capital Punishment, with some of his own characteristic
notes in the margin. Carlyle does not like capital punishment,
because he wishes men to live as much and as long as
possible; he rejoices in the increasing feeling that it is a right
solemn thing for one man to say to another, 'Give over living!'
But on my characterising it as a declaration that though God
could bear with the criminal, man could not, he said, 'Why,
there are many things in this world which God bears with:—
He bears with many a dreary morass and waste, yet He gives
to man the will and the power to drain and to till it and make
oats grow out of it. But you'll make no oats grow out of men's
corpses. This pamphlet-author is oddly inconsistent; with all
his enthusiastic feeling for the value of individual life, he is

* Indian political officer killed in the massacre at Kabul.
† Influential, though short-lived, organ of the Transcendentalists of New England,
  edited by Emerson.

quite in favour of going to war with England, thus willing to
sacrifice thousands of brave fellows, while he would save the
life of a miserable rascal like Good, who cut his wife into
pieces and stuffed them into a coach-box.' Carlyle's laughs
are famous fellows, hearty and bodily. He was interested in
hearing of Sterling's Polytechnic lecture, and amused to learn
the horror which the mention of his (Carlyle's) name aroused.
'I suppose they took me for Richard Carlile, but they say that
even Richard has taken another turn and become a religious
character. I remember when his father was a bookseller and
his shopmen were constantly being taken up for selling the
sort of book he kept, yet there was such an enthusiastic feeling
towards him, such a notion that he was supporting the right
cause, that no sooner was one taken up than another offered
himself from the country, and so he was always kept supplied.
Edward Irving fell in with one of them at Newgate, who
appealed to him as to whether it was not very hard to be
imprisoned for disseminating views which he honestly
believed to be true. Irving rather agreed with him, and he
afterwards paraded Irving's opinion in a somewhat morti-
fying manner.' He (Carlyle) spoke on politics and bribery,
and the deep and wide influence of money, which seems now
the one recognisable claim to human esteem. 'But that can't
last long,' quoth I. 'No, it can't last,' he replied, 'unless God
intends to destroy the earth at once and utterly.' He looks to
Parliament for some great vital change in our condition, and
expects that ere long some sincere, earnest spirit will arise and
gradually acquire and exert influence over the rest. Not that
he supposes it will ever again take the form of Cromwell's
Revolution. [John Arthur] Roebuck,* he thinks, would very
much like the place of the Lord Protector of England,
Scotland, and Ireland! The other day he was talking with
him about bribery, when Roebuck said, 'Really if you so
remove temptation, you will take away opportunity for
virtue.' 'Then,' said Carlyle, 'we must acknowledge as a great
encourager of virtue, one who certainly has not got much
credit for it yet—namely, the Devil.' He thinks it would have
a wonderful effect in the House if Roebuck was to raise his
small curious person, and with his thin, shrill voice give

* Independent MP. Chairman of the Committee formed to enquire into the conduct
of the Crimean War.

utterance, 'Either bribery is right or wrong: if wrong, let us give up practising it and abuse it less; if right, let it go on without outcry.' They were very kind, and pressed us to spend an evening with them, which I trust we shall be able to do.

May 29.—The Derwent Coleridges have given up the school at Helston and settled near London, at St. Mark's College . . . Their object is to train up a class of teachers intermediate between the present aristocratic constitution of the Church, and the extremely ignorant set who have now to fulfil its inferior offices. This link is in the way to be supplied, as this is a sort of college. where they not only study, but practise teaching and reading subordinate parts of the service. He sees that a similar plan has been of wonderful use among the Methodists, and has long been a desideratum in the Church . . .

Steamed away to London Bridge and saw the Maurices, and liked them much. [The Rev. Frederick Denison Maurice]* is not at all dogmatic in his manner, but kind and conciliating. He thinks that Carlyle has much more real sympathy with moral excellence than intellectual force, thus that he raves a great deal, but never really sympathises with Goethe as he does with Dante. He has just been with Wordsworth, who is now in town and seems in force and vigour.

May 30.—A very pleasant chatty tea with the Owens, talking over phrenology, mesmerism, and interpersonal influence. [Michael] Faraday† is better, but greatly annoyed by his change of memory. He remembers distinctly things that happened long ago, but the details of present life, his friends' Christian names, &c., he forgets . . .

May 31.—Dined at the Mills'—a biennial jubilee; John Mill in glorious spirits; too happy to enter much into deep things. He alluded to the indescribable change and growth he experienced when he made the discovery that what was right for others might not be right for him. Talked of Life not being all fun, though there is a great deal of fun in it . . .

---

* Founder of Christian Socialism. He was dismissed from his Professorship of Modern History at King's College, London, in 1853 for his unorthodox views on Eternal Punishment. He inaugurated the Working Men's College, London, 1854.

† Discoverer of magneto-electricity and originator of the theory of the atom as 'centre of force'.

He said, 'My family have no idea how great a man I am!!' He
is now saving up his holidays for a third journey to Italy; he
had serious hopes of an illness in the winter, but was
conscientious enough not to encourage it! He is inclined to
agree with Wordsworth in the defence of capital punishments, but I am glad to say has not quite made up his mind.
He thinks Carlyle intolerant to no class but metaphysicians;
owing to his entire neglect of this mode of thought, he is
persistently floored by Sterling in argument . . . John Mill
had designed writing a book on the French Revolution, when
he heard of Carlyle's purpose, and accordingly made over his
books of reference to him; the world has also been deprived of
a History of Greece from his pen, because Thirlwall was just
beforehand with him.

June 1.—Visit from the Edward Sterlings [parents of John],
who were much excited at another attempt at shooting the
Queen, which happened last evening in the Park. The day
before, the man had been there ready for action, but was
unavoidably prevented; this was mentioned to Her Majesty,
who ordered a double number of police in their plain clothes
to be stationed in the Park, and forbade her ladies to attend
her, and expose themselves to danger from which she would
not shrink. The man raised the pistol within three paces of
the carriage, when a policeman struck it down harmless. The
Queen and Prince stood up in the carriage and were greeted
with the utmost enthusiasm.

June 2.—Amelia Opie* to breakfast. Two of the themes she
wrote for our Schoolroom are published, or to be published,
in America. She is having her swing of London excitement.

Hampstead, June 4.—Gurney Hoare brought us the good
news that William Wordsworth was staying at old Mrs.
Hoare's†; so thither he took us. He is a man of middle height
and not of very striking appearance, the lower part of the face
retreating a little; his eye of a somewhat French diplomatic
character, with heavy eyelids, and none of the flashing which
one connects with poetic genius. When speaking earnestly, his
manner and voice become extremely energetic; and the
peculiar emphasis, and even accent, he throws into some of

---

* Novelist, wife of the fashionable portrait painter John Opie (known as 'the
  Cornish Wonder'). She became a Quaker.
† Louisa, née Gurney; first cousin of Caroline's mother.

his words, add considerably to their force. He evidently loves
the monologue style of conversation, but shows great candour
in giving due consideration to any remarks which others may
make. His manner is simple, his general appearance that of
the abstract thinker, whom his subject gradually warms into
poetry. Now for some of these subjects:—

Mamma spoke of the beauty of Rydal, and asked whether
it did not rather spoil him for common scenery. 'Oh no,' he
said, 'it rather opens my eyes to see the beauty there is in all;
God is everywhere, and thus nothing is common or devoid of
beauty. No, ma'am, it is the *feeling* that instructs the *seeing*.
Wherever there is a heart to feel, there is also an eye to see;
even in a city you have light and shade, reflections, probably
views of the water and trees, and a blue sky above you, and
can you want for beauty with all these? People often pity me
while residing in a city, but they need not, for I can enjoy its
characteristic beauties as well as any.' I said that Lamb's
rhapsody on London might not then have been sent to him in
a spirit necessarily ironical. 'Oh no,' he answered, 'and
Lamb's abuse of the country and his declared detestation of it
was all affected; he enjoyed it and entered into its beauties;
besides, Lamb had too kindly and sympathetic a nature to
detest anything.' Barclay asked him about Hartley Coleridge.
He thinks that there is much talent but no genius in his
poetry, and calls him an eminently clever man. One thing he
has learnt—that poetry is no pastime, but a serious earnest
work, demanding unspeakable study. 'Hartley has no originality; whenever he attempts it, it is altogether a mistake; he is
so fond of quaintness and contrariety, which is quite out of
keeping with a true poet: and then he is of that class of
extreme Radicals who can never mention a bishop or a king,
from King David downward, without some atrabilious prefix
or other. Surely this is excessively narrow and excessively
vain, to put yourself in opposition to the opinions and
institutions which have so long existed with such acknowledged benefit; there must be something in them to have
attracted the sympathies of ages and generations. I hold that
the degree in which Poets dwell in sympathy with the Past,
marks exactly the degree of their poetical faculty. Shelley,
you see, was one of these, and what did his poetry come to?'
'But,' said I, 'some would not be true to themselves unless

they gave voice to their yearnings after the Ideal rather than the Actual.' 'Ah, but I object to the perpetual ill-humour with things around them,' he replied; 'and Ill-humour is no spiritual condition which can turn to poetry. Shakespeare never declaimed against kings or bishops, but took the world as he found it.' He spoke of S. T. Coleridge, and the want of will which characterised both him and Hartley; the amazing effort which it was to him to will anything was indescribable: but he acknowledged the great genius of his poetry. Talked of Superstition and its connection with a young state of society: 'Why, we are all children; how little we know! I feel myself more a child than ever, for I am now in bondage to habits and prejudices from which I used to be free.' Barclay quoted Emerson's advice to imitate the independence of the schoolboy who is sure of his dinner, which greatly pleased him. We got, I forget how, to the subject of the Divine permission of Evil, which he said he has always felt the hardest problem of man's being. When four years old he had quaked on his bed in sharp conflict of spirit on this subject. 'Nothing but Faith can keep you quiet and at peace with such awful problems pressing on you—Faith that what you know not now, you will know in God's good time. It is curious, in that verse of St. Paul's about Faith, Hope, and Charity or Love, that Charity should be placed the highest of the three; it must be because it is so universal and limitless in its operations: but Faith is the highest individual experience, because it conquers the pride of the understanding—man's greatest foe. Oh, how this mechanical age does battle against the Faith: It is altogether calculated to puff up the pride of the understanding, while it contains no counteracting principle which can regulate the feelings; the love of the beautiful is lost in notions of shallow utility, and men little think that the thoughts which are embodied in form around them, and on which the peasants' shoon can trample, are worth more than all their steam-engines and railroads.' 'But this cannot last, there must be a reaction,' said I. 'No,' he said, 'it cannot last; God is merciful and loves His earth, and it cannot last. I have raised my voice loudly against it, particularly in the poem on the treaty of Cintra; and others have taken up the sound and under many forms have given the World to know that there are thoughts in man by which he holds communion with his God, of far higher moment that any outward act or circumstance whatever.' We took a truly affectionate leave; he held my hand in both of his for some time, which I consider a marked fact in my existence! Mrs. Wordsworth was there, but we were too much absorbed for any collateral observations.

June 6.—To the Carlyles', where we were received with great cordiality in the library, which looks well suited to the work performed there. Wax medallions of Edward Sterling and his son hang over the chimney-piece. Thomas Carlyle came in in his blouse, and we presently got, I know not how, to Swedenborgianism. Swedenborg was a thoroughly practical, mechanical man, and was in England learning ship-building. He went into a little inn in Bishopsgate Street, and was eating his dinner very fast, when he thought he saw in the corner of the room a vision of Jesus Christ, who said to him, 'Eat slower.' This was the beginning of all his visions and mysterious communications, of which he had enough in his day. He gave exactly the date—I think it was the 5th of May 1785—when Christianity died out, that is to say, when the last spark of truth left its professors, which is truly the death of anything; and that, he thought, was the Day of Judgment; not our old notions of it at all, but a sort of invisible judgment, of which he got informed in his visions. 'There was a great deal of truth in the man, with all his visions and fancies, and many hold with him to this day . . .' Then he continued:—

"'Tis an odd thing this about Queen Victoria. After having had a champion to say before the whole assembly of them, "O Queen, live for ever!" a little insignificant fellow comes up, points his pistol at her, and says, "Chimera! die this minute!" Poor Little Queen! I have some loyalty about me, and have no wish to see her shot; but as for her having any right to hold the reins of government if she could not manage them, all the cart-loads of dirty parchment can't make that clear. There are thousands of men about her made of the same flesh and blood, with the same eternities around them, and they want to be well governed and fed. It is something to get it recognised that the ablest man should be the one to guide us, even if we may never see it carried out.' Something led us to John Mill: 'Ah, poor fellow! he has had to get himself out of Benthamism; and all the emotions and sufferings he has endured have helped him to thoughts that never entered Bentham's head. However, he is still too fond of demonstrating everything. If John Mill were to get up to heaven, he would hardly be content till he had made out how it all was. For my part, I don't much trouble myself about the machinery of the place; whether there is an operative set of angels or an industrial class, I'm willing to leave all that. Neither do I ever quake on my bed like Wordsworth, trying to reconcile the ways of Providence to my apprehension. I early came to the conclusion that I was not very likely to make it out clearly: the notions of the Calvinists seem what you cannot escape from, namely, that if it's all known beforehand, why, it all must happen. This does not affect your actual work at all; and if you have faith that is all just and true, why, it won't harm you to shape any notions about it. I don't see that we do any good by puzzling our poor weak heads about such things while there is plenty of clear work before them in the regions of practicability. In the meantime, I know that I have uncontrolled power over one unit in creation, and it's my business in life to govern that one as well as possible. I'm not over-fond of Bolingbroke's patronising Providence, nor of Voltaire's—"If there were no God, we should be forced to invent one for the completion of the system." '

On finding out what one's path in life really is, he said, 'You're better judges of this than any one else, yet you must often waste half your life in experimenting, and perhaps fail after all! There is a set of people whom I cannot do with at all—those who are always declaring what an extremely perfect world this is, and how very well things are conducted in it; to me it seems all going wrong and tending irresistibly to change—which can't but be for the worse.' I asked if there was a single institution existing which was as he would have it. 'Why, I can't say there is, exactly.' Asked him concerning his early history, as compared with Teufelsdröckh's.* 'Why, my advent, I believe, was not at all out of the common; one extraordinary fact of my childhood was that after eleven months' profound taciturnity, I hear a child cry, and astonished them all by saying, "What ails wee Jock?" A small

* Imaginary German Professor in Carlyle's *Sartor Resartus*.

acquaintance of mine was looking at some soldiers, and turned solemnly to his father: "Papa, these were once men!"—it is his last speech on record.' The description of Entepfuhl is identical with that of his (Carlyle's) native village; also the indivisible suit of yellow serge is historical, into which he had daily to insinuate himself. Talked of 'Hermann and Dorothea,' which Mrs. Carlyle says he likes to read on a warm day; he thinks Wordsworth might have written it, but there are thoughts in Goethe, and particularly in 'Wilhelm Meister,' which a dozen Wordsworth's could not see into. Their two maids got hold of his translation of the book and were always at it, scrubbing with one hand and holding the book with the other. Talked much on the misery of the Scotch poor: he feels a great jealousy of the quantity of black benevolence which goes out of the country, when so much yellow and green benevolence is wanted at home—at Paisley and elsewhere; people should sweep clean before their own door. He spoke vehemently in favour of emigration. He told us of having once been with Elizabeth Fry at Newgate, where she read the story of Mary Magdalene in those silver tones of hers: it went from the heart, and therefore to the heart: there was nothing theatrical about it. Mrs. Fry and one or two Quakeresses who were with her looked like a little spot of purity in a great sweltering mass of corruption. We then talked on self-forgetfulness, how attainable? You can soon ascertain whether there is any affection about you, and get rid of that first, and then the faults you are continually falling back into keep down your vanity and help to hold the balance fair. His wife was very affectionate; her health and spirits are deeply depressed by what she has gone through.

Carlyle's conversation and general views are curiously dyspeptic, his indigestion colouring everything. There was something particularly engaging in his reprobation of a heartless caricature of the execution of poor Louis XVI., which he desired us not to look at, but introduced a beautiful one of himself smoking in his tub, which John Sterling compares to one of Michael Angelo's prophets. He stood at the window with his pipe to help us to draw a comparison.

June 10.—John Mill told us that he sent 'Arthur Coningsby,' with other books, some years ago to Carlyle in Scotland, which so interested him that he wished to know the author, and thus he and Sterling began their friendship. Called on Sir W. Hooker [Director] at Kew Gardens; his enthusiasm for his New Holland shrubs and plants knew no bounds. They are in many respects totally distinct in general character from what we are accustomed to, presenting the edge of the leaf to the sun, and other fantastic arrangements. His son is with Captain Ross.

June 11.—Elizabeth Fry took us to Coldbath Fields Prison. Asked her concerning her experience of solitary confinement: in one prison, where it was very limitedly used, she knew of six who became mad in consequence of it. Met the Duchess of Saxe-Weimar (sister to our Queen Dowager), her two pretty daughters, and Lady Denbigh. The survey of the prison was exceedingly interesting. It is on the whole the best of our Houses of Correction, though a severe one, as whipping and the treadmill are still allowed. It was sad to see the poor exhausted women ever toiling upward without a chance to progress. The silent system is enforced with as much strictness as they can manage, but of course it is sometimes evaded. It was beautiful to hear Cousin Fry's little conversations with them; her tone of sympathy and interest went to their hearts. She had no reading, owing to the High Church principles of the directors and chaplains of the prison, but she craved leave to tell them a story of the effect of one passage from the Bible on a poor prisoner, which melted many of them to tears. The tact with which she treated the two chaplains who went round with us was inimitable, telling them that if the Duchess was very anxious for a reading, she would propose to turn out all the gentlemen except her brother, for they had said it would be impossible to be present at worship which they did not conduct. The Duchess was much pleased, and with her unaffected daughters drove off to Chiswick.

June 16.—Met John Sterling, fresh from Italy, at Temple Bar, and proceeded by appointment to the rooms of William Smith [philosopher], a quiet, recluse, meditative, abstract-looking man, somewhat like F. D. Maurice. It was pleasant to see the warm and surprised meeting between him and Sterling after a separation of many years. Progressed to the [Templars'] ... W. Smith obtained admission for us by means of a weak brother-Bencher, who was not aware of a recently issued prohibition, consequent on the rush of visitors. They are endeavouring to restore it to its antique gorgeousness by painting the ceiling in arabesque after contemporary patterns, inserting beautiful coloured glass windows, relieving the marble from the stucco by which it had been concealed in the days of the Puritans. The Mills joined us in the survey. This was the opening scene of the 'Onyx Ring' [tale by Sterling]. It was much to listen to him and John Mill on Italy and the thoughts it inspired . . . Visited the grand old Templars, all lying in state under a shed waiting for readjustment. Sterling expressed all the feeling one has about them in quoting Coleridge's lines:

'Their bones are dust,
Their good swords rust,
Their souls are with the saints, I trust'

which just gives the middle-age spirit of chivalry and religious faith. It is said that all monuments of Templars have the legs crossed, but as the opposite case has been equally proved, Smith remarked, 'I am gradually coming to disbelieve everything that has ever been asserted.' John Mill talked about his book on Logic, which he is going to give us; but he declares it will be more intelligible than interesting—how intelligible he will find out in two years. He forbids my reading it, though, except some chapters which he will point out. 'It would be like my reading a book on mining because you live in Cornwall—it would be making Friendship a burden!'

June 18.—To Bridgewater House to see the pictures, where we met Sterling. His criticisms very useful and illuminating. A fine ecclesiastical head suggested the following story:—A Protestant Bishop was declaiming to a Roman Catholic on the folly of a belief in Purgatory. 'My lord,' was the reply, 'you may go further and fare worse.'

We then went to [Sir Richard] Westmacott's* studio, introduced by Fanny Haworth. He is a man of extreme energy and openness of countenance, real enthusiasm for his art, and earnest to direct its aim as high as heaven. He and Sterling had several spirited discussions on Greek feeling for

* Professor of Sculpture, Royal Academy. Best known for his bronze Achilles, Hyde Park Corner.

Art, and how far we may benefit by studying from such models. Westmacott . . . delights in [John] Flaxman,* and pointed out a bas-relief of his Mercury and Venus 'as a little piece of music.' 'A most pagan illustration by a most Christian artist,' said Sterling.

June 19.—Saw the — Foxes. They are very full of Deville, the phrenologist, with whom they have had some intercourse. He told them of an anonymous lady, whom he had to caution against sensitiveness to the opinion of others. Some years afterwards she came again and brought a daughter, who, when finished, was sent into another room, and the lady consulted him upon her own cranium. He found the sensitiveness so fearfully increased as almost to require medical treatment. He afterwards met her at a party, when she introduced herself to him as Lady Byron. Her third visit to him was made whilst Moore's Life of her husband was being published, and, in accordance with his prescription, she had not allowed herself to read it.

June 21.—At the African Meeting; Lady Parry [wife of Sir William Edward Parry, Arctic explorer] with us, and very amusing. We sat in a little gallery with the Duchess of Sutherland, her three daughters, and Lady John Russell, all very striking women. The meeting was not very interesting, with the exception of a brilliant speech from Samuel Wilberforce, full of eloquence from the heart; and a capital one from Lord John Russell, in which he thoroughly committed himself to measures of justice, humanity, and civil progress.

June 22.—Met Samuel Gurney† at Paddington, and reached Hanwell [Asylum] in a few minutes. Were most kindly received by Dr. [John] Conolly; he has had the superintendence for two years, and at once introduced the system of non-coercion in its fullest sense, though feeling that it was a very bold experiment and required intense watching; but he dared it all for the sake of a deeply suffering portion of humanity, with most blessed result. It was delightful to observe the pleasure with which he was greeted by the patients and their anxious inquiries after his health, for he has been ill lately; and the extreme kindness, gentleness, and

---

* Preceded Westmacott as Professor of Sculpture, Royal Academy.
† Philanthropist, known as 'the banker's banker'; worked for reform of the criminal code. Brother of J. J. Gurney and Elizabeth Fry.

patience of his manner towards them was the triumph of sympathy, forbearance, and love. All the assistants seemed influenced by his spirit, and it is a most delightful and heart-cheering spectacle to see madness for once not treated as a crime.

June 27.—A charming visit from M. A. Schimmelpenninck,* who looks bright, handsome, and active. We soon got to Roman Catholicism and a book of Miss [Grace] Agnew's, 'Geraldine,' which sets forth the sunny side of the doctrine. Mrs. Schimmelpenninck would define the principle of Roman Catholicism as Belief, that of Protestantism as Examination, and a just mixture of these two she conceives to be the true article. As for any one party getting at the whole truth, she justly considers this preposterous enough, and illustrated her view by the account an Indian missionary gave her of a Christian native, whom he had been asking, how the diversity of Christian belief which had come before them from the settlement of some fresh missionaries, had affected them. 'Why,' he said, 'it is like a city of the blind, when an elephant is brought amongst them for the first time. Each tries to give an account of it. One says it is like the tail of a thing, another, it is like a hoof, and so on; and then they begin to quarrel, a seeing man tells them, "It's quite true that part is like a tail, part like a hoof, but none of you have any idea how large the elephant is, and how impossible it is for any of you to have felt it all." ' Thus she is always anxious that we should not condemn others for their views, however little we can see with them. She talked with a good deal of poetical truth on Quakerism, and she loves the conventual effect of our costumes.

Falmouth, July 12.—Capital walk with John Sterling . . .

On Goethe's character: the more Sterling examines, the less he believes in his having wilfully trifled with the feelings of women; with regard to his selfishness, he holds that he did but give the fullest, freest scope for the exercise of his gift, and as we are the gainers thereby, he cannot call it selfishness. On Carlyle and their recent expedition together to Hampton Court: Carlyle was in gloomy humour and finding fault with everything, therefore Sterling defended with equal universality. At last Carlyle shook his head and pronounced, 'Woe

* For this writer's descriptions of visits to Penjerrick see Introduction.

to them that are at ease in Zion.' Sterling was reminded of a poem which Goethe has translated, which introduces the carcase of a dead dog, which one after another approaches, expressing disgust at the smell, the appearance, &c.; at last Christ passes, looks on it, and says, 'What beautiful white teeth it has!'

July 14.—Tea at the Sterlings'. I did not notice in its right place the admirable living sketch of Carlyle which Mrs. Carlyle told Sterling of, saying it was the best that had been done, and that she thought the artist, Samuel Laurence,* meant to give it her. Sterling went to Laurence, found that he had no such intention, bought it, and with much triumph displayed it to the lady. It is a thoroughly satisfactory portrait.

July 21.—Visit to the Sterlings . . . He is devouring the new and greatly improved edition of Maurice, whose notion of Quakerism is, that it is all included in the belief of the Church of England, and therefore that George Fox mistook his calling when he separated himself and followers into a sect. Sterling would fain abolish all sects, and desires that all might concentrate their light into one pure Crystal. But I fear that this Crystal will never be discovered but in Utopia or—Heaven.

July 27.—John Sterling is interesting himself much about George Fox, whose life he means to write. He sadly misses his earnest, prophetic spirit in the present day, and thinks Carlyle the only one who at all represents it. He read us a grievous letter from the latter, complaining of finding great difficulty in doing his work, 'his right hand having forgotten her cunning.' . . . Speaking of the old Puritan preachers, Carlyle comments on the excessive fun which bursts out even in their sermons, and says that he believes all really great men were great laughers too, and that those who have the gravest capacity in them have also the greatest fun; therefore he cordially hails a hearty guffaw even from a Puritan pulpit.

July 28.—Sterling, commenting on some Essays by a clever young man of twenty, and finding a want of solidity in them, remarked, 'Why, I was once a clever young man of twenty, and I know the quantity of inefficient thought which possesses you at that age. Not that any true effort at thought is

* Herkomer's etching of Caroline is after Laurence's portrait.

useless, though you have often to think yourself out of it
again. You frequently come to your original position, but on
principles how different from what before possessed you!'

August 3.—John Sterling and Samuel Gurney were talking
over Quaker peculiarities of language, S. Gurney going to the
derivation of words to prove that truth was our object . . .

August 22.—Sterling has finished George Fox's Journal,
which has interested him much, though he does not find it as
remarkable as he had expected—less originality and out-
flashing of the man's peculiar nature. He is greatly amused at
Fox's placid conviction that he has never committed a fault
or made a mistake; also his undoubting belief in the most
astounding judgments pronounced and executed around him
on his account. Thus—'A Judge treated me very cruelly;
accordingly God smote him with a fever, so that he died the
next day!'

September 4.—Saw John Sterling: he has heard from Carlyle, who has been greatly interested by two interviews with
Professor Owen, from whom, he says, he has learnt more than
from almost any other man. He is charmed by his natural-
ness, and the simplicity he has preserved in a London
atmosphere.

September 16.—Floated in the harbour with the Sterlings, a
very calm, thoughtful, and merry opportunity, as fancy led
us. Books and men engaged us more to-day than angels or
speculations. Sterling is truly an invaluable person to consult
on any literary or logical difficulties, and his ready friendship
seems really rejoiced to be able to help any who desire it in
earnest. He read us some admirable letters from Carlyle, who
has just been making a pilgrimage to Ely, and enjoyed the
music in the Cathedral so as to wish it might always last, and
whenever the spirit of worship inspired one, he might go in
there and worship with congenial tones from invisible sources.
He smoked a pipe sitting on Cromwell's horse-block, and felt
it a sort of acme in possible human positions.

John Sterling rather impertinently compared [Clarkson]
Stanfield's* colouring to a literary Quakeress, all drab and
blue!

September 27.—This morning Sterling gave a capital sketch
of Carlyle. The occasion of his first publishing was this:

* Marine and landscape artist; scene-painter at Drury Lane.

Edward Irving was requested by the editor of the *Gentleman's Magazine* to contribute an article; he looked into the magazine and discovered in one of the papers the expression, 'Good God!' This he said must prevent his having anything to do with it, but he had a friend not so scrupulous, who would be glad to send a paper and was well qualified for it. This friend was Thomas Carlyle, who continued in connection with this magazine (in which the 'Essays of Elia' first appeared) until Jeffrey induced him to write for the *Edinburgh*,* where his 'Life of Schiller' first made him notorious. Sterling read these papers with the strongest interest, which he once expressed in the presence of Charles Buller. 'Oh,' said he, 'he was a tutor of ours'; and from that time Buller got prettily pumped for information concerning this said tutor of theirs.

October 4.—At the Falmouth Polytechnic; met Anthony Froude, who was thoughtful, speculative, and agreeable. He was interesting in analysing character. From Sterling's handwriting he calls him enthusiastic but not sanguine, rather desponding; an amazing flow of ideas and great choice of language. Defined Affectation as an attempt to Seem. Thus the high are as affected in imitating the low, as the low in aping the high. On the study of history: he is as delighted with [Thomas] Arnold as I am; on his remarking to Dr. Pusey on the beauty of Arnold's comparing the Church and State to the Soul and Body, Pusey quietly but most solemnly said, 'I consider the Church belongs to a much higher Body.'

October 10.—. . . Herman Merivale [later Under-Secretary for India] has been at Falmouth and spent some time with Sterling; he has a clever head and much good sense.

October 16.—A. B. went with us to see some of the old women; he shrank from it on the ground of not being a clergyman, but was reassured by Sterling reminding him that St. Paul was not a clergyman either.

October 17.—A discussion between William Edward Forster and Sterling on the purity of motive in martyrdom—whether any would yield his life for the sake of an abstract moral truth, if there were no prospect of reward or punishment in the background. Sterling said, 'Life would not be worth living

---

* Carlyle's *Schiller* actually appeared in *The London Magazine*, though he also contributed to *The Edinburgh Review*.

without such a faith in the entire devotion to Truth being experienced by some high minds.' Both parties argued well, and it was continued for the evening, William admitting that all actual martyrs were probably actuated by both motives, and that in this, as in most cases, a mixed theory was the true one . . .

November 4.—Carlyle writes complaining of the mighty dust-mountain which he has to dig into, as yet with little result, in his Cromwellian researches. Laments the death of Allan Cunningham,* as one face that has ever looked kindly on him and will look on him no more—'A loss,' Sterling says, 'which he can little afford, such is the warmth and exclusiveness of his affection.' Anna Maria heard also in the evening from Mrs. Carlyle, who thanks her for a copy of Laurence's portrait of her husband. She speaks of her husband's present subject being a particularly toilsome one, if you may judge from the spluttering he makes; he is trying whether some teeth and a shin-bone dug up from the field of Naseby may not inspire him.

November 14.—Note from Carlyle begging Sterling to make inquiries about the miner at Caradon, who so heroically devoted himself to the saving of his comrade, and suggesting whether anything, and what sort of thing, might be done for him. 'At all events,' he says, 'let me know whether there is one other such true brave workman living and working with me at this time on this earth; there is help and profit in being sure of that.'

November 19.—Heard that the Caradon miner Verran is saving up his money, till he has got £30 or £40, in order to leave off work and get six months' learning—a good fact.

December 17.—John Sterling brought a letter from Carlyle, written in the spirit of his 'Essay on Burns,' together with the following petition:—

'To Michael Verran, seemingly a right brave man, and highly worthy of being educated, these small gifts of money, if they can assist him therein, are, with all hopefulness and good regard, presented by certain undersigned fellow-wayfarers and wayfarers of his.'

In his letter to Sterling he says:—

* Collector of old songs and tales; produced 'old ballads' of his own composition.

'This man Verran is evidently a hopeful person; one of those rare human beings whom it is not very difficult to help. Decidedly he ought to be tried to a certain extent. In what way, with what precautions, pre-inquiries, &c., I will leave you and our benevolent Friends altogether to decide. A sum of forty or fifty pounds to aid him in his noble purpose of schooling himself might at any rate be useful. I put down my sovereign on the adjoined leaf (the post-office order goes along with it); do you and other kind men add what more you can in the shape of money or of better than money: my poor faculty in regard to the matter is as good as out. But just men beholding such a thing are *bound* to acknowledge it, to cherish it and the like of it, as Heaven's sacred fire on the altar of this our common earth, not too copiously supplied with fire at present! I have rarely fallen in with a more assistable-looking man than this same most meritorious Verran. Tell the Misses Fox that I specially recommend him to them. Tell all people that a man of this kind ought to be hatched—that it were shameful to eat him as a breakfast egg! And so Heaven prosper him and you, and all the benefactors he can find; and may some blessing come out of this inquiry, and not a curse to any one.'

December 22.—Barclay had a letter from J. S. Mill: he speaks of his growing conviction that individual regeneration must precede social progress, and in the meantime he feels that the best work he can do is to perfect his book on Logic, so as to aid in giving solidity and definiteness to the workings of others.

1843

Falmouth, January 6.—I was made somewhat conceited this morning by a kind note from Thomas Carlyle. He makes amusing reference to my saying 'thou' to him, and threatens to say 'thou' to me too, but must not venture at present. Speaking of Verran, he says, 'We are not to neglect such when they offer themselves among the half or wholly useless things so enormously copious among us.'

January 9.—Another characteristic note from Carlyle:—

'Dear Caroline,—Thanks for your excellent news. We will not scold the poor fellow much, at least not till he get fully well again. As to the Hero Verran, I wish you to understand that, at such a distance, and with such friends' eyes close on the very scene, I cannot presume to form any further judgment of his interests, but will leave them altogether to the eyes and hearts of said friends. Do, therefore, what seems to *you* wisest. Perhaps if there be, as it seems there is, in Verran's personal neighbourhood a good discerning man who will take charge of this £20, to do his best therewith for the poor miner's behoof, it will be wiser in several ways to give it up to that man at once and for altogether; saying merely, "Do thy best with it for him." Verran may thus gain another friend and occasional guide and patron, which may be worth more to him than several guineas. "Twenty," I think, is no bad result. To find twenty persons, in any locality, who reverence worth to the extent of paying one pound sterling to it, is verily something in these days. Days (as I sometimes feel, when I reflect sorrowfully on them) altogether unexampled since the creation of the world in that respect! Even the fickle Athenians did at least put Socrates to death, had at least the grace to hate him, did not merely seek to amuse themselves with him! It is unutterable, and will lead to conclusions by and by.

'Meanwhile, what the good Caroline has to do is happily utterable enough; not abstruse or fearful at all! What I have to do is also, alas! too plain: namely, to go about my business, and, with many wishes and salutations, vanish, as one in haste and double haste,—subscribing myself cordially once more, Caroline's friend,

T. Carlyle'

January 21.—Fanny Allen sends a very interesting account of a visit she and her father paid to Michael Verran. He is a thorough Methodist, who sometimes feels so full of joy that his skin seems too small for him, and he is obliged to lie down and pray that he may be enlarged, to make room for his bursting happiness. He gave a simple, quiet account of the Caradon affair, during which, it seems, his mind was so full of the prospect of being so soon with his Saviour, that the idea of death and its suffering hardly occurred to him; and on coming to the surface, he fell down on his knees in the shed and 'gave glory.' He is not getting on very brilliantly at school, but is steady and persevering, and means to be a dairyman or an ore-dresser.

February 3.—Aunt Charles Fox told us of an American

Friend who once felt a concern to go somewhere, he knew not where. He ordered his gig, his servant asking where he was to drive. 'Up and down the road,' said his master. At last they met a funeral. 'Follow this funeral,' said the master. They followed in the procession until they came to the churchyard. Whilst the service was being performed the Friend sat in his gig; at its conclusion he walked to the grave, and exclaimed solemnly, 'The person now buried is innocent of the crime laid to her charge!' and then returned to his gig. An elderly gentleman in deep mourning came up to him in great agitation, and said, 'Sir, what you said has surprised me very much.' 'I can't help it, I can't help it,' replied the other; 'I only said what I was obliged to say.' 'Well,' said the mourner, 'the person just buried is my wife, who for some years has lain under the suspicion of infidelity to me. No one else knew of it, and on her deathbed she again protested her innocence, and said that if I would not believe her then, a witness to it would be raised up even at her graveside!'

February 9.—Sir Edward Belcher dined with us to-day, and sailed when the post came in. He has a high appreciation of Papa's Dipping Needle. He talked of the Pacific Islanders he has visited: they all appear to have a common origin, and their languages to be derived from, and very analogous to, Hebrew . . .

February 11.—Strong Methodist letter from Michael Verran—very grateful to God and man. Three years ago he found peace, a month later he received the second blessing, and the day following the third; his path is now like that of the Just, shining brighter and brighter to the perfect Day. He finds spelling 'asier than at first, and has got to the Rule of Three in refimatic.'

February 20.—John Sterling . . . says that Carlyle is bringing out a thirty-pounder of a book on the Northern troubles [*Past and Present*].

February 26.—Letter from Carlyle. His present work is one that makes him sad and sick; it is likely to be ready in about three weeks, and then he expects to be ready for the hospital. He says that John Sterling was the first to tell him that his tendencies were political, a prophecy which he feels is now being strangely verified. Terrible as it is to him to pronounce the words which he does, he feels that those and no others are given him to speak; he sees some twenty thousand in pauper-Bastilles looking for a Voice, inarticulately beseeching, 'Speak for us!' and can he be silent? His book is on the sorrows in the North, and will probably consist of the Facts of the French Revolution connected with his theory of the present misgovernment of England.

March 9.—J. S. Mill's book arrived yesterday—'A System of Logic.' I read the chapter on Liberty and Necessity. Sterling spoke of the gradual development which he had watched in him . . .

March 24.—Sterling talked about the men he has seen in his visit to London.—Carlyle very unhappy about the times, thinking everything as bad as ever, and conducted on the least happiness for the greatest number principle; the only thing good is, that people are made to feel unhappy, and so prove that enjoyment is not the object of life. His book is now being copied, and is to be printed simultaneously in England and America, so that he, being the Prophet to both lands, may receive the Profits from both. With Julius Hare he had uniting intercourse, and it was particularly interesting after their long separation to see how much common ground they still had to walk and love upon. He gave him Tieck's last book, which he thinks shows more genius than anything lately published . . .

March 31.—Sterling talked this morning about the Apocalypse, which he believes refers principally to Pagan Rome, and the actual life which the Apostle saw around him, and which he felt must be denounced and punished by a God of holiness and truth. This he believes to be the feeling of all the prophecies.

May 3.—After dinner I was writing to Aunt Charles, and on running upstairs for more paper, I was startled to find myself spitting blood. It proved to be only from the throat, but I, for half an hour, took it entirely as a signal of death, and shall, I believe, often look back with satisfaction to the solemn quietness which I felt at that time. I finished Aunt Charles's note, and then lay down alone, and felt altogether rather idle about life, and much disposed to be thankful, or at any rate entirely submissive, whatever might be the result.

May 6.—Called on the W. Molesworths.* He is threatened

* Sir William Molesworth was proprietor of the *London Review*.

with total blindness, and his excellent wife is learning to work in the dark in preparation for a darkened chamber. What things wives are! What a spirit of joyous suffering, confidence, and love was incarnated in Eve! 'Tis a pity they should eat apples.

May 25.—John Sterling wandered out and dined with us; he was calm and sad, and feels the idea of leaving Falmouth. His London time was an extremely bustling one. Carlyle does not seem quite happy; though he has blown so loud a blast, and though it has awakened so many deep echoes in the hearts of thoughtful men, there are other trumpets yet to sound before Truth can get itself fully recognised, even by those who have gone far. Sterling gives a very bright description of their Isle of Wight habitation; I wish it may prove the land of promise to them.

May 29.—Sterling dwelt with delight on Mrs. Carlyle's character—such hearty sympathy in the background, and such brilliant talent in front; if it were merely 'eternal smart' with her, it would be very tiresome, but she is a woman as well as a clever person. She and her husband, though admiring each other very much, do not in all things thoroughly sympathise; he does not pay that attention to little things on which so much of a woman's comfort depends.

May 30.—Sterling dined here . . . He went off in the rain, looking quite his old self.

June 13.—I had the luxury of a solitary evening at Grove Hill—yet not solitary. I took up Emerson again, which I had not read in for many months, and was quite startled at the deep beauty and truth that is in him . . .

June 14.—How I like things to be done quietly and without fuss. It is the fuss and bustle principle, which must proclaim itself until it is hoarse, that wars against Truth and Heroism. Let Truth be done in silence 'till it is forced to speak,' and then should it only whisper, all those whom it may concern will hear.

June 18.—No news from Barclay. Well, silence is doubtless safe, and patience is good for us. I think Heaven will bless him, but how, it does not suit me even to wish; I've no notion of giving hints to providence.

August 5.—Finished that wondrous 'Past and Present,' and felt a hearty blessing on the gifted Author spring up in my soul. It is a book which teaches you that there are other months besides May, but that with Courage, Faith, Energy, and Constancy, no December can be 'impossible.'

August 14.—Schleiermacher is a very fine fellow, so far as I can yet discern; a noble, large-hearted, courageous, clear-sighted, thoughtful, and generous Christian, in the deepest as well as the popular sense of the terms, a nourishing writer, whose whole reasoning and discerning speaks irrefutably to one's own holiest convictions. Then what knowledge of human nature he has! He ferrets out our high, noble, self-sacrificing sins, and shows no more mercy to them than to the vulgar fellows which smell of garlic.

August 20.—Barclay had a long interview yesterday with Espartero, the ex-Regent of Spain. He has just had to escape from a Rebellion aided by France, which he could not repress, and now resigns himself to becoming an Englishman until Spain is ready for him again.

August 21.—Tea at Trebah. Aunt Charles sends brilliant accounts of her present environment—Hartley Coleridge on one side, Wordsworth on the other. She says the latter is very sensible and simple about the Laureateship; he speaks of it very kindly, but has quite declined doing any work connected with it on compulsion. He says it is most gratifying to fill the same station that Dryden and Southey have done.

September 10.—Barclay and his beloved W. E. Forster cheered our day. Barclay showed us letters from a bookseller in London to F. D. Maurice, which exhibit most touchingly, most vividly, most truly, the struggle of doubt, the turbulence of despair, the apathy of exhausted effort, so frightfully general among the mechanics of large towns; a something which tells that at the present attempts at teaching do not meet the wants of the time . . .

September 13.—Embarked on the railroad at Bristol* and reached London at four o'clock; our only companion was a weary young man, who complained of this tedious mode of travelling!

Norwich, September 21.—Called at the Palace with Anna Gurney. Catherine Stanley said the Bishop [Edward Stanley] would be so charmed, and ran down for him. He is as active as usual. He was very affectionate, and charged Anna to use

* The railway did not reach Falmouth until 1863.

her endeavours to make us follow her example and remain in Norfolk. He says there is no chance of his coming into Cornwall unless they make him Bishop of Exeter . . .

Cromer, September 24.—Our first visit at Northrepps Hall, a droll, irregular, unconventional-looking place, which must have had some share in shaping the character of its inhabitants . . . A wild horseback party of eleven, with Sir Fowell Buxton at our head, scampered over everything in tremendous rain, which only increased the animation of our party. Then dined with the Buxtons. Sir Fowell is capital now and then, but not at all to be depended upon as a man of society. Most pleasant intercourse with the family, individually and collectively, but there is little of steady conversation to record. Sir Fowell Buxton has never recovered his old tone of joyous mental energy since the failure of the Niger Expedition, and looked sometimes very sadly. He was most kind and affectionate to us, and we greatly valued being with them. During the night a storm told most seriously on the little fishing-boats, and there was sad loss of life. In his prayer the next morning this affliction was most beautifully named, and the suffering and sorrowing fervently petitioned for. Lady Buxton gave us each a Prayer-book, thinking it probable that no one else had done so. He likes to tell absurd stories about her, in the face of her emphatic protestations, and he enjoys being impertinently treated himself. His frolics with his grandchildren are charming.

October 9.—Lieutenant Hammond dined here. He was with Captain Fitz-Roy on the *Beagle*, and feels enthusiastically towards him. As an instance of his cool courage and self-possession, he mentioned a large body of Fuegians, with a powerful leader, coming out with raised hatchets to oppose them: Captain Fitz-Roy walked up to the leader, took his hatchet out of his hand, and patted him on the back; this completely subdued his followers.

Norwich, October 21.—Catherine Gurney gave us a note to George Borrow, so on him we called,—a tall, ungainly, uncouth man, with great physical strength, a quick penetrating eye, a confident manner, and a disagreeable tone and pronunciation. He was sitting on one side of the fire, and his old mother on the other. His spirits always sink in wet weather, and to-day was very rainy, but he was courteous and not displeased to be a little lionised, for his delicacy is not of the most susceptible. He talked about Spain and the Spaniards; the lowest classes of whom, he says, are the only ones worth investigating, the upper and middle class being (with exceptions, of course) mean, selfish, and proud beyond description. They care little for Roman Catholicism, and bear faint allegiance to the Pope. They generally lead profligate lives, until they lose all energy and then become slavishly superstitious. He said a curious thing of the Esquimaux, namely, that their language is a most complex and highly artificial one, calculated to express the most delicate metaphysical subtleties, yet they have no literature, nor are there any traces of their ever having had one . . .

October 22.—Dined with Amelia Opie: she was in great force and really jolly. Exhibited her gallery containing some fine portraits by her husband, one being of her old French master, which she insisted on Opie painting before she would accept him. She is enthusiastic about Father Mathew,* reads Dickens voraciously, takes to Carlyle, but thinks his appearance against him; talks much and with great spirit of people, but never ill-naturedly.

October 23.—Dined very pleasantly at the Palace. The Bishop was all animation and good-humour, but too unsettled to leave any memorable impression. I like Mrs. Stanley much—a shrewd, sensible, observing woman . . .

London, October 30.—An early call in Cheyne Row. Jane Carlyle was very brilliant, dotting off, with little reserve, characters and circumstances with a marvellous perception of what was really significant and effective in them, so that every word told. She spoke of some Americans who called yesterday to take leave, and her hand got such a squeeze that she almost screamed, 'for all my rings are utilitarian and have seals.' She says that Carlyle has to take a journey always after writing a book, and then gets so weary with knocking about that he has to write another book to recover from it. When the books are done they know little or nothing of them, but she judges, from the frequent adoption of some of his phrases in books of the day, that they are telling in the land.

Met John Sterling and H. Mill, and went to Professor Owen's, where W. E. Forster and Barclay joined us. Here we

* Champion of temperance in Ireland; he did relief work during the famine.

saw the great bone—the actual bone—of a bird which a sailor
brought to Owen from Sydney, and out of which he has
mentally constructed an immense Ostrich. And we saw the
series of vast bottles, each filled with a fixed Idea. Sterling
said he was quite awe-struck at the thought of being with a
man who knew them all! Owen gave us a little lecture on the
brain: that when it is much worked a certain portion is
actually lost; adding, that [Browning's] 'Strafford,' he supposed, cost its author about two ounces. He and Sterling then
got into a delicate little discussion upon Dr. Johnson's taste
for a good hater. Mrs. Owen supposed that differences in
opinion would be settled by definition, so Sterling defined it
as the sort of feeling which Owen would entertain towards Sir
Everard Home, who destroyed John Hunter's* papers; he
would not do him any harm, but he would not go out of his
way to prevent his being well punished. This led to discussion
on the wicked waste of Thought which Home had thus
committed. Facts and results of positive worth have been
irrevocably lost. Sara Coleridge [daughter of S. T. Coleridge]
is writing a defence of her father's theology, proving how very
orthodox he was and how well he deserved to be the pet son
of the Church. Sterling remarked that she shows the limited
nature of a woman's mind in her 'Phantasmion'; she does not
make Ariel an element, but the whole thing is Ariel, and
therefore very wearisome and unsubstantial.

1844

Falmouth, January 9.—Fanny Allen sends a glorious letter
from Verran. He says: 'I have three cows, three slip pigs; I've
plenty of grass, and a good sale for butter and cream. I've the
pleasure to tell you that I've also got a wife, and my wedding-
day was yesterday.'

Some boys to dinner; interested them and ourselves with
Dickens' beautiful human-hearted 'Christmas Carol.'

January 12.—Finished my week's work at the Infant School,
and wrote in the Visitors' Report Book, that as many eminent

* Surgeon and anatomist, he built a large museum in Leicester Square; though his
manuscripts were lost his collection was acquired by the College of Surgeons.

men were very stupid at school, there was every hope for the sixty-three there.

January 16.—I have had a treat in the following kind letter from Carlyle:—

Chelsea, 15th January 1844

'Dear Miss Caroline,—Your message is far from an intrusion; such a musical little voice coming out of the remote West, in these dull days, is not unwelcome to me, is rather apt to be too welcome! For undue praise is the poison of human souls: he that would live healthily, let him learn to go along entirely without praise. Sincere praises, coming in a musical voice in dull times, how is one to guard against them!

'I like Verran's picture of himself somewhat better this time. It is good that he has got a wife: his manner of announcing that great fact, too, is very original! 'Four cows, with plenty of grass, three slip pigs.' What are slip pigs? Pigs that have slipt or left their dam, and now feed on spoon-meat? All these things are good. On the whole, it was a benefit to lift this poor man out of the dark subterranean regions into the upper daylight, to the sight of the sky and green world. But it was not I mainly; no, it was another than I. The poor man, if well let alone, I think will now do well. Well let alone: it is an invaluable rule in many things—apt to be miserably forgotten in the case of Grace Darlings and such like!

'By the by, ought not you, with your swift neat pen, to draw up, on half a sheet of paper, and exact narrative of this man's act of heroism—authentic, exact in every detail of it—and reposit it in some safe place for a memorial of the same? There is no more genuine use that the art of writing can be turned to than the like of this. Think of it.

'I am about writing upon Oliver Cromwell—still *about* it; for the thing will not stir from the spot, let me shove it never so desperately! It approaches the impossible, this task of mine, more nearly than any task I ever had. How awaken an oblivious world, incognisant of Cromwells, all incredulous of such; how resuscitate a Hero sunk under the disastrous wrecks of two such centuries as lie dead on him?

'If I had a Fortunatus' Hat, I would fly into deepest silence,—perhaps into green Cornwall towards the Land's End, to meditate this sad problem of mine, far from Babylon and its jarrings and its discords, and ugly fog and mud, in sight of the mere earth and sea, and the sky with its stars. But I have not such a hat, there is none such going, one must learn to do without such.

'Adieu, dear Miss Caroline. Salute your brother in my name,—your brother and sister, and all that have any remembrance of me. My wife, pretty well in health, sends you her kindest regards.—I remain, ever yours, most sincerely,

T. Carlyle'

February 7.—Eliza Dunstan died to-day. It was such a child's deathbed, so innocent, so unpretending. She loved to hold her father's hand, he, poor fellow, kneeling by her in silent agony. She thought none could nurse her so well as father. Her spirit was most tenderly released. It is a wonderful thought, that sudden total change of hers. Has Heaven its Infant Schools? Who can tell?

March 8.—Mr. Dew told us much about Dr. Arnold, one of whose pupils he was. Such was his power over the hearts of the boys that they dreaded doing anything wrong lest it should pain him; they looked forward to his weekly sermons with as much delight as to a holiday, and as they were quite private, if anything remarkable had taken place in the week, they knew that it would be noticed on the Sunday. The class books they had to study were rich in marginal notes from his pencil, which made them live and become a pleasure, instead of a weariness, to flesh and spirit.

March 11.—Mrs. Carlyle told W. E. Forster that 'Hyperion'* answered, and Longfellow has married the young lady he wrote it at. Bon!

April 2.—I finished 'Deerbrook' with much regret. It is a brave book, and inspires trust and love, faith in its fulness, resignation in its meekness. One has a vicious desire to know Miss [Harriet] Martineau's private history.

April 4.—On reading [John Pringle] Nichol's 'Solar System,' Papa said, 'That Light only comes to those objects capable of receiving it.' A truth purely physical, it is to be observed.

April 8.—Read a letter from Harriet Martineau, describing the irresistible influence under which she uttered her 'Life in the Sick-Room,' and the numerous deeply interesting responses and echoes it has awakened, proving how much such a book was needed.

---

* Through *Hyperion* Longfellow did in fact transparently woo Frances Appleton who became his second wife. (See the entry for July 30, 1846.)

London, May 25.—Overtook John Mill in the Strand, and had a pleasant little chat with him . . .

May 27.—Called on the Carlyles. He was poorly, and asleep on the sofa when we went in. We told them of Barclay's engagement. 'Well, they must club together all the good sense they've got between them; that's the way, I suppose,' was the valediction bestowed. He groaned over Oliver Cromwell, for his progress in that memorial is slow and painful: all that had been said or written in his favour was destroyed or ignored when Charles II. came to reign; as a Calvinistic Christian he was despised, and as a Ruler and Regicide he was hated; the people would not forgive him for having seemed to deceive them, and so they dug up his body and hanged it at Tyburn, and have been telling the most abominable lies about him ever since; lately there has been some better feeling, but the case is still very bad. 'Upon the whole,' he added, 'I don't believe a truer, more right-hearted Englishman than Oliver ever existed. Wherever you find a line of his own writing you may be sure to find nothing but truth there.' . . . Then, speaking of the wretched mistakes which different ages make concerning their Greatest, he said, 'Why, the Jews took Jesus for a scoundrel, and thought all they could do with Him was to nail Him up on a gallows. Ah! that was a bad business; and so He has returned to Heaven, and they go wandering about the streets buying old clothes!'

Falmouth, July 21.—We were delighted to watch Uncle Joshua in his sweet companionship with Nature; the little birds are now so intimate and trustful that they come when he calls them and eat crumbs out of his mouth . . .

August 12.—Sir Charles Lemon and Lady De Dunstanville to lunch. Sir Charles has been with Bunsen lately, and both heartily share our enthusiasm about Dr. Arnold. Sir Charles says he is a man whom he always loved and valued; how sad it was that his friends not only did not understand but would not trust him, fancying he would run wild on politics or something else.

August 21.—Andrew Brandram, the very respectable and respected Secretary of the Bible Society, appeared before us once more with his shaggy eyebrows. He held a large Bible Meeting here, and told us many good things. There is a glimpse of an opening for the Bible in China, which it will be highly interesting to watch. In India the demand and supply is most satisfactory; about fifty years ago they could not find a Bible in Calcutta, and in Madras were obliged to swear on a scrap of a Prayer-book at the opening of a court-martial. In New Zealand the natives held a council before the last miserable war, when one of them entreated the rest to 'Remember the Book, remember the Book: it tells us not to fight; so if we do, mischief must come of it.' But the majority found it expedient to forget it as completely as the English had done . . .

August 22.—Andrew Brandram gave us at breakfast many personal recollections of curious people. J. J. Gurney recommended George Borrow to their Committee; so he stalked up to London, and they gave him a hymn to translate into the Manchow language, and the same to one of their own people to translate also. When compared they proved to be very different. When put before their reader, he had the candour to say that Borrow's was much the better of the two. On this they sent him to St. Petersburg to get it printed, and then gave him business in Portugal, which he took the liberty greatly to extend, and to do such good as occurred to his mind in a highly executive manner.

September 19.—We are told of Stephen Grellet once preaching to the Friends of a certain meeting, saying, 'You are starched before you are washed!'

Windermere, September 28.—Hartley Coleridge came to us whilst Anna Maria was sketching near Fox How, and talked of Dr. Arnold. He is just now reading his 'Life and Letters' with extreme interest. He used seldom to be with him in his mountain rambles, because he walked always so far and so fast. When Hartley Coleridge was at College, the Rugby boys were proverbially the worst, their moral training had been so neglected; but now Dr. Arnold's influence has reformed not only that, but raised the tone of the other public schools.

September 30.—Thought much on those stimulating lines of John Sterling's:—

> '"Tis worth a wise man's best of life,
> 'Tis worth a thousand years of strife,
> If thou canst lessen but by one,
> The countless ills beneath the sun.'

So in the strength of this feeling we helped a damsel to collect her calves and drive them into a field.

October 1.—We floated about Windermere with Hartley Coleridge. It was all very, very beautiful. Hartley Coleridge sparkled away famously, but I have preserved little. He showed us the house where Charles Lloyd* lived, and where he with Coleridge and Lamb used to dash away their thoughts and fancies. His remembrances of Lloyd were truly pathetic: he believes that much which is attributed to him as madness was simply his own horrible imaginations, which he would regard as facts, and mention to others as things which he had himself done. Query: Is not this of the essence of madness? His wife was one of the best of women, and it was a cruel task to her to give hints to strangers of his state, which she often had to do, in order that injustice might not be done him. Tennyson he knows and loves. He said, 'My sister has some real power; she was a great deal with my father during the latter years of his life.' He admires her 'Phantasmion,' but wishes it cut up into shorter stories. He thinks her thoroughly equal to her subject when she treats of Rationalism. He is a most affectionate brother, and laments her weak, overdone state of health. He hopes to bring out his own second volume of Poems this year or next, and rejoices to hear of any who sincerely sympathise with them. Speaking of the Arnolds, he said they are a most gifted family. I asked what specially in their education distinguished them. He rose from the dinner-table, as his manner is, and answered, 'why, they were suckled on Latin and weaned upon Greek!' He spoke of his father being one day in company with some celebrated man, and some man who was not celebrated; the latter wore leather breeches, and S. T. Coleridge had the delight of observing him taking notes of their conversation with a pin in the creases of the leather! . . . He talked of Wordsworth with high respect, but no enthusiasm . . . The reason for his not permitting the Prologue to the 'Excursion' to be published till after his death is, he believes, that the benefit of copyright may be enjoyed longer. He talked funnily of the necessity of every woman having two names, one for youth and one for mature age . . .

October 5.—We wandered forth by the Lake, and were

---

* Poet; author of *Desultory Thoughts on London*, 1831.

overtaken by a shower, and sheltered ourselves in a shed. Hartley Coleridge saw us, and begged us to come into his cottage—'The Knbbe,' as he endeavours to have it spelt. It was a snug little *room*, well furnished with books, writing affairs, and MSS. Anna Maria said, in answer to some deprecatory remark of his, 'One might be very happy here.' *'Or very miserable,'* he answered, with such a sad and terrible emphasis . . .

October 6.—Anna Maria and I paid a visit to the Words-worths. He was in great force, and evidently enjoyed a patient audience. He wanted to know how we came from Cornwall, which naturally brought us to railroads and a short lament over the one they mean to introduce here. He grieves that the ravens and eagles should be disturbed in their meditations, and fears that their endeavours after lyric poetry will be checked. However, he admits that railroads and all the mechanical achievements of this day are doing wonders for the next generation; indeed, it is the appropriate work of this age and this country, and it is doing it gloriously. That anxious money-getting spirit which is a ruling principle in England, and a passion and a law in America, is doing much by exhausting itself; we may therefore look forward with hopeful trust. Nothing excellent or remarkable is done unless the doer lays a disproportionate weight on the importance of his own peculiar work; this is the history of all sects, parties, cliques, and stock-jobbers whatsoever.

He discoursed on the utter folly of sacrificing health to books. No book-knowledge in the world can compensate you for such a loss; nothing can excuse your trifling with health except duty to God or to your neighbour. All that is needful is to understand your duty to God and to your neighbour, and that you can learn from your Bible. He heard with some indignation of Aunt Charles's party having been at Kis-singen. 'Why don't they take our own baths and not spend their money abroad?' Then we asked about his Solitary's Valley—whether it had a real or only a poetical existence? 'Why, there is such a valley as I have described in that book of the "Excursion," and there I took the liberty of placing the Solitary.' He gave the outline of a beautiful tour for us amongst the Lakes, and assured us that the guides would not treat us to passages from the 'Excursion,' as they probably did not know of the existence of such a poem. Told him of our Wednesday evening readings of the 'Excursion.' 'I hope you felt much wiser for it when you had finished,' he said laughingly. When we told him who had been the genius of those bright starry evenings, he said, 'John Sterling! Oh, he has written many very beautiful poems himself; some of them I greatly admire. How is he now? I heard that he was in poor health.' When told.—'Dead!'* he exclaimed; 'that *is* a loss to his friends, his country, and his age. A man of such learning and piety! So he is gone, and [William Lisle] Bowles and [Samuel] Rogers† left, who are so much older!' and the poor old man seemed really affected. He said, 'I was just going to have sent him a message by you to say how much I had been admiring his poetry.' I read him the lines—

> 'Regent of poetic mountains,
> Drawing from their deepest fountains
> Freshness, pure and everlasting,
> Wordsworth, dear and honoured name,
> O'er thee pause the stars, forecasting
> Thine imperishable fame'—

which he begged me to transcribe for him.

Wordsworth then spoke of having written to Bowles on the death of his wife, and found that his sympathy had been very welcome, though he had feared that it would be all confusion in the mind of the imbecile old man. It was Amy Fisher‡ who encouraged him to write. Spoke of her with enthusiasm: after what she wrote when a child, it was impossible she could go on progressing; her poetry was pure inspiration showered down direct from heaven, and did not admit of any further perfection. She is a very modest, womanly person, not allowing herself to come forward in society, nor abandoning herself to the eloquence of which he believes her very capable. Spoke of Archdeacon Hare as very excellent and very learned; more valued by Wordsworth for his classical than for his German attainments. Talked of the effect of German literature on the English mind: 'We must wait to find out what it

---

* See Introduction.
† Poets; Rogers declined the Laureateship on Wordsworth's death.
‡ Correctly, Emmie Fisher, whose youthful poems Wordsworth (her mother's cousin) regarded as the work of a prodigy.

is; my hope is, that the good will assimilate itself with all the good in the English character, and the mischievous element will pass away like so much else.' The only special criticism which he offered on German literature was,—'That they often sacrifice Truth to Originality, and in their hurry to produce new and startling ideas, do not wait to weigh their worth. When they have exhausted themselves and are obliged to sit down and think, they just go back to the former thinkers, and thus there is a constant revolution without their being quite conscious of it. Kant, Schelling, Fichte; Fichte, Schelling, Kant: all this is dreary work and does not denote progress. However, they have much of Plato in them, and for this I respect them: the English, with their devotion to Aristotle, have but half the truth; a sound philosophy must contain both Plato and Aristotle.' He talked on the national character of the French and their equalising methods of education: 'It is all formal, military, conventional, levelling, encouraging in all a certain amount of talent, but cramping the finer natures, and obliging Guizot and the few other men of real genius whom God Almighty is too good to leave them entirely destitute of, to stoop to the common limits, and teach their mouths to flatter and conciliate the headstrong, ardent, unthinking multitude of ordinary men, who dictate to France through the journals which they edit. There is little of large stirring life in politics now, all is conducted for some small immediate ends; this is the case in Germany as well as France. Goethe was amusing himself with fine fancies when his country was invaded; how unlike Milton, who only asked himself whether he could best serve his country as a soldier or a statesman, and decided that he could fight no better than others, but he might govern them better. Schiller had far more heart and ardour than Goethe, and would not, like him, have professed indifference to Theology and Politics, which are the two deepest things in man—indeed, all a man is worth, involving duty to God and to man.'

He took us to his Terrace, whence the view is delicious: he said, 'Without those autumn tints it would be beautiful, but with them it is exquisite.' It had been a wet morning, but the landscape was then coming out with perfect clearness. 'It is,' he said, 'like the human heart emerging from sorrow, shone on by the grace of God.' We wondered whether the scenery had any effect on the minds of the poorer people. He thinks it has, though they don't learn to express it in neat phrases, but it dwells silently within them. 'How constantly mountains are mentioned in Scripture as the scene of extraordinary events; the Law was given on a mountain, Christ was transfigured on a mountain, and on a mountain the great Act of our Redemption was accomplished, and I cannot believe but that when the poor read of these things in their Bibles, and the frequent mention of mountains in the Psalms, their minds glow at the thought of their own mountains, and they realise it all more clearly than others.'

Thus ended our morning with Wordsworth.

October 8.—We went up to Wordsworth with a copy of the 'Beadroll of Scamps and Heroes' for which he had asked. He was just going out, so we joined him in walking about the garden. He was consulted about the lines of Dedication for our Bride's Album, which Barclay had sent us . . . He made only one criticism, and withdrew it directly on understanding the line better. He praised the verses, and made various gratifying inquiries about the dear writer. He brought us in to see Mrs. Wordsworth, who was getting tea ready, and then we had an affectionate parting.

The old man looks much aged; his manner is emphatic, almost peremptory, and his whole deportment is virtuous and didactic.

1845

Falmouth, January 1.—Life is ceaselessly repeating itself, yet anything but monotony is the result. The beginning of our New Year was an epitome of our last year's experience—a marriage and a funeral.

January 13.—S. Rigaud, Lecturer from the Peace Society, came to dinner; he told us of an interview with Louis Philippe, who expressed his strong sympathy with the principle of Peace, declaring that when he was in America he was often asked for a toast, and always gave, 'Universal Peace throughout the World.' He said that since he came to the throne, he had been endeavouring to maintain the peace of

Europe, and had succeeded so far as to make it improbable that war should be again known, and that if he should be spared a few years longer, he quite hoped to be able to make war impossible! Bravo! most modest King.

January 18.—Charles Johns,* the Botanist, spent the morning with us. The earliest botanical fact concerning him is, that a biscuit was given him over which carraway seeds were sprinkled; he picked out the seeds, planted them, and waited, alas! vainly, for a crop of biscuits!

January 24.—A walk with Papa, in which he bore his testimony to the depth, perseverance, and far-seeing nature of the German mind in the way of science . . .

March 17.—Reading 'Wilhelm Meister.' It is a marvellous book, with its infinity of sharply drawn, perfectly distinct personalities . . .

June 6.—Reading a brilliant book by a nameless man[†]— 'Eothen, or Eastern Travel.' Full of careless, easy, masterly sketches, biting satire, and proud superiority to common report. It is an intellectual egotism which he acknowledges and glories in. He has remarkably freed himself from religious prepossessions, and writes as he feels, not as he *ought* to feel, at Bethlehem and Jerusalem.

June 12.—Spent the evening at Penmere, and met Professor Airy [Astronomer]. His subjects were principally technical, but he handled them with evident power and consciousness of power. Perhaps his look and manner were sometimes a little supercilious, but his face is a very expressive and energetic one, and lights up with a sudden brightness whilst giving lively utterance to clear expressive thoughts. He spoke with evident astronomical contempt of the premature attempts of Geology to become a science; all but mathematically proved Truth seems to him a tottering thing of yesterday. He delights in the Cornish miners, whom he has long known, and attributes their superior intelligence and independence partly to their having themselves an interest in the mining specula-tions and adventures of their employers—an arrangement unknown in other parts. The virtues of the dousing-rod he wholly attributes to the excitability of the muscles of the wrist. He totally ignores all inhabitants of the Moon, and says

* Succeeded Derwent Coleridge as headmaster of Helston School.
† Alexander William Kinglake (1809-91), historian of the Crimean War.

there is no more appearance of life there than in a teacup. And he seems to shun everything like undemonstrable hypotheses. He says the difference which Herschel's telescope makes in the appearance of the Moon is by giving it shade, and therefore the globular, instead of the flat look, which it has through ordinary glasses. There was a comet visible this evening, but very pale and hazy.

1846

Falmouth, January 4.—I have assumed a name to-day for my religious   principles—Quaker-Catholicism—having   direct spiritual teaching for its distinctive dogma, yet recognising the high worth of all other forms of Faith; a system, in the sense of inclusion, not exclusion; an appreciation of the universal, and various teachings of the Spirit, through the faculties given us, or independent of them.

February 18.—Teaching in Infant School. By way of realising a lecture on affection and gratitude to parents, I asked each of the little class what one thing they had done for their mothers that morning; and I confess I felt humbled and instructed to discover that one of these tiny creatures had worked some pocket-handkerchief, another lighted the fire, another helped to lay the breakfast, whilst most of them had taken part in tending the baby whilst mother was busy.

March 18.—Papa zealously defended this age from the charge of languor. He thinks there never was such activity— so much so, that men live twice as long now as formerly, in the same number of years. In mechanics, in shipping, in commerce, in book-making, in education, and philanthropy, this holds good.

London, May 17.—To Samuel Laurence's studio to be drawn. Admirable portraits in his rooms of Hare, Tennyson, Carlyle, Aubrey de Vere, and others. Of Laurence himself, more anon. Saw the Mills afterwards, who were infinitely cordial, and John Mill most anxious that we should come and see them in the spirit of self-mortification.

May 18.—Interesting time with Laurence. Tennyson strikes him as the strongest-minded man he has known. He has

Caroline Fox aged 27; etching by Herkomer
after a drawing by Samuel Laurence

William Wordsworth at the time Caroline Fox
met him: painting by H. W. Pickersgill

much enjoyed F. D. Maurice's sittings lately, and dwelt
especially upon the delicate tenderness of his character. Went
to South Place to luncheon, and met Dean Trench there—a
large melancholy face, full of earnestness and capacity for
woe. Under a portrait of himself he once found the name
'Ugolino' written, he looked so starved. He spoke of the two
Newmans,* who are alike in person, and he sees a likeness in
their intellectual results.

Called on the Derwent Coleridges at St. Mark's. Spoke of
F. D. Maurice: whatever country clergymen may think of
him, he is appreciated in London and recognised as a Leader
in the exposition of fundamental eternal Truth. He feels the
likeness between Maurice's method and aim and that of S. T.
Coleridge, and devoutly loves it accordingly.

May 19.—In the evening enter F. D. Maurice, who spent
two or three hours with us in varied conversation. Of the
Newmans: he thinks John Henry has far more imagination
than Frank. He (Maurice) was so little prepared for John's
last change, that he hardly feels sure it will now be a final
one . . . F. D. Maurice then spoke of Carlyle's 'Cromwell,'
in which he rejoices: the editorial labour in it is enormous;
there was such confusion, now brought into perfect clearness
by different punctuation and an occasional connecting word.

May 23.—To the College of Surgeons, where we found
Professor Owen enjoying his Museum. On looking at the
Dodo, he said that he believes the Dutch, on their way to
Amboyna, used to call at New Zealand and lay in a stock of
these birds; that the poor natives used themselves to eat them,
and when they were all gone, they were reduced to feed on
each other . . .

May 28.—To the Coleridges' examination by [Henry Hart]
Milman [formerly Professor of Poetry at Oxford]; he is a man
with great black eyebrows, and a strongly expressive
countenance, displaying more of strength than sensibility,
more of the critic than the poet.

May 29.—Went to the Mills. John Mill produced [J. D.]
Forbes's book on the Glaciers, and descanted thereon with all
the enthusiasm of a deep love. Talked of Blanco White,†

---

* J.H., later Cardinal Newman, and his brother F.W., scholar and writer.
† Theological writer. Originally a priest in Spain, he rejected Catholicism and
    became a Unitarian.

whom he once met at dinner. He did not seem a powerful man, but full of a morbid conscientiousness. None who knew him could avoid thinking mildly of him, his whole nature was so gentle and affectionate. As to Cromwell, he does not always agree with Carlyle, who tries to make him out ever in the right. He could not justify the Irish Massacres, though he fully believes that Cromwell thought it was right, as a matter of discipline, or he would not have done it. Mill says that he scarcely ever now goes into society, for he gets no good there, and does more by staying away.

June 2.—Called on the Maurices. He talked of Emerson as possessing much reverence and little humility; in this he greatly differs from Carlyle. He gave me, as an autograph, a paper on the philosophy of Laughter; he thinks it always accompanied with a sense of power, a sudden glory. From this he proceeded to dilate on Tears, and then to the triumph over both.

June 3.—Paid the Carlyles a visit. He looks thin but well, and is recovering from the torment of the sixty new Cromwell letters: he does not mean to take any more fresh ones on any terms . . . Talked of our projected tour in Switzerland, where we said Barclay was to go to grow fat. This he thinks exceedingly unnecessary: 'It's not a world for people to grow fat in.' Spoke of his first vision of the Sea, the Solway Firth, when he was a little fellow eighteen inches high: he remembers being terrified at it all, and wondering what it was about, rolling in its great waves; he saw two black things, probably boats, and thought they were the Tide of which he had heard so much. But in the midst of his reverie an old woman stripped him naked and plunged him in, which completely cured him of his speculations. If any one had but raised him six feet above the surface, there might have been a chance of his getting some general impression, but at the height of eighteen inches he could find out little but that it was wet. He asked about Yearly Meeting and the question of dress. I told him that the Clothes-Religion was still extant; he rather defended it, as symbolising many other things, though of course agreeing on its poverty as a test. He said, 'I have often wished I could get any people to join me in dressing in a rational way. In the first place, I would have nothing to do with a hat; I would kick it into the Serpentine, and wear some kind of cap or straw covering. Then, instead of these layers of coats one over the other, I would have a light waistcoat to lace behind, because buttoning would be difficult; and over all a blouse'—*ecce* Thomas Carlyle!

'My American acquaintance proceeded from vegetable diet to vegetable dress, and could not in conscience wear woollen or leather, so he goes about Boston in a linen dress and wooden shoes, though the ice stands there many feet against the houses. I never could see much in him, but only an unutterable belief in himself, as if he alone were to bear the weight of the Universe. So when he said to London, with all its businesses and iniquities and vast machinery of life, "Be other than thou art!" he seemed quite surprised that it did not obey him.' I remarked on its being rather a tendency amongst American thinkers to believe more intensely in Man than in God; he said, 'Why, yes; they seem to think that Faith in Man is the right sort of Faith.'

June 4.—Called on the Owens, and their just-arrived portrait of Cromwell. It was as of one resting after a long hard fight, and in the calmness of his evening, recalling and judging some of its stern incidents. The Carlyles had been to see it, and spent a characteristic evening there; he grumbling at all Institutions, but confessing himself convinced by Owen's 'Book on Fossils.'

Geneva, June 15.—Called on M. Merle d'Aubigné [theologian and ecclesiastical historian], and were interested by his beautifully curved lips and strong self-asserting look and manner . . .

Madame Janssen tells us that D'Aubigné has lost a child just as he finished each volume of his Reformation History, except the last and then his mother died! Will he venture on a fifth?

Merle d'Aubigné is a tall, powerful-looking man, with much delicacy of expression and some self-consciousness, very shaggy overhanging eyebrows, and two acute, deep-set, discriminating eyes . . .

July 13.—At Hattwyl we dined at the table-d'hôte, and had Merle d'Aubigné opposite us. He was very gracious, and gladly received a promise of a set of Anna Maria's illustrations of his works . . .

July 30.—Made the acquaintance of two American ladies,

and was much pleased with them. Mary Ashburnham, *alias* Fanny Appleton, was a near neighbour and friend of theirs— a most beautiful girl, whom thirty bold gentlemen sought to win! She came to Europe, and met Longfellow in the Black Forest, and there transacted the scenes described in 'Hyperion.' She returned to America, and her father on his deathbed expressed his wish that of all her suitors she should fix her choice on Longfellow, as the person most worthy of her and most able to sympathise with her feelings. After a little time she married him, settled in the country in poetic simplicity, and speaks of herself as the happiest woman possible.

London, August 12.—Jacob Bell* took us to Landseer's, who did not greatly take my fancy. Some one said he was once a Dog himself, and I can see a look of it. He has a somewhat arrogant manner, a love of contradiction, and a despotic judgment. He showed us the picture he has just finished of the Queen and Prince Albert in their fancy ball-dresses. He deeply admires the Queen's intellect, which he thinks superior to any woman's in Europe. Her memory is so very remarkable, that he has heard her recall the exact words of speeches made years before, which the speakers had themselves forgotten. He has a charming sketch of her on horseback before her marriage. His little dogs went flying over sofas, chairs, and us—brilliant little oddities of the Scotch terrier kind. Count d'Orsay was with him when we came; Landseer's ambition is to make a picture for the next exhibition of Count d'Orsay and John Bell,† in the same frame as Young England and Old England. Saw the Fighting Stags, the Belgian Pony, and a capital sketch of his father done at one sitting.

August 13.—Another sitting to Laurence. He has given his portrait of Carlyle to Carlyle's old mother. He thinks Mrs. Carlyle fosters in him the spirit of contradiction and restlessness. He regrets the jealous feeling existing among so many artists, keeping them apart, and leading them to deprecate each other like petty shopkeepers . . .

August 14.—Breakfast with Ernest de Bunsen‡ and his wife. Both so bright, merry, and affectionate . . . Called on the

---

* Quaker; life-long friend of Landseer; founder of the Pharmaceutical Society.
† Sculptor; the Guards' Memorial in Waterloo Place, London, is his work.
‡ Prussian Ambassador's son; married Elizabeth Gurney.

Maurices. He took us to see his Chapel with the beautiful
windows, also the new Dining Hall in Lincoln's Inn [of which
he was Chaplain] containing Hogarth's picture of Paul before
Felix; the quiet irony of the Apostle evidently talking down
the Orator Tertullus, very funny in a picture painted for the
lawyers . . .

Falmouth, September 5.—Dr. Lloyd introduced his Dublin
friend, Dr. [Robert] Ball, who dined with us to-day. He is a
most erudite naturalist, and was, moreover, very clever and
interesting on Irish subjects, including Archbishop Whately,
that torment of intelligent young men at dinner parties. 'Do
you think there can be a sixth sense?' 'Yes; and it is called
Nonsense,' said Dr. Ball. He feels genially on Church and
State politics in Ireland. 'Why don't the noblemen live on
their Irish estates?' asked some one. 'Because they are not
noble men,' was his reply.

September 20.—Dr. Lloyd with us: he threw out many of his
own large comprehensive views and feelings on religious
matters; his untractarian and unsectarian convictions, and his
broad charity, which longs for all to enter the fold . . . He
talked of Whately, who is much injured by being the centre
of a clique who flatter and never contradict him, hence he
becomes very despotic. He is a most generous creature and
full of knowledge. He wriggles his limbs about in an extraordinary manner, and once pronounced the benediction with
one leg hanging over the reading-desk in church; and in
society he will sit balancing his chair, occasionally tipping
over backwards. One of his chaplains, during a walk with
him, stated that fungus was very good eating, upon which the
Archbishop insisted on his then and there consuming a slice,
which the poor chaplain resisting, the Archbishop jerked it
into his mouth. A Doctor who was with them was in ecstasies
of mirth at the scene, which the Archbishop perceiving, said,
'Oh, Doctor! you shall try it too; it is very important for you to
be able to give an opinion.' 'No, thank you, my lord,' said the
Doctor; 'I am not a clergyman, nor am I in your lordship's
diocese.'

September 29.—W. E. Forster writes from Daniel O'Connell's house, where he is much enjoying himself. His family
and all call the old man the Liberator. He lives in a simple
patriarchal style, nine grandchildren flying about, and kissing

him, on all sides.

October 5.—Dr. Lloyd rejoined us this evening. He looks at science with the ardour of a lover and the reverence of a child . . .

October 6.—A luminous talk with Dr. Lloyd on Men and Books . . . He wants us to know his friend, Aubrey de Vere, a poetical, pure-minded, high-souled creature.

October 13.—Dined at Carclew; met Sir Roderick and Lady Murchison. He gave me a little lecture on Geology, which he regards as an accomplished fact: all the principles of terrestrial arrangements clearly made out, only details to be looked after: mineral veins, however, a quite different case; infinite scope therein for Papa and all Magneticians . . .

October 24.—Heard that Archdeacon Hare is likely to bring out John Sterling's prose works before Christmas. There is to be a portrait either from the medallion or Delacour's picture.

December 31.—Dinner at Carclew. Herman Merivale spoke of John Sterling with enthusiastic admiration, as one quite unlike any other, so deeply influential in the earnest eloquence of his conversation. At Cambridge he had a most loving band of disciples, who, after he left, still felt his opinion a law for themselves.

1847

Falmouth, January 1.—Samuel Laurence with us. He thinks James Spedding* the most beautiful combination of noble qualities he has ever met with. He is collecting letters of Bacon's, by which he hopes to do as much for him as Carlyle has for Cromwell. A bust of Bacon which Laurence has seen is so entirely free from everything mean, that on the strength of it he rejects Lord Campbell's† Memoir, believing it to be inaccurate.

February 18.—A damsel belonging to Barclay's establishment being here, I thought it right 'to try and do her good'; so I asked her, after many unsuccessful questions, if she had not heard of the Lord's coming into the world. 'Why,' she said, 'I

---

* Editor of Bacon's works; friend of Tennyson and FitzGerald.
† Lord Chancellor. The memoir of Bacon occurs in his *Lives of the Lord Chancellors.*

may have done so, but I have forgot it.' 'But surely you must have heard your master read about it, and heard of it at school and church and chapel.' 'Very likely I have,' said she placidly, 'but it has quite slipped my memory!' and this uttered with a lamb-like face and a mild blue eye.

Dublin, April 7.—Spent part of our morning with Robert Ball in his den at the College, seeing beasts, birds, and bottles innumerable. When he put on a breast-plate of dogs' teeth he looked like a curious preparation ready to walk into a glass case; and when he put on some other unpronounceable sheath-like garments, he exclaimed, 'Coleoptera!' and replaced them. He is gradually putting the Museum into order, an Herculean task. Poor man, he has not yet recovered from the sunstroke he got in Gerrans Bay, but has been seeing spectres, particularly a very troublesome gentleman in black like a clergyman; but his ghosts are getting better . . . Dined at Mrs. Lloyd's; met, amongst many others, Dr. [John] Anster, the admirable translator of 'Faust,' who fell to my share, and we had plenty of talk on German and other matters. He is weary of translations, and thinks that except S. T. Coleridge's 'Wallenstein,' no poem has ever come of any such attempts . . .

Dr. Anster is a great burly man, awkward in his ways, occasionally making a deep utterance, the voice rising from the lowest depth within him. There is some beauty in his profile and in the sudden lighting up of his countenance . . .

April 9.—Dr. Lloyd told us that one night, during the British Association Meeting in Dublin, when he was utterly fagged with his duties as Secretary, and had fallen into an intense sleep, he was aroused by tremendous knocking, and in came Sir William Hamilton with, 'My dear Lloyd, I'm so sorry to disturb you, but this Norwegian noble and I have become great friends, and he must not leave Dublin until we have had a glass of wine together. Unluckily I have none left; will you lend me a bottle?' So the poor Doctor had to turn out to promote friendly relations between scientific bodies.

Bristol, May 12.—A visit to M. A. Schimmelpenninck: symbolic as ever, and teeming with imaginative Facts . . .

London, May 14.—Met Ernest de Bunsen at Ham House. He was very pleasant, talked rapturously of Archdeacon Hare and the Maurices (a sure passport to our regard) . . .

May 16.—Ernest de Bunsen and his wife went to Meeting with us this evening. Ernest would like Meeting far better if he might take his Testament and read when he was not better employed, he so dislikes the idea of appearing to worship when he is not worshipping. At church he always contrives a little silent service for himself before the sermon by a not difficult effort of abstraction . . .

He sang us some old German hymns. The rich sustained quality of his voice, and its wonderfully beautiful tones, were a rare treat to listen to . . . The other day Sarah Gurney heard him sing and Mendelssohn accompany him. Mendelssohn is beautiful, poetical, and childlike, clinging to those he loves; his playing is like Ariel in the 'Tempest.'

May 17.—Archdeacon Hare joined us; as nervous, dragged-looking a man as in his portrait, but far more genial and approachable than that would lead you to expect. Plenty of pleasant talk, but nothing extremely marked. We were presently on the footing of old friends. Walter Savage Landor had been with him this morning, intolerant of everything as usual; some of his views very amusing:—'The only well-drawn figure in existence, a female by Overbeck in his picture of "Children brought to Christ"; Milton wrote one good line, but he forgot it; Dante perhaps six, his description of Francesca; Carlyle's "French Revolution" a wicked book, he had worn out one volume in tossing it on to the floor at startling passages,' &c., &c. His old age is an amalgam of the grotesque and forlorn.

May 18.—Ernest de Bunsen took us to town, and told us a plenty by the way . . .

Well, we arrived at Carlton Terrace at ten o'clock, and were soon made known to this remarkable family, who received us like old friends and said they seemed to have long known us. Madame is a very foreign-looking lady, with plenty of dignity but more heart, so that Ernest was at once for leading her off in a wild dance, 'because you are so vwerry glat to see your son.' She is practical and clear-sighted, and has done much in the education of the family. The Chevalier [the Prussian Ambassador] has far more real beauty than I expected, exquisite chiselling about the mouth and chin, large grey eyes, a certain vagueness and dreaminess, but also a general decision of character in the expression of the face, and a fine glow of genial feeling over all. His wife showed us a bust of him taken 'just the last moment before his face filled out so,' quite ideally beautiful. I sat by him at breakfast and enjoyed his profile as well as his conversation. Frederick Maurice was also there, and the Henry Bunsens and the sweet sister Mary. We had much talk on the German Hospital at Dalston, the Chevalier's peculiar pet . . . They have a splendid portrait of the King of Prussia, painted on china, and presented by himself. Ernest tells us of his father's intimacy with our Queen, whom he finds highly principled, religious, and judicious. In the course of the morning he took us to George Richmond's studio, who showed us his life-like portrait of Bunsen, and then exhibited one of an English Judge as an extreme contrast: the one dreamy and beautiful, the other solid, self-satisfied, and practical. George Richmond is a mild, unassuming, easy, agreeable man, with a large, open eye, and a look of as much goodness as intelligence. He talked of John Sterling and his merits, and he regrets that he never got even a sketch of him.

May 20.—Went to Chelsea, where we soon settled into an interesting talk with Mrs. Carlyle. She has been very ill, and the doctors gave her opium and tartar for her cough, which induced, not beautiful dreams and visions, but a miserable feeling of turning to marble herself and lying on marble, her hair, her arms, and her whole person petrifying and adhering to the marble slab on which she lay. One night it was a tombstone—one in Scotland which she well knew. She lay along it with a graver in her hand, carving her own epitaph under another, which she read and knew by heart. It was her mother's. She felt utterly distinct from this prostrate figure, and thought of her with pity and love, looked at different passages in her life, and moralised as a familiar friend. It was more like madness than anything she has ever experienced. 'After all,' she said, 'I often wonder what right I have to live at all.' She talked sadly of the world's hollowness, and every year deepening her sense of this: half-a-dozen real friends is far too magnificent an allowance for any one to calculate on—she would suggest half-a-one; those you really care about, die. She gave a wondrously graphic and ludicrous picture of an insane imagination, cherished by a poor invalid respecting her. Carlyle is not writing now, but resting—reading English history and disagreeing with the age. She told of M. F.— [Margaret Fuller], an American transcendentalist. She came here with an enthusiasm for Carlyle. She has written some beautiful things, and is a great friend of Emerson's, of whom she speaks with more love than reverence. Mrs. Carlyle does not see that much good is to come of Emerson's writings, and grants that they are arrogant and shortcoming. He came to them first in Scotland with a note from John Stuart Mill in his pocket, and was kindly welcome in a place where they saw nothing but wild-fowl, not even a beggar. She talked of her own life and the mistake of over-educating people. She believes that her health has been injured for life by beginning Latin with a little tutor at five or six years old, then going to the Rector's school to continue it, then having a tutor at home, and being very ambitious she learnt eagerly. Irving being her tutor, and of equally excitable intellect, was delighted to push her through every study; then he introduced her to Carlyle, and for years they had a literary intimacy, and she would be writing constantly and consulting him about everything, 'and so it would probably have always gone on, for we were both of us made for independence, and I believe should never have wanted to live together, but this intimacy was not considered discreet, so we married quietly and departed.' She laughs at him as a nurse; he peeps in and looks frightened, and asks, 'How are ye now, Jeannie?' and vanishes, as if well out of a scrape. Talked of her brilliant little friend Zoë (Miss Jewsbury), [novelist and author of children's books], who declares herself born without any sense of decency: the publishers beg she will be decent, and she has not the slightest objection to be so, but she does not know what it is; she implores Mrs. Carlyle to take any quantity of spotted muslin and clothe her figures for her, for she does not know which are naked. She is a very witty little thing, full of emotions, which overflow on all occasions; her sister, the poetess, tried to bring them into young-ladylike order, and checked her ardent demonstrations of affection in society and elsewhere. The sister died, so did the parents, and this wild creature was thrown on the world, which hurled her back upon herself. She read insatiably and at random in an old library, alchemy, physiology, and what not, and undraped

'Zoë' is the result. Dr. Chalmers' coadjutor, as Leader of the Free Church, came in one day when she was here: she said, 'He looked the incarnation of a Vexed Question.'

Carlyle wandered down to tea, looking dusky and aggrieved at having to live in such a generation; but he was very cordial to us notwithstanding. Of Thomas Erskine [advocate and theologian], whom they both love: 'He always soothes me,' said Mrs. Carlyle, 'for he looks so serene, as if he had found peace. He and the Calvinistic views are quite unsuited to each other.' Carlyle added, 'Why, yes; it has been well with him since he became a Christian.' We had such a string of tirades that it was natural to ask, 'Who *has* ever done any good in the world?' 'Why, there was one George Fox; he did some little good. He walked up to a man and said, "My fat-faced friend, thou art a damned lie. Thou art pretending to serve God Almighty, and art really serving the devil. Come out of that, or perish to all eternity." ' This—ay, and stronger language too—had he to say to his generation, and we must say it to ours in such fashion as we can. It is the one thing that *must* be said; the one thing that each must find out for himself is that he is really on the right side of the fathomless abyss, serving God heartily, and authorised to speak in His name to others. Tolerance and a rose-water world is the evil symptom of the time we are living in: it was just like it before the French Revolution, when universal brotherhood, tolerance, and twaddle were preached in all the market-places; so they had to go through their Revolution with one hundred and fifty a day butchered—the gutters thick with blood, and the skins tanned into leather: and so it will be here unless a righteous intolerance of the devil should awake in time. Utter intolerance of ourselves must be the first step—years of conflict, of agony—before it comes out clearly that you have a warrant from God to proclaim that lies shall not last, and to run them through or blow them into atoms. 'Tis not, truly, an easy world to live in, with all going wrong. The next book I write must be about this same tolerance, this playing into the hands of God and the devil—to the devil with it! Then another man who did some good was Columbus, who fished up the island of America from the bottom of the sea; and Caxton—he too did something for us indeed, all who do faithfully whatever in them lies, do something for the

Universe.' He is as much as ever at war with all the comfortable classes, and can hardly connect good with anything that is not dashed into visibility on an element of strife. He drove with us to Sloane Square, talking with energetic melancholy to the last.

May 21.—Just heard of the death of Daniel O'Connell . . .

May 22.—Called on Frank Newman, and were soon in the presence of a thin, acute-looking man, oddly simple, almost quaint in his manner, but with a sweetness in his expression which I had not at all expected. He was as cordial as possible, but in a curiously measured way.

May 24.—Went with Mrs. Carlyle and Samuel Laurence to see Thomas Hope's Gallery in Duchess Street. She is delightfully unaffected in her appreciation of pictures, and will not praise where she does not feel. The Francias in the National Gallery are more to her than all the rest.

May 26.—Called on Dr. Southwood Smith,* who exhibited Jeremy Bentham to us, and talked much of the bland-looking old philosopher, whom he had 'prepared,' dissected, and lectured upon, as well as loved.

May 27.—F. D. Maurice and Samuel Laurence spent the evening with us. The former on Ireland, deeply trusts that much of her evil will be consumed in this sorrow [the Famine], and that she will come out purified. O'Connell could not have been a permanent benefactor; he never told his countrymen one unpalatable truth, and his death now makes little or no sensation in a political sense. Maurice looks for a season of sharp proving for us all,—physical calamity, and moral trial, which must always accompany it. A prophecy is current in many counties—'The blight is for the first year on the potatoes, for the second on the corn, and for the third on the bodies of men.'

May 28.—Called on the Bunsens in Carlton Terrace. Madame Bunsen and Anna Maria erudite on the old Greeks; daughters and I sharp-sighted on the modern Europeans. Their first impression of the English was that they were a formal and heartless people, but this got itself corrected in time, and they now value the forms as all tending to lead to

---

* Sanitary reformer to whom Bentham left his body.

something better—as a safety-valve, or else a directing-post for religious feeling when it comes, which is just what they think the Germans lack . . .

Then to the Dean of Westminster (Dr. Buckland) in his solemn habitation. He took us through the old Abbey, so full of death and of life. There was solemn music going on in keeping with the serious Gothic architecture and the quiet memory of the great dead. The Dean was full of anecdote—historical, architectural, artistic, and scientific. The new-found planet is now recognised as a joint-discovery, and is to be called Neptune. On Prince Albert condoling with Professor [John Couch] Adams* on the vexatious incidents of the affair, he answered, 'Oh! I hope we shall find another planet during your Royal Highness's Chancellorship.' We got a far grander and truer notion of Westminster, both inside and out, than we ever had before.

Falmouth, June 18.—Read Archdeacon Hare's dedication to [Cardinal] Manning on the true principle of Unity: delightfully large and deep, and full of Faith.

July 19.—A. Murray to dinner. He told us of his having had an interview with Napoleon when he was First Consul: he was then thin, sharp-featured, and with such an eye; he wore long hair, and a General's uniform. Murray was a great agriculturist, and had then some thoughts of settling in France, but Napoleon advised him not to do so, and not to bring a large stock of sheep, because the Government was still in too unsettled a state; however he promised, in case he persisted in his intentions, to afford him every facility and protection. Napoleon's manner throughout the interview was affable and kind.

September 15.—Mrs. Buchanan talked about Mrs. Carlyle, whom she had known at Fort Augustus as Jeannie Welsh. She and her very pretty widowed mother were staying there; a clergyman went to call one morning, and finding Greek and Hebrew books scattered about the parlour, he asked, 'What young student have you here?' 'Oh, it is only Jeannie Welsh,' was the answer. Another who called reported that the mother would get two husbands before the daughter had one; however, this was a mistake, for news came before long that

---

* For Caroline's account of his discovery, almost simultaneously with the French astronomer Leverrier, see the entry for October 7.

Jeannie had married, 'just a bookish man like herself.' . . .

October 4.—[Nevill Northey] Burnard, our Cornish sculptor, dined with us. He is a great powerful pugilistic-looking fellow of twenty-nine; a great deal of face, with all the features massed in the centre; mouth open, and all sorts of simplicities flowing out of it. He liked talking of himself and his early and late experiences. His father, a stone-mason, once allowed him to carve the letters on a little cousin's tombstone which would be hidden in the grass; this was his first attempt, and instead of digging in the letters, he dug around them, and made each stand out in relief. His stories of [Francis Leggatt] Chantrey very odd: on his death Lady Chantrey came into the studio with a hammer and knocked off the noses of many completed busts, so that they might not be too common—a singular attention to her departed lord. Described his own distress when waiting for Sir Charles Lemon to take him to Court; he felt very warm, and went into a shop for some ginger-beer; the woman pointed the bottle at him, and he was drenched! After wiping himself as well as he could, he went out to dry in the sun. He went first to London without his parents knowing anything about it, because he wished to spare them anxiety, and let them know nothing until he could announce that he was regularly engaged . . . He showed us his bust of the Prince of Wales—a beautiful thing, very intellectual, with a strong likeness to the Queen—which he was exhibiting at the Polytechnic, where it will remain.

October 7.—Dined at Carclew, and spent a very interesting evening. We met Professor Adams, the Bullers, the Lord of the Isles, and others. Adams is a quiet-looking man, with a broad forehead, a mild face, and a most amiable and expressive mouth. I sat by him at dinner, and by gradual and dainty approaches got at the subject on which one most wished to hear him speak. He began very blushingly, but went on to talk in most delightful fashion, with large and luminous simplicity, of some of the vast mathematical Facts with which he is so conversant. The Idea of the reversed method of reasoning, from an unknown to a known, with reference to astronomical problems, dawned on him when an Undergraduate, with neither time nor mathematics to work it out. The opposite system had always before been adopted. He, in common with many others, conceived that there must be a planet to account for the disturbances of Uranus; and when he had time he set to work at the process, in deep, quiet faith that the Fact was there, and that his hitherto untried mathematical path was the one which must reach it; that there were no anomalies in the Universe, but that even here, and now, they could be explained and included in a Higher Law. The delight of working it out was far more than any notoriety could give, for his love of pure Truth is evidently intense, an inward necessity, unaffected by all the penny trumpets of the world. Well, at length he fixed his point in space, and sent his mathematical evidence to Airy, the Astronomer-Royal, who locked the papers up in his desk, partly from carelessness, partly from incredulity—for it seemed to him improbable that a man whose name was unknown to him should strike out such a new path in mathematical science with any success. Moreover, his theory was, that if there were a planet, it could not be discovered for 160 years; that is, until two revolutions of Uranus had been accomplished. Then came [Urbain Jean Joseph] Leverrier's equally original, though many months younger, demonstration; [Johann Gottfried] Gall[e]'s immediate verification of it by observation; and then the astronomers were all astir. Professor Adams speaks of those, about whom the English scientific world is so indignant, in a spirit of Christian philosophy, exactly in keeping with the mind of a man who had discovered a planet. He speaks with warmest admiration of Leverrier, specially of his exhaustive method of making out the orbits of the comets, imagining and disproving all tracks but the right one—a work of infinite labour. If the observer could make out distinctly but a very small part of a comet's orbit, the mathematician would be able to prove what its course had been through all time. They enjoyed being a good deal together at the British Association Meeting at Oxford, though it was unfortunate for the intercourse of the fellow-workers that one could not speak French nor the other English! He had met with very little mathematical sympathy, except from Challis* of the Cambridge Observatory; but when his result was announced, there was noise enough and to spare. He was always fond of star-gazing and speculating, and is already on the watch for another planet. One moon

* Astronomer who on August 6, 1846 observed Neptune without knowing it.

has already been seen at Liverpool wandering round Neptune. Papa suggested to him the singularity of the nodes of the planets being mostly in nearly the same signs of the Zodiac, a matter which he has not considered, but means to look into.

Burnard told us that when Professor Adams came from Cambridge to visit his relations in Cornwall, he was employed to sell sheep for his father at a fair . . .

October 8.—Professor Adams' talk yesterday did me great good, showing in living clearness how apparent anomalies get included and justified in a larger Law . . .

October 12.—Burnard tells amusing stories of his brother sculptors, and their devices to hide their ignorance on certain questions. Chantrey, after sustaining a learned conversation with Lord Melbourne to his extremest limits, saved his credit by, 'Would your Lordship kindly turn your head on the other side and shut your mouth.' . . .

December 3.—Long letters from Julius Hare detailing difficulties in the Sterling Memoir, which we had foreseen and could well enter into. He seems almost forced to publish more than he would wish in order to leave Mill and Carlyle no pretext for an opposition portrait.

1848

Falmouth, January 4.—Such a beautiful day, that one felt quite confused how to make the most of it, and accordingly frittered it away.

January 25.—Most animated visit from W. Cocks.* Lithography, benevolence, anatomy, and religion were all unpacked, arranged, systematised, and lectured upon, with keen insight and most lively illustration. His parting words, after mentioning his present ill-health, his 'butter-headed condition,' were: 'When I am called to appear before God Almighty, I shall not go in the character of an apothecary's shop; no, no medicine, thank you!'

This evening Archdeacon Hare's 'Life of John Sterling' arrived. The portrait is very unsatisfactory, the volumes full

* Naturalist who lived in Falmouth for many years.

of exquisite interest, though of a very mixed kind. Julius Hare has, I believe, done his part admirably well, but F. D. Maurice has (by his letters) quite spoiled us for any other handling of such a subject.

February 1.—Read and was thankful for [Richard] Cobden's speech,* declaring this was not the time to lose faith in principles so boldly asserted and toiled for: now we must prove that we believe them, and not shriek at the French as a nation of pirates. He read extracts from French speeches just delivered, one by a member of the Chamber, in the best tone of an English Peace Advocate.

February 23.—Clara Mill writes a brave note in answer to my cautious entreaties [on her brother's then intention of writing a life of John Sterling]: 'Publish what you will, and all you can, it can only do him honour.' She is frightened at the prospect of the Paris Reform Banquet, lest it should not go off quietly.

February 24.—Her doubt is soon answered—the Banquet was forbidden by Government. Odilon Barrot† protested in the Chamber against the interference, and placarded an entreaty to the people to be quiet, although they gave up the Banquet. But they would not be quiet, and crowds assembled; troops were called out, collisions and slaughter followed. The Chamber of Deputies and Guizot's house are the chief points of attack. I have been so familiar of late with the French Revolution, through Carlyle and Burke, that all this fills one with a horrid dread of what next.

February 26.—Louis Philippe and Guizot have both abdicated, and the Royal Family have quitted Paris. Arago, Odilon Barrot, and [Alphonse de] Lamartine‡ are the new administration, desperately revolutionary. How far will they go? And how long will they last? The Tuileries has been taken, furniture thrown out of windows and burnt, and the throne paraded through the streets. Uncle Charles summing up the recent French rulers: Louis XVI. beheaded, Louis XVII. done away with, Napoleon abdicated, Charles X. abdicated, Louis Philippe abdicated; truly a most difficult

---

* First of a series of speeches advocating Universal Peace through Arbitration. See the entry for June 12, 1849.
† French reformist statesman; president of the Council under Louis Napoleon.
‡ Poet and moderate Liberal in politics.

people to govern.

February 29.—Duc de Nemours* and his sister Clementine have arrived in London, without even a change of raiment. No news of the King, Guizot, or the others. Louis Bonaparte has reached France from London to see what is toward. Lord John Russell states his determination not to interfere with any government which France may deem most fitting for herself, and Lord Normanby remains in Paris. M. Van der Weyer, the Belgian ambassador, has offered the Royal Family his father-in-law's house at East Sheen.

March 4.—Poor Louis Philippe and his Queen arrived at Newhaven; they have been skulking in different farms near Eu, in strange disguises. Guizot, too, is come; he crossed from Ostend to Folkestone. His safety is a great comfort.

March 8.—Dinner at Penmere, when who should appear but Mr. Froude. The only thing specially characteristic of his name that fell from him was a solemn recognition of the vitality existing in the Church of Rome, or rather, that if the Pope succeeds in maintaining his spiritual supremacy in conjunction with all these remarkable reforms, it will prove that a real vitality must exist. He also spoke of Miss Agnew's second work, 'The Young Communicant,' as likely to be a still more perplexing and influential book than 'Geraldine.'

March 18.—Plenty to do, and plenty to love, and plenty to pity. No one need die of *ennui.*

May 8.—Old Samuel Rundell has ended his weary pilgrimage, with his old wife sitting by his side: 'he departed as one who was glad of the opportunity.' He, far more than any I have seen, carries one back centuries in the history of opinion and feeling. He was a perfect Quaker of the old George Fox stamp, ponderous, uncompromising, slow, uninfluenced by the views of others, intensely one-sided, with all the strength and weakness of that characteristic; a man to excite universal esteem, but no enthusiasm; simple and childlike in his daily habits, solemn and massive in his ministry; that large voice seemed retained to cry with ceaseless iteration, 'The Kingdom of God is within you.' Last of the Puritans, fare thee well! There was a certain Johnsonian grandeur about him, and one would have lost much insight into a bygone

---

* Second son of Louis Philippe; he lived in England from 1848 to 1870.

time and an obsolete generation by not having known him.

May 15.—Read Carlyle's article on the 'Repeal of the Union.' Terrible fun and grim earnest, such as a United or other Irishman would writhe under, it gives them such an intense glimpse of their smallness, their folly, their rascality, and their simple power of botheration . . .

May 23.—Twenty-nine years came to an end with this evening,. and left me pondering on the multiform and multitudinous blessings in disguise with which I have been acquainted . . .

June 1.—Barclay dined at the Buxtons', and met M. Guizot and his daughter, Arthur Stanley [Dean of Westminster], and others. He had much chat with Guizot on French matters, who expects sharper work in France, and a collision between the National Guards and the National Workmen.

September 2.—R. Buxton writes of a charming coterie she has been in at Lowestoft—Guizot, the Bishop of Oxford, and Baron Alderson. Young Guizot told her of having gained the first prize at the Bourbon College this spring, but when the Revolution came the Professors refused to give it. His two hundred fellow-students processed to them, demanding justice, and the authorities had, after all, to send the prize to him in England.

September 5.—Professor Lloyd and his wife came to stay. She spoke of some one's dictum on Carlyle, 'That he had a large capital of Faith not yet invested.' Had a stroll with the Professor . . . The anxiety about Sir John Franklin is now almost despair, though he may still be in some snug corner of Esquimaux land. He hopes that this will be the last expedition of the sort.

September 6.—When Captain Ross was with the Lloyds, he told them such pleasant things about some of the Greenlanders who had come under missionary influence. He had asked a large party to dine on board his ship, and they came in full native costume, and when they assembled at the table they all stood for a while and sang a Moravian hymn, to the delighted surprise of their hosts. He finds some vestiges of what he supposes to be a traditional religion amongst the most remote Esquimaux, a sense of right and wrong, and an expectation of future state, though this takes the grossest form of enjoyment—'plenty of whales.' One of his sailors married a Greenlander, and as she approached England she was very curious to learn if seals were to be found there. 'Yes, a few, but you will hardly meet with them.' This was sad; however, she tried the country for a time, till the *mal du pays* and the longing for seals seized her so fiercely, that there was no comfort but in letting her return home.

September 7.—When [Baron Alexander von] Humboldt* came through Paris to see the Lloyds, he spoke of Elizabeth Fry having been in Berlin, and that she had a religious service there, and herself addressed the company, when, Humboldt said, he had the honour of translating for her, which was, he added, with a twinkling sense of incongruity, '*très bon pour mon âme.*'

September 8.—Professor Lloyd told us of Jenny Lind, her nobility and simplicity of character. The only time he heard her talk of her singing was when she had got up a concert impromptu, for the sake of an hospital which they feared must be abandoned for want of funds . . .

October 23.—A wet day and all its luxuries.

October 24.—A fine day and all its liabilities.

October 26.—Read of the thrice-noble [Johann Gottlieb] Fichte† till I cried, for love of him. Concluded that 'My mind to me a kingdom is' was a masculine sentiment, of which 'My heart to me a kingdom is' is the feminine. My mind, I fear, is a Republic. Was also led to consider that Love has no tense, it must always be Now or Never . . .

1849

Penjerrick, January 8.—M. H— gave me some curious and graphic particulars of an execution he had attended for purely moral purposes. He wanted to see the effect on the individual of the certainty of approaching death, and he saw that the fellow was reckless, and elated as a mob-hero; the hangman, a little wretch, intent on doing his job neatly; and when he walked home, sickened at what he had seen, he

---

* Prussian naturalist and explorer, a founder of modern physical geography.
† German idealist philosopher (1762-1814).

heard one man ask another, 'Weel, hast been to th' hanging?' 'No, I've been at my work.' 'Why, thee never dost go to see any pleasuring.' Thus much for its effect on society.

January 12.—Accounts reached us of the 'humble and prayerful' death of Hartley Coleridge. His brother Derwent has been with him three weeks . . .

January 18.—Attended George Wightwick's lecture on 'Macbeth.' It was most forcibly done, and some of the criticisms extremely valuable. One of his grand objects in these Shakespeare Studies is to correct the impression of characters made by actors and actresses. Thus Lady Macbeth is always conceived as a magnificent unapproachable woman—in fact, as Mrs. Siddons; whilst he, and Mrs. Siddons too, think she was small, delicate, almost fragile, with the quickest, sharpest of ferret eyes, as such is the ordinary build of women greatly gifted for intrigue. The witches too, and specially Hecate, should be wild, unearthly beings, not ugly old women: Hecate the palest of ghosts, with a little spirit to do her bidding. He thinks the gist of the play to lie in the manifold utterance of 'Fair is foul, and foul is fair,'—a play of wicked, magical contradictions; the witches ever present in spirit, and presiding over the double-faced picture of life. He was ill with rheumatism, but said that an enthusiastic evening with Shakespeare had done him more good than all the pills and rubbings, and this, unlike any other social stimulant, leaves no weary depression after it. On being asked that common question as to your favourite amongst Shakespeare's Plays, he said, 'Oh, the one you know best.' . . .

January 21.—Driving to Falmouth, a pig attached itself to the cortège and made us even more remarkable than usual. Piggy and Dory (the dog) scampering on side by side, and playing like frolicsome children, spite of all we could do to turn the incipient Bacon back to his former path in life.

February 4.—Aunt Charles read us some striking letters from Derwent Coleridge from the Knbbe, whilst his brother Hartley was breathing forth his last suffering sighs . . . Then she read a clever letter from Harriet Martineau, combining the smoker, the moralist, the political economist, the gossip, and the woman.

March 1.—Found a kindly note from Thomas Carlyle. He has seen 'my gigantic countryman,' Burnard, and conceives that there is a real faculty in him; he gave him advice, and says he is the sort of person whom he will gladly help if he can. Burnard forwarded to me, in great triumph, the following note he had received from Carlyle with reference to a projected bust of Charles Buller: '*February 25. 1849* . . . Nay, if the conditions *never* mend, and you cannot get that Bust to do at all, you may find yet (as often turns out in life) that it was *better* for you you did not. Courage!' . . .

March 12.—Our friend [G. T.] Edwards* gave me some private memories of Emerson. He is most quiet in conversation, never impassioned; his ordinary life is to sit by a brook some miles from Boston, and gaze on the sky reflected in the water, and dream out his problems of existence.

March 21.—S. Sutton came in, and we had a talk about Anthony Froude's astonishing book, 'The Nemesis of Faith,' which has made an ugly stir, and has been publicly burnt at Oxford, and so on . . .

April 2.—Read the horrid details of Rush's trial [a murder case], and felt bitterly for the poor chief witness, Emily Sandford, who still evidently has compassion towards him, but whose evidence will doubtless hang him. She lived formerly at Truro.

April 6.—Rush's trial concluded as it could not but do. Baron Rolfe, before pronouncing sentence, remarked that if Rush had fulfilled his promise to poor Emily Sandford and married her, her evidence could not have been demanded, and thus the crime could not have been so mightily brought home to him.

May 5.—William Ball staying with us. He produced these graceful lines on this passage in Anna Maria's Journal: 'W. B. falls into the ways of the house capitally':—

> 'Into such ways who would not fall
>   That ever rightly knew them?
> It were a dull and wayward Ball
>   That would not roll into them . . .'

[To Mrs. Lloyd] *May 8.*—Yesterday we parted with a remarkable little person who has been spending a few days

---

* An Evangelical Friend who sent a copy of the *Journals* to Cardinal Newman whose opinion of them is quoted in the Introduction.

John Stuart Mill with his step-daughter Helen
Taylor

F. D. Maurice, founder of Christian Socialism
and pioneer of adult education: portrait from
The Illustrated London News

with us—Dr. Guggenbühl, who founded the Institution for
Cretins on the Abendberg, near Interlaken. Do go and see
him and his protégés when you are next in Switzerland, if the
moral sublime is (as I fancy) more interesting to you than the
most glorious scenery. He is a very young man, highly
educated, full of sense as well as soul, eminently a Christian—
indeed, he is quite a saint for the nineteenth century—uniting
action with thought, and explaining thought by action. His
face is one of the most serene and happy I have ever beheld,
expressing a fulness of faith, hope, and charity, with all the
liveliness and simplicity of the Swiss character. Moreover, as
Thomas (our old servant) says, 'He would be very good-
looking if the gentleman would but trim himself!' The offence
in Thomas's eyes is long hair waving over his shoulders,
moustaches, and a cherished little beard . . .

London, May 21.—Samuel Gurney with us. I never saw him
in greater force than now—more continuous in conversation,
more sunny and happy. Large and liberal he always was, but
now he is more mellow than ever. Sunshine on granite tells
but half the tale of the beaming cordiality and unflinching
strength and energy of his present countenance.

May 22.—To Queen's College, to F. D. Maurice's Lecture
on Theology. He was much exhausted after it, for he was
thoroughly in earnest; but after the refreshment of a cup of tea
he went off with us towards Carlton Terrace, talking with his
usual quiet depth and loving compassionate soul . . . Paid
the Bunsens a visit and lunched there, and visited the
Chevalier in his snuggery, and enjoyed his dramatic, enthusiastic reading of the news that Rome is saved, and the
French fraternising there as fast as they can. Drove to J. M.
W. Turner's house in Queen Anne's Street, and were
admitted by a mysterious-looking old housekeeper, a bent
and mantled figure, who might have been yesterday released
from a sarcophagus. Well, she admitted us to this dirty,
musty, neglected house, where art and economy delight to
dwell. In the gallery was a gorgeous display of haunted
dreams thrown on the canvas, rather in the way of hints and
insinuations than real pictures, and yet the effect of some was
most fascinating. The colouring almost Venetian, the imagination of some almost as grand as they were vague; but I
think one great pleasure in them is the opportunity they give

for trying to find out what he can possibly mean, and then
you hug your own creative ingenuity, whilst you pretend to
be astonished at Turner's. This especially refers to the Deluge
and the Brazen Serpent.

May 25.—Dined with the Gurneys in Lombard Street. The
Chevalier Bunsen, Elizabeth, and others were there. His face
and Samuel Gurney's were fine studies of genial humanity.
He told us that the deputation of Friends to Sir Robert Peel
had much to do with the settlement of the Oregon question;
the earnestness of their appeal struck him deeply . . .

After dinner we went with the Bunsens to the German
Hospital, and were charmed with the order, cleanliness, and
comfort of the whole establishment, but above all, with the
dear Sisters from Kaiserswerth, who are in active ministry
here by night and by day. One of them, in particular, might
have sat to Fra Angelico . . .

May 26.— . . . F. D. Maurice with us in the evening. He
spoke of Edward Irving, and the blessing he proved, spite of
all his vagaries . . . Stumbled somehow on War. 'Won't the
world some day come to think with us?' quoth I. 'They will
come to think rightly,' was the reply, 'no doubt, but perhaps
very differently to you or I.' 'But would any nation dare to
attack another which resolved under no circumstances to do
them anything but kindness?' 'Well, I find that whenever I
am most right, I may always expect to be most bullied, and
this, I suppose, will go on; it brings home to one very strongly
the meaning of the words, "Woe unto you when all men
speak well of you." ' . . .

June 1.—Went to call on poor Lady Franklin,* who was
out. She spends most of her days in a room she has taken in
Spring Gardens, where she sees all the people who can tell or
suggest anything. She is just going to America, which is
thought very good for her, as she is in such a restless, excited
state of feeling.

June 5.—Went to Harley Street to hear Maurice's lecture.
It was so full and solemn that it left us all trembling with
emotion. Then we passed into the presence of Richard

* Second wife of Sir John, polar explorer. She sent out the last of many expeditions
searching for him: Sir Leopold McClintock found boats, skeletons and papers
which established that Franklin had died on June 11, 1847 after discovering the
North West Passage.

Trench, whose great sorrowful face seemed to fill the room. We sat round a table with about thirty young disciples, and listened to his comments on the chapter of Saint John which was then read.

June 7.—The Buxtons, the Guizot party and their friend, Mademoiselle de Latour Chabaud, came here, and we went together to the Joseph Frys at Plashet Cottage—a long and interesting drive. Mademoiselle de Latour was born in prison during the former Revolution, just after her father had been beheaded. Old Madame Guizot, who was in attendance on her imprisoned husband, looked after the poor lying-in lady, and finally adopted the child, who has turned out admirably, addicting herself to all sorts of philanthropies, schools, &c., in Paris, and renouncing them all to share and soothe her friends' exile now. She spoke with warm affection of the old Madame Guizot; it was beautifully ordered that she should believe a report true that her son had reached England four days before he actually arrived. Mademoiselle de Latour knew that it was false, but did not think it necessary to undeceive the dear old lady—the days were then like months. Pauline Guizot gave very interesting accounts of their and their father's escape. They left their house at the beginning of the Revolution and took refuge at the houses of their friends, and the girls were very soon able to come over to England with no great difficulty. Their brother came as son to an American gentleman, and began by remembering he must always *tutoyer*, which he felt very awkward. 'How d'ye do?' was his entire stock of English, and for a whole hour he had the fright of totally forgetting his assumed name. Their father escaped in a woman's dress, into which he had a good deal of difficulty in insinuating himself; and when he arrived at his friend's house, the portress looked into his face, and said, 'You are M. Guizot.' 'Yes,' he said: 'but you'll do me no injury?' 'Certainly not,' said she, 'for you've always protected honest men.' So she took him upstairs and hid him, and for the rest of the day entertained him with an account of the difficulties she and her husband had in bringing up their four children. Then he was arrayed as a livery servant and attached to a gentleman who was in anguish at his carrying his carpet-bag. They had to wait two terrible hours at the railway station before they could get off. On arriving in England, a railway director gave him instantly the blessed news that his daughters and all his dear belongings were safe. They none of them have any patience with Lamartine, thinking him an altogether would-be great man, attempting impossibilities and failing utterly, yet still considering himself the greatest of his age. I had a most interesting drive home with Guizot, his eldest daughter, and Mademoiselle Chabaud . . . Mademoiselle Guizot was the really interesting one—earnest and clear; her quiet, large dark eyes set the seal to every worthy word, and every word was worthy. She spoke of the solid education which their father had chosen for them, which in France is so rare that they kept their classical attainments a strict secret . . .

In France, women now take far less part in politics than they used to do, because parties have for long been too excitable and distinct to be safely meddled with. Not a new feature! Guizot is shorter than my remembrance of him in 1840, when he was at the meeting preliminary to the fatal Niger Expedition; he looks about sixty, a face of many furrows, quiet, deep-set, grey eyes, a thin expressive face, full of quiet sagacity, though very animated in conservation, hands and all taking their share. His little bit of red ribbon seems the only relic of official greatness left.

June 8.—We met Bunsen and Guizot at an out-of-doors party at the Frys'. The two politicians walked up and down the lawn in long and earnest discourse; the character of their faces as unlike as that of two men whose objects in life have been in many respects so similar, can well be . . .

June 9.—Went to Laurence's, and he took us to see Samuel Rogers's pictures. He has some capital drawings, a letter of Milton's, and the rooms are decorated with all sorts of curiosities. A large dinner-party at Abel Smith's. C. Buxton spoke of a day's shooting in Norfolk with Sir Robert Peel, when he was by far the best shot of the party. He talked incessantly of farming, and with a knowledge far deeper than they had met with before; in fact, he was the whole man in everything, and yet so cold and unapproachable that they felt quite frightened at him.

June 12.—Went to the House of Commons and heard Cobden bring on his Arbitration Motion to produce Universal Peace. He has a good face, and is a clear, manly speaker . . . We were much pleased with the debate; it showed that there was much more willingness to listen to moral argument, and much less disposition to snub and ridicule such a proposal, than we had expected. Lord Palmerston's was a very manly speech . . .

June 13.—Steamed to Chelsea, and paid Mrs. Carlyle a humane little visit. I don't think she roasted a single soul, or even body. She talked in rather a melancholy way of herself and of life in general, professing that it was only the Faith that all things are well put together—which all sensible people *must* believe—that prevents our sending to the nearest chemist's shop for sixpennyworth of arsenic; but now one just endures it while it lasts, and that is all we can do. We said a few modest words in honour of existence, which she answered by, 'But I can't enjoy Joy . . . ' Carlyle is sitting now to a miniature-painter, and Samuel Laurence has been drawing her; she bargained with him at starting not to treat the subject as an Italian artist had done, and make her a something between St. Cecilia and an improper female. She caught a glimpse of her own profile the other day, and it gave her a great start, it looked such a gloomy headachy creature . . . She talked with much affection and gratitude of W. E. Forster, and cannot understand his not marrying; remarking, 'I think he's the sort of person that would have suited me very well!' She talked of the Sterling Memoir by Julius Hare, and of Captain [Anthony, brother of John] Sterling's literary designs: in these her husband means to take no part . . .

June 20.—To Wandsworth, and met Elihu Burritt* at dinner. Exceedingly pleased with him; his face is strikingly beautiful, delicately chiselled, bespeaking much refinement and quiet strength. He is a natural gentleman, and seems to have attained the blessed point of self-forgetfulness, springing from ever-present remembrance of better things. That Cobden evening was the happiest in his life; he felt it a triumph, and knew how it must tell on Europe that in the midst of all the wars and tumults of most nations, the greatest legislative body in the world should put all their policies aside, and for hours be in deliberation on a vast moral question. Cobden got a larger number of votes than on the introduction of any other of his great subjects, and yet he

* American blacksmith who campaigned for universal brotherhood.

came out of the House, after his speech, earnestly apologising
for having done so little justice to their subject . . .

July 2.—Dined at St. Mark's College. Derwent Coleridge . . . had been dining at a whitebait party where the
toastmaster successively proclaimed each toast behind the
speaker's chair; and soon after, preaching at a friend's church,
he was startled by hearing the responses and the Amen given
in the very same tone and twang which had so lately uttered,
'Gentlemen, fill your glasses.' Spoke of Macaulay's brilliant
talking . . . Mary Coleridge told us much of Helen Faucit
[classical actress]. She is full of strength and grace, and
though cold in surface there is a burning Etna beneath. Of S.
T. Coleridge and her earliest intercourse with him: when in
the midst of the highest talk he would turn to her, smooth her
hair, look into her face, and say,—'God bless you, my pretty
child, my pretty Mary!' He was most tender and affectionate,
and always treated her as if she were six years old. They tried
hard to bring him to Cornwall, but the Gilmans would not
suffer it, though the old man wished it much . . .

July 4.—We joined Professor Owen in his Museum [Hun-
terian Collection, Royal College of Surgeons]. He showed us
some of the vertebrae of the genuine sea-serpent; the commonly reported ones are really a very long species of shark,
and when a pair are following each other, and appearing
from time to time above water, they look of course wondrously long . . .

We looked in on Laurence on our way home, and admired
his sketch of Aunt Backhouse, which looks hewn out of
granite.

Falmouth, September 4.—Dined at Carclew; met Henry Hallam,* his son, Henry, and daughter. The historian is a fine-
looking, white-haired man, of between sixty and seventy . . . Sir Charles Lemon is just come from Paris, where
he finds them at the theatres making infinite fun of their pet
Republic. 'What shall we try next?' asked De Tocqueville one
evening when Sir Charles was taking tea there. 'Oh, try a
Queen, to be sure; we find it answer famously, and the
Duchesse d'Orléans would do it to perfection.' The difficulty
seems that they would have to alter the Salic law. Young

---

* Historian. Father of Arthur, close friend of Tennyson and the subject of *In
Memoriam.*

Henry Hallam was breakfasting somewhere in London with Louis Blanc,* who for two hours talked incessantly and almost always about himself. He is a very little man, and though eloquent on his one idea, gives you no feeling of power or trustworthiness, there is so much showy declamation instead. Carlyle was there, and it was the veriest fun to watch their conversation. Carlyle's French was a literal translation of his own untranslatable English, uttered too in his own broad Scotch. Louis Blanc could not at all understand him, but would listen attentively and then answer very wide of the mark. Henry Hallam is very agreeable, sensible, and modest, and at dinner asked if I knew anything of a man of whom he had heard much though he had never met him—Sterling. He spoke of the peculiar affection and loyalty which all who had ever known him at all intimately seemed to cherish towards him, and their criticism on Hare's Memoir—that it portrayed a mere book-worm always occupied with some abstruse theological problem, rather than the man they delighted in for his geniality and buoyancy of feeling. Henry Hallam knows Tennyson intimately, who speaks with rapture of some of the Cornish scenery. At one little place, Bude, where he arrived in the evening, he cried, 'Where is the sea? show me the sea!' So after the sea he went stumbling in the dark, and fell down and hurt his leg so much that he had to be nursed for six weeks by a surgeon there, who introduced some of his friends to him, and thus he got into a class of society totally new to him; and when he left, they gave him a series of introductions, so that instead of going to hotels he was passed on from town to town, and abode with little grocers and shopkeepers along his line of travel. He says that he cannot have better got a true general impression of the class, and thinks the Cornish very superior to the generality. They all knew about Tennyson, and had heard his Poems, and one miner hid behind a wall that he might see him! Tennyson hates being lionised, and even assumes bad health to avoid it . . .

September 14.—The Bishop of Norwich is almost suddenly dead.

September 23.—Aunt Backhouse ministered at Meeting very

---

* French revolutionary historian; his *Histoire de Dix Ans 1831-40* shook Louis Philippe's throne.

strikingly; to us her prayer was quite grand . . .

September 26.—Took Field Talfourd to see the Grove Hill pictures, some of which seemed to fascinate him: the mouth he considers the criterion in portraits . . .

October 10.—Reading [Mrs. Gaskell's] 'Mary Barton' a most stirring book, which ought to stimulate one in many ways to a wiser sympathy with others, whose woeful circumstances are apt to beget bitter thoughts and mad deeds. It opens the very floodgates of sympathy, yet directs it into its wisest channel.

October 17.—Heard of a poor woman in Windsor Forest who was asked if she did not feel lonely in that exceeding isolation. 'Oh no; for Faith closes the door at night and Mercy opens it in the morning.'

October 25.—We attended a very good lecture on Female Influence, by Clara Balfour, at the Polytechnic Hall. There was nothing to annoy by its assumptions for our sex; and even in the perilous art of lecturing the lady did not unsex herself . . . She concluded with Wordsworth's beautiful little epitome of Woman, and was immensely applauded by her audience, from which she had the good sense to escape at once, by disappearing from the platform.

October 26.—Clara Balfour called on us. She spoke a good deal of Alexander Scott,* who, after his connection with Edward Irving, continued to officiate in the Scotch Church, until one day he felt such a stop in his mind on the subject of prayer, that he was unable to proceed at that moment with its expression. This he explained to the astonished congregation, and was soon dismissed from the Scotch Church, and had his own small but earnest and sincere audience at Woolwich, and then came to London . . .

I asked Clara Balfour about the effort of lecturing. She said the work came so gradually and without premeditation that the way was made easy for her. She was thrown alone upon her subject and carried through. She began at a sort of friendly party at Greenwich on a similar subject to last evening's, and in all her course she has met with nothing but kindness. Carlyle once asked her, 'Well, Mrs. Balfour, have ye got over your nervousness concerning that thing (*i.e.*, lecturing)?' 'Oh no, and I believe I never shall.' 'I'm very glad to

---

* First principal of Owens College, Manchester, the forerunner of Manchester University.

hear ye say so,' he replied. She told us pleasant things of Jane
Carlyle; her thoroughgoing kindness, without any attempt at
patronage. Clara Balfour was very poor, and most thankfully
assisted in correcting the press for the *London and Westminster
Review*. Carlyle's article on 'Mirabeau' fell to her portion one
day, which haunted her; she disliked but was fascinated by it,
and had no idea by whom it was written: her press-correcting
superior was a very matter-of-fact man, who held Addison the
immutable standard in English writing, so anything of Carlyle's drove him half mad, and he was thankful enough to
make it over to his subordinate. Her temperance friend, Mr.
Dunlop, is a cousin of Carlyle's, and he asked her if she had
ever seen the 'French Revolution.' 'No, but she longed to do
so.' The next day, to her delighted surprise, Mrs. Carlyle
called on her, with the volumes under her arm; and this was
the first of an untiring succession of acts of kindness and
consideration. A little before her mother died, Jane Carlyle
yearned to go and see her, but her wish was opposed; at length
she said, 'go she would, in spite of the world, the flesh, and
the devil,'—but, poor thing, she was too late.

After tea we went together to the Lecture Hall, which was
immensely crowded. Her subject was the Female Characters
in our Literature, especially those of Scott . . .

November 4.—Finished that brilliant, bitter book, 'Vanity
Fair'; it shows great insight into the intricate badness of
human nature, and draws a cruel sort of line between moral
and intellectual eminence, as if they were most commonly
dissociated, which I trust is no true bill.

November 8.—Sir John Ross returned.* No news. Poor Lady
Franklin, I wonder how much of the Greenland Report she
had received. Sir John's has been a most adventurous expedition, walking 230 miles over the ice, and so forth.

November 10.—Papa sent forth a Magnetic Deflector to
[Antoine] L'Abbadie, the Basque African explorer.

December 5.—Read W. E. Forster's manly, spirited answer
to Macaulay's libels on William Penn . . .

December 29.—Aunt Charles, writing of a visit to the now
patriarchal-looking Poet at Rydal Mount, says, 'The gentle
softened evening light of his spirit is very lovely, and there is a

---

* From an expedition in search of Franklin. Ross was discoverer of the magnetic
pole.

quiet sublimity about him as he waits on the shores of that Eternal World which seems already to cast over him some sense of its beauty and its peace.'

1850

Falmouth, February 1.—Heard many thoughts and things of the times discussed in the evening by George Dawson in his lecture on the tendencies of the age. It consisted of a string of weighty and brilliantly illustrated truths, which very few are in a sufficiently advanced condition to call truisms. He is a little, black-eyed, black-haired, atrabilious-looking man, full of energy and intensity, with an air of despising, if not defying, the happiness which he wished to make us all independent of.

March 27.—Heard a lecture of Clara Balfour's on Joanna of Naples, Isabella of Castile, Elizabeth of England, and Mary of Scotland. It was excessively well done . . .

April 1.—This evening Clara Balfour's picture-gallery included Christina of Sweden, Anne of England, Maria Theresa, and Catherine of Russia . . .

April 13.—Evening at Rosemerryn; Mary Anne Birkbeck told me a good deal about her grandmamma, Lord Byron's Mary Chaworth.* Lord Byron used often to be with her, but would never sleep at Annesley, saying that the house felt as if it had a grudge against him. This was owing to the duel having been fought by two members of the families in the preceding generation. Byron was a very sulky boy of nineteen, and felt quite savage when she danced, because his lameness made it impossible for him to do the same. She had no idea that his fancy for her was anything serious, and, moreover, she had at that time a *penchant* for the Mr. Musters whom she married. He saw her once again, when he wrote in her album, unknown to her, those touching lines† which she did not discover until some time afterwards. Mary Anne's mother was that 'favourite child' who had its mother's eyes. When Newstead had to be sold, he had the greatest horror of Mr.

---

* Heiress of Annesley Hall, Nottinghamshire, to whom Byron proposed.
† In Byron's 'Well! Thou Art Happy' (1808).

Musters buying it . . .

May 5.—Visited the Laundry School. The good teacher was taking most patient pains with an endlessly stupid little girl, who meekly and respectfully whispered the most heterogeneous answers to the simplest questions. 'Who did Adam and Eve sin against when they ate the fruit?' 'Their parents and friends, ma'am!' 'Were Adam and Eve happy when they left the garden?' 'Holy and happy, ma'am!'

May 24.—My birthday: it seems as if my future life might well be spent in giving thanks for all the mercies of the past.

June 7.—Tea with Barclay at the Farm; he was all a host could be to his large party, but a day of pleasure is not half so pleasant as other days.

June 25.—Met some very pleasant O'Reillys. They knew Mezzofanti, a little, bright-eyed, wiry man, who greeted them in pure Milesian, which they knew only in fragments; then he tried brogue, and succeeded admirably, and then in the most perfect London English. Mr. O'Reilly, to puzzle him, talked slang, but only got a volley of it in return. He knew sixty-four, and talked forty-eight, languages. But he told them a fact which gave moral interest to his acquirement. When a young Priest, he was visiting an hospital, and found a poor foreign sailor dying, and longing to confess, but finding no priest who could understand him. The sadness of this struck him, and he turned his attention forthwith to languages.

September 11.—Much interested about the mobbing which J. J. von Haynau, the Austrian [general], got at the Barclays' Brewery the other day, when he was most unhandsomely whipped and otherwise outraged in memory of his having flogged Hungarian women. He has found it expedient to leave England, cursing, doubtless, the gallantry of the English burghers.

October 2.—Dined at Carclew; met Professor [Lyon] Playfair . . . He is come as Commissioner about the great Exhibition next year, and tells wonders of their preparations—a great glass-house half a mile long, containing eight miles of tables . . .

1851

London, May 24.—Visited Ernest and Elizabeth de Bunsen at Abbey Lodge, their pretty house in Regent's Park. They gave us breakfast at eleven, the little Fritz and Hilda acting as kellners. They are soon expecting [Augustus] Kestner, the Hanoverian Minister of Rome, the son of Goethe's Charlotte; he is a genial and kindly man . . .

May 27.—Drove to the Lloyds and found the dear old Chevalier Neukomm there. We had a capital talk. He is an adept in all the sciences of the imagination, including phrenology, mesmerism, and homoeopathy, and talked with earnest zeal. The lastingness of an individual conviction is with him a pledge for its truth.

Whilst dining at Uncle David's, Captain Barclay of Ury* walked in. He is so striking a Fact in the family, that one is very glad to have realised it whilst it lasts. It is a decrepit Fact now, for an illness has much broken him down, but there is a slow quiet Scotch sagacity in his look and manner which declares him quite up to his present business in London viz., selling a vast grey horse. His conversation was not memorable, but his great strength was never supposed to lie in that direction. He looks now upwards of seventy.

May 30.—Dined with the Priestmans [John† and Helen]. John Bright was there, fighting his Parliamentary battles over again like a bull-dog. It was quite curious to watch his talk with his quiet father-in-law.

June 1.—Anna Braithwaite told us of her last interview with William Wordsworth: he spoke of having long had a great desire for Fame, but that that had now all ceased, and his sole desire was to become 'one of the poor in spirit' whom our Lord had declared to be blest.

June 4.—A charming story of F. Cunningham,‡ coming in to prayers, just murmuring something about his study being on fire, and proceeding to read a long chapter, and make equally long comments thereupon. When the reading was over and the fact became public, he observed, 'Yes, I saw it

---

* Well known for his walking feats.
† Quaker philanthropist; father of John Bright's first wife.
‡ The Rev. Francis Cunningham, vicar of Lowestoft; married Richenda Gurney of Earlham.

was a little on fire, but I opened the window on leaving the room!'

June 5.—Attended a Ragged School Meeting; Lord Kinnaird* in the chair, instead of Lord Ashley (who has become Lord Shaftesbury by his father's death). A great deal of good sense was spoken, and encouraging stories told. Dr. [John] Cumming† was on the platform, and made an admirable speech, with perfect ease, choice language, and excellent feeling, so as to modify my prejudice against him most notably . . . Described the origin and progress of the Ragged Schools in his parish, and asked the audience for £500, assuring them that at his chapel he always got what he asked for, large sums just as easily as small ones; the great thing being to ask boldly, and you are paid boldly. He is a younger man than I had expected—about thirty-six, with dark hair and eyes, rather Jewish, wearing spectacles, and very energetic in voice and manner.

June 7.—A bright dinner at Abbey Lodge. Kestner was there; a dry, thin gentleman of the old school, who looks as if he had had his romance done for him long before his birth. He has a most interesting correspondence between his mother and Goethe, who had greatly admired and loved her, but as she was betrothed to his friend, he had the prudence to retire from the great peril he felt himself in; and even after her marriage he left Frankfort whenever they were coming there. These experiences, and the awful death of a friend who had not been so self-controlled, were combined into the Wertherian romance. But of all this Kestner said nothing; he is quite happy when talking of his six Giottos, the gems of his collection . . . The Chevalier and Madame Bunsen were there, also George de Bunsen the Philologist,‡ Dr. [Reinhold] Pauli, Amelia Opie, and others. The Chevalier and Dr. Pauli were my dinner comrades, of whose discourse I remember some fragments . . . Dr. Pauli is just bringing out a Life of our Alfred: he has found some very precious MSS. concerning him at Oxford, many of his translations from monkish Latin poems, which were evidently first translated for him into easy

---

* One of the founders of the YWCA.
† Divine; appointed to the Scottish Church, Crown Court, Covent Garden; took part in Maynooth controversy.
‡ Son of the Chevalier. Dr Pauli, a historian, was the Chevalier's secretary.

Latin; and one original poem, a Thanksgiving (I think) for the coming of St. Augustine and the introduction of Christianity into England; in which his arrival, &c., is minutely described. I suggested the propriety of an English translation being published at the same time, when both my gentlemen waxed very scornful concerning the reading public in England. No one would read it unless it had some such title as, 'Alfred the Great, or the Papal Aggression Question Considered,' or unless it had pictures of the costumes of the people running down amongst the letterpress! . . . Ernest and George de Bunsen sang gloriously: at one time they were nightingales, the one merry, the other sentimental; but George de Bunsen's 'Wanderer' was beyond all compare. [Richard] Ford, the writer of the Handbook of Spain, joined the party. A son of Brandis was there, quiet and silent as a statue; and the dear old Chevalier Neukomm, who became rapt over the singing.

June 9.—Spent a charming evening at the Chevalier Bunsen's. They were alone, and the Chevalier talked much of their Universities as compared with ours. His son is gone to-day to take his Doctor's degree, which is just a certificate that he is *able* to lecture on subjects of philosophy, history, and philology. He is much amused to think how little the English Universities educate for the times we live in, though he rejoices in some of the reforms at Cambridge and Dublin, and wishes all success to the Government Commission. But the spirit of the evening was Neukomm. The inventor of a silvery lute of some sort came to introduce his instrument, and its breathings were indeed exquisite; and very marvellous was it, when the two musicians improvised together, just taking the 'Ranz des Vaches' as a motive, to hear how they blended their thoughts and feelings in true harmony. But I was glad when the lute was silent and Neukomm poured out his own heart through the voice of the organ . . .

June 11.—Went to the Associated Trades' Tea at St. Martin's Hall. Our chairman, F. D. Maurice, is at his post behind the urn, but he springs up to welcome his friends. He seemed nervous, for there was no arranged plan of the evening. In listening to the workmen's speeches, especially Walter Cooper's (cousin to the author of the 'Purgatory of Suicides'), we could not help feeling very thankful that such fiery spirits had been brought under such high and holy

influences, leading them to apprehend self-sacrifice as the
vital principle on which all successful co-operation must be
founded . . .

June 12.—Went to Thackeray's lecture on the 'Humorists'
at Willis's Rooms [King Street, St James's]. It was a very
large assembly, including Mrs. Carlyle, Dickens, Leslie, and
innumerable noteworthy people. Thackeray is a much older-
looking man that I had expected; a square, powerful face, and
most acute and sparkling eyes, greyish hair and eyebrows. He
reads in a definite, rather dry manner, but makes you
understand thoroughly what he is about. The lecture was full
of point, but the subject was not a very interesting one, and
he tried to fix our sympathy on his good-natured, volatile,
and frivolous Hero rather more than was meet. 'Poor Dick
Steele,' one ends with, as one began; and I cannot see, more
than I did before, the element of greatness in him.

June 13.—We went to Faraday's lecture on 'Ozone.' He
tried the various methods of making Ozone which [Christian
Friedrich] Schönbein* has already performed in our kitchen,
and he did them brilliantly . . .

June 27.—Saw George Wightwick, who, with wife and
other furniture, is just starting for Clifton to live. He showed
us two portraits of himself: one by young Opie, so good that
he says if he saw a fly on its nose he should certainly scratch
his own; the other by Talfourd, catching a momentary
passionate gleam of dramatic expression—a fine abstraction.
Talked of [William Charles] Macready† and his retirement
from the stage to Sherborne, where he is in perfect happiness,
with wife and children, and all joyousness. He begs Wightwick sometimes to tell him something about theatrical
matters, as he hears naught.

[To Aunt Charles Fox] *Penjerrick, July 19.*—Anna Maria
says you wish to see this book (Carlyle's 'Life of Sterling'), so
here it is. That it is calculated to draw fresh obloquy on the
subject of it, is a very secondary consideration to the fact that
it is a book likely to do much harm to Carlyle's wide
enthusiastic public. It is painful enough to see the memorial
of his friend made the text for utterances and innuendoes
from which one *knows* that he would now shrink even more

---

* German chemist who discovered gun-cotton.
† Tragedian and manager of Drury Lane.

than ever, and God alone can limit the mischief. But He can.
That the book is often brilliant and beautiful, and more
human-hearted than most of Carlyle's, will make it but the
more read, however little the world may care for the subject
of the memoir. The graphic parts and the portraiture are
generally admirable, but not by any means always so; however, you will judge for yourselves.

December 3.—Great news stirring in that volcanic Paris. The
President has dissolved the Assembly and appealed to the
people and the army; he establishes universal suffrage, and has
arrested his political opponents . . . How will it end? Shall
we have a Cromwell Junior, or will blood flow there again
like water? One learns to give thanks for being born in
England.

December 29.—C. Enys told us of Sir John Franklin, shortly
before leaving home the last time, lying on a sofa and going
to sleep. Lady Franklin threw something over his feet, when
he awoke in great trepidation, saying, 'Why, there's a flag
thrown over me; don't you know that they lay the Union Jack
over a corpse!'

1852

[To Elizabeth T. Carne*] *Penjerrick, April 14, Easter Tuesday.*—I wish I could as fully enter into the conclusion of thy
sentence, 'To me Easter is an especially cheerful time—a
remembrance and a pledge of conquest over death in every
shape.' I wish I could always *feel* it so for we may without
presumption. But human nature quails under the shadow of
death, when those we dearly love are called hence at even
such a time as this. And but one Easter Tuesday passed
between the departure of two most attached sisters on this
very day, and as it comes round year by year the human
sorrow *will not* be entirely quenched in the resurrection joy.

Thanks many and warm for thy dear little apropos-of-a-
scold note: I so liked what thou said of the caution which
should always be observed in writing, because I had never
distinctly thought of it before, and have been grieved at being

* Geologist and from 1858 head of the Penzance Bank.

taken quite *au pied de la lettre* sometimes, when I meant my lecture to have a smile and a kiss at each end, and two in the middle.

Excellent news,* first from Vigo, then from Lisbon, has set our hearts a-dancing. They had a long voyage, thanks to adverse winds, but suffered far less than they or we had feared. They had pleasant fellow-voyagers, and were able to read, write, and draw, and digest deep draughts of Scandinavian archaeology from the Portuguese Minister to Denmark and Sweden, with whom they seem to have fraternised . . .

Of Slavery matters more anon of course, there is not much to report on yet, but things look cheery in some quarters.

[To Elizabeth Carne] *May 11.*—How pleasant it is to go on abusing each other, instead of being always on one's Ps and Qs, with one's hair brushed and one's shoes on one's feet . . .

[To Elizabeth Carne] *June 25.*— . . . We have one of the best, if not the absolutely best (excuse me), women in England now staying with us—sound, clear-headed, thoughtful, religious; she has performed the difficult duties of a sad-coloured life with thankful and cheerful energy, and a blessed result in the quarter which lay next her heart. Of course she is one of our family, but *any one* might hug Louisa Reynolds, for she is worthy of all honour and love. It may be very stimulating or very humbling to come in contact with such people, or, better still, it may lead one to forget self for half an hour . . .

Are you in for any election interests? A curious Purity-experiment is being tried here, which a good deal engages speculative minds just now. The young candidate, T. G. Baring,† the subject or object of this experiment, is very popular.

[To Elizabeth Carne] *August 11.*—But thou dost not absolutely forbid our telling thee that we *do* enter into your sorrow, . . . and would commend it and you to the compassion of Him who knows all the depths, and in His own way

---

* Robert Were Fox and other Friends were hoping to persuade the Portuguese Government to abolish the slave trade in their African colonies.
† First Earl of Northbrook, Whig MP for Penryn and Falmouth, 1857; governor-general of India, 1872-76.

and time will either relieve the suffering, or else enable you to bear it in that deep and awful and trustful submission to His will, in which alone the spirit can be taught and strengthened to endure. 'He openeth the ear to discipline,' and oh how endlessly does He bless the docile learner!

A very dear friend of ours, who was called on to resign, first her husband, then one grown-up child after another, and who did resign them, as one who knew that her Lord loved them more than she could do, heard suddenly that her youngest son had died at Malta after a day or two's illness. The others she had lost had long known the beauty of holiness; but this youngest—oh! this was hard to bear. She almost sank under it; still her faith did not fail her; all her prayers for him *could* not have been wasted; what she knew not now, she might be permitted to know hereafter. And so, though well-nigh crushed, she would not lose her confidence that the Hand of Love had mixed this cup also. About a year passed, when a little parcel reached her containing this son's Bible which he had with him to the last, and in it were many texts marked by him, which spoke such comfort to her heart as she had little dreamed was ever meant for her.

My dear Elizabeth, God has fitting consolation for every trial, and He will not withhold that which is best for you. Coleridge says in one of his letters, 'In storms like these, that shake the dwelling and make the heart tremble, there is no middle way between despair and the yielding up the whole spirit unto the guidance of faith.' May He who pities you be very near you all, in this time of earnest need.

Dublin, August 18.—We landed safely on Dublin Pier after a very pleasant passage. A thunderstorm marched grandly over the Wicklow Mountains as we approached. We soon found ourselves at the Lloyds' hospitable home, the Chevalier Neukomm being a new feature among them.

August 19.—He brought down to breakfast a little canon he has composed for the ceremony of to-day—the laying the foundation-stone of Kilcrony (the Lloyds' new house). The words chosen are, 'Except the Lord build,' &c.; and this he has arranged for four voices. There is a great contrast between Professor Lloyd and the Chevalier in their principle of judgment on large subjects. The texts of the latter are from the gospel of Experience, those of the former from the New

Testament. But Neukomm's judgment of individuals is noble and generous, only to the masses everywhere he denies the guidance of any principle: self-interest and ambition he thinks the motive power of every national movement to which we would give a higher origin, and he thinks he sees distinctly that a nation is always the worse for it. But then he lived for twenty years with Talleyrand—twenty years of the generous and hopeful believing part of his life . . .

August 21.—The Lloyds took us to Mullagh Mast, where Daniel O'Connell held his last monster meeting just before he was arrested; it is a large amphitheatre, on very high ground commanding the view of seven counties.

August 23.—Went to Parsonstown. Lord Rosse* was very glad to see the Lloyds, and very kind to all the party. It was a great treat to see and hear him amongst his visible powers, all so docile and obedient, so facile in their operations, so grand in aim and in attainment. We walked about in the vast tube, much at our ease, and examined the speculum, a duplicate of which lies in a box close by: it has its own little railroad, over which it runs into the cannon's mouth. There are small galleries for observers, with horizontal and vertical movements which you can direct yourself, so as to bring you to the eye-piece of the leviathan. This telescope takes cognisance of objects fifteen degrees east and west of the meridian, which is more than usual in large instruments, but observations near the horizon are worth little on account of the atmospheric influences. The three and a half foot telescope goes round the whole circle, and there is a third instrument at hand, under cover, for the most delicate results. Then Lord and Lady Rosse showed us the foundry, the polishing-shop, &c., and Professor Lloyd gave the story of the casting . . . We had tea, and were shown a multitude of sketches of nebulae taken on the spot. Sir David Brewster† was there, with his sagacious Scotch face, and his pleasant daughter. Whilst we were over our tea, news came of a double star being visible; so we were soon on the spot and gazing through the second glass at the exquisite pair of contrasted coloured stars, blue and yellow. The night was hazy, and the moon low and dim, which was a disappointment; but Lord Rosse kindly showed us a cluster of

* Astronomer; discovered spiral nebulae. MP for King's County, 1823-34.
† Natural philosopher; edited *Edinburgh Magazine.*

stars and a bit of the Milky Way through the great telescope: the very movement of its vast bulk in the darkness was a grand sight. After the British Association, a little party are coming here to inquire into the geology of the moon, and compare it with that of the earth, and in six weeks Otto Struve* is expected, when they mean to begin gauging the heavens. We left after midnight full of delight.

They tell all manner of charming stories of Lord Rosse: of his conduct as a landlord, his patriotic employment of a multitude of people in cutting for an artificial piece of water, because work was very scarce; of his travelling in England long ago as Mr. Parsons, visiting a manufactory, and suggesting a simpler method of turning, so ingenious that the master invited him to dinner, and ended by offering him the situation of foreman in his works.

Killarney, August 25.—This evening we went into the coffee-room of our hotel, and enjoyed the minstrelsy of old Gaudsey the piper . . . There is something very touching in the remembrance of this old man, who looks as if intended for higher things than playing jigs and hornpipes for dancing waiters.

August 30.—Heard a pleasant story of the origin of one of the London Ragged Schools. Miss Howell took a room in a miserable district, and had her piano settled there; as she played plenty of little faces would come peering in, and she would ask them in altogether and play on to them. This went on day after day, until she had some books likewise on the spot, and easily coaxed her musical friends to take a little of her teaching, and the school soon became so large that it had to be organised and placed under regular teachers.

Belfast, September 2.—I was a good deal with the Sabines, who had a torrent of things to tell. The fourth volume of 'Cosmos' will be coming out soon. Humboldt sends Mrs. Sabine [English translator] sheet by sheet as it comes from his printer . . .

September 4.—Colonel Sabine took us into the Ethnological Section of the B. A. Meeting whilst [Augustus] Petermann was reading his paper on the amount of animal life in the Arctic regions. As this had close reference to the probable fate

* German astronomer; he made the first estimate of the sun's velocity, and calculated the orbits of several comets.

of Franklin and his party, the interest was intense. Murchison, Owen, Sabine, and Prince de Canino all expressed themselves most earnest that the national search should be continued. It was a great treat to be present at this discussion, and to watch the eager interest with which they claimed their friend's life from science and from England. Canino, or Prince Bonaparte as he now chooses to be called, is a short man of ample circumference, a large head, sparkling good-humoured eyes, a mouth of much mobility, and a thorough air of *bonhomie.*

September 12.—On a beautiful starry night we steamed into Falmouth Harbour, which, with the earthly and heavenly lights reflected on its surface, looked as beautiful as Cornish hearts could desire. And then on reaching Penjerrick we had a welcome from our beloved Ones, on whom, too, earthly and heavenly light shines visible.

[To Julia and Hester Sterling*] *Falmouth, September 29.*—The story of your journey was very diverting; a severe test for the Equality and Fraternity theory certainly, but it is well to bring one's principles up hardy. Social Reforms, born, nurtured, and matured in a boudoir, are very apt to die there too, I fancy.

We are in the thick of a very pleasant Polytechnic. The Art Exhibition is better, they say, than in any previous year; nevertheless, they have not hesitated to give Anna Maria two bronze medals—one for a wave in the Bay of Biscay, the other for her Lisbon Sketch-Book; and, moreover, a public compliment was paid them, which I am almost apt to fancy well deserved. A great attraction is a vast working model of a mine, which has taken the poor man eight years to execute, and cost him £200. There are a prodigious number of figures, all duly engaged in mining operations, and most of them with distinct movements of their own. It is extremely ingenious and entertaining.

Yesterday we had a crowd of pleasant visitors, too numerous to mention, but almost all adjourned early to a Polytechnic Conversazione . . .

I wish you could all see the submarine experiences of Professor Blank, which have received a Polytechnic medal.

---

* Daughters of John Sterling. They settled at Maenporth, near Falmouth.

They are deliciously witty thoughts, most beautifully executed in little pen-and-ink sketches . . .

Falmouth, November 30.—At the Bank House, when enter Elihu Burritt, looking as beautifully refined an American Indian as ever. He has formed a little Peace Society here, with meetings, funds, books, and a secretary; and has cleverly managed to persuade the editors of many influential foreign newspapers to give constant insertion to its little 'Olive leaf,' which is well. He gave a lecture at the Polytechnic on the extension of the penny-postage system. It was conclusively argumentative and well buttered with facts, statistical, financial, and social. Our ragged boys in the gallery quite agreed with him, and the feeling of the meeting crystallised into a petition.

1853

[To Elizabeth Carne] *Falmouth, January 19.*—My dear E.,— It's only I, but never mind. Neither do I like either to be or to appear ungrateful, and so with all my heart thank thee for my share in the two last despatches. It is a long time to go back to the first of them, with its triumphant refutation of [Charles] Kingsley's 'Miracles Made Easy,' Ireland's claims on the best feelings of England, and several other popular fallacies, with neither the pros or cons of which I am sufficiently acquainted to enter the lists with thee. As for 'Alton Locke,' I totally forget all the miraculous part, and only read it as an intensely, frightfully practical book, and bought a more expensive pair of boots in consequence!

And as for Ireland, poor dear impracticable Ireland, let us be thankful that we are not made governors over one city. The state of the North, especially as we saw it around Belfast, proved that the problem of introducing order into that chaos is not one for absolute despair; a mixture of races, and steady employment, and energetic wills, and benevolent hearts, have done wonders there in a very few years, without many Staffordine executions or despotisms, as far as I could hear of . . .

I wish thou wouldst always choose Monday for writing to

us, and then we should get those Sunday thoughts which surely ought to have a vent before those woeful account-books give a comfortless direction to thy idea. I feel for thee amongst them from the bottom of my heart—for am not I the Treasurer of the Industrial Society, and do my accounts ever balance?

We have just had a long visit from a Prussian sailor-friend of ours from the Sailors' Home, called Kisting: he is a ship's carpenter, who fell from the mast and broke leg and hand, but is now nicely mended. He is quite a man of education, and is delighted to have books; moreover, we have taught him to read as well as talk a little English during his dreary confinement, and I was excessively charmed at receiving a lovely, graceful little note from his sister, thanking us for the small kindnesses shown to him. He is thoroughly with *us* in thinking the manufacture of war machines 'unnatural and unchristian,' and he said when he saw two cannons taken on board ship, with great circumstance, and heard the clergy pronouncing their blessings on them, 'I felt that it was not right.' . . .

Does Friendship really go on to be more pain than a pleasure? I doubt it; for even in its deepest sorrows there is a joy which makes ordinary 'pleasure' a very poor meaningless affair. No, no; we need never be scared from the very depths of Friendship by its possible consequences. The very fact of loving another more than yourself is in itself such a blessing, that it seems scarcely to require any other, and puts you in a comfortable position of independence. . . .

January 29.—Barclay is at the Manchester Peace Conference, which is going on capitally; it is in a practical tone, though held in a very financial atmosphere. He followed Cobden unexpectedly in a speech, and got through it well, describing the origin of the Peace Society, and telling the story of a French Privateer letting a captured ship loose on finding that its owner was a Friend.

February 7.—Kisting (from the Sailors' Home) is staying with us. He talked of Humboldt, and how, during the uproar of '48, the mob rushed from house to house taking possession, at last came to Humboldt's; he opened wide the door and answered, 'Oh yes, come in and take what you can find. I have always been glad to do what I can for you; I am

Humboldt.' It acted like magic to see the simply clad, white-haired old man, standing there with his kind arms extended . . .

March 10.—As we turned the corner of a lane during our walk, a man and a bull came in sight; the former crying out, 'Ladies, save yourselves as you can!' the latter scudding onwards slowly but furiously. I jumped aside on a little hedge, but thought the depth below rather too great—about nine or ten feet; but the man cried 'jump!' and I jumped. To the horror of all, the bull jumped after me. My fall stunned me, so that I knew nothing of my terrible neighbour, whose deep autograph may be now seen quite close to my little one. He thought me dead, and only gazed without any attempt at touching me, though pacing round, pawing and snorting, and thus we were for about twenty minutes. The man, a kind soul but no hero, stood on the hedge above, charging me from time to time not to move. Indeed, my first recollection is of his friendly voice. And so I lay still, wondering how much was reality and how much dream and when I tried to think of my situation, I pronounced it too dreadful to be true, and certainly a dream. Then I contemplated a drop of blood and a lump of mud, which looked very real indeed, and I thought it very imprudent in any man to make me lie in a pool—it would surely give me rheumatism. I longed to peep at the bull, but was afraid to venture on such a movement. Then I thought, I shall probably be killed in a few minutes, how is it that I am not taking it more solemnly? I tried to do so, seeking rather for preparation for death than restoration to life. Then I checked myself with the thought, It's only a dream, so it's really quite profane to treat it in this way; and so I went on oscillating. There was, however, a rest in a dear will of God which I love to remember; also a sense of the simplicity of my condition—nothing to do to involve others in suffering, only to endure what was laid upon me. To me the time did not seem nearly so long as they say it was: at length the drover, having found some bullocks, drove them into the field, and my bull, after a good deal of hesitation, went off to his own species. Then they have a laugh at me that I stayed to pick up some oranges I had dropped before taking the man's hand and being pulled up the hedge; but in all this I acted as a somnambulist, with only fitful gleams of consciousness and memory.

April 3.—Cobden is so delighted with Barclay's tract, 'My Friend Mr. B.,'* that he requests it may be printed on good paper and sent to every member of the two Houses, which is to be done.

Interesting letter from Henry F. Barclay from Paris, with an account of the dinner at the Tuileries given to the Deputation from the Commercial Community of London to the Emperor.† It was a small party; the Emperor and Empress, with three ladies, joined them in the Empress's drawing-room, and they were not at all prepared to see so lovely a creature. Their Majesties preceded them in to dinner and sat side by side, Lord and Lady Cowley flanking them; it was a real pleasure to see the husband and wife quite flirting together, as happy as birds. After dinner, when they all returned to the drawing-room, the Emperor and Empress separately went about conversing pleasantly with all the different guests; the Empress on the Exhibition and the improvements around Paris, and the Emperor and Samuel Gurney on the state of the country, the good the Deputation had done, the difficulty of understanding the state of things around you until cleared up by inquiring of Ministers, the mischief of the tone taken by some of the English papers; the difference between the nature of the two countries. 'In France,' said the Emperor, 'revolutions are easy, but reforms slow, almost impossible; in England reforms are steady and certain, but revolutions can never be accomplished.'

London, May 4.—To the Bible Meeting. Dr. Cumming was most felicitous in language and illustration; Hugh M'Neile very brilliant and amusing on Tradition *versus* Scripture; then an American Bishop and his friend spoke as a deputation. Dr. [Thomas] Binney, in a clever, free-and-easy speech, sympathised with them (on slavery being still an institution in their country); and Mrs. H. B. Stowe, being present in a side gallery, gave great piquancy to these remarks, and the room was in a tumult of sympathy.

* A peace tract, in which John Bull keeps many uniformed servants he can ill afford to protect his estate.
† Representing 4,000 merchants, bankers, and traders of London who wished to emphasise that, in spite of rumours, the English people harboured no feelings of unfriendliness towards the French.

May 8.—Charles Gilpin took us to a presentation of Shakespeare, by 9000 working Englishmen, to Kossuth.* We were in a little orchestra with Madame Kossuth, who is an anxious, care-worn, but refined-looking woman, with very prominent eyes. Her husband is a very manly-looking Saxon, with clear blue eyes and much openness of expression; he was in his Hungarian dress, and the people were in uncontrollable excitement at his entrance. Lord Dudley Stuart† was in the chair, and contrived cleverly to bespeak a loyal tone to the meeting, which was certainly in a most democratic spirit. Then old, rather crabbed-looking Douglas Jerrold presented Shakespeare's house and works in a very good, though, of course, intensely eulogistic, speech. Kossuth replied wonderfully; his language so well chosen, and pronounced with such emphasis and point; his attitudes were quiet and unstudied, and he impressed one with vastly more respect than we had ever felt for him before. He described his first introduction to our language when in prison and utterly alone, not seeing the trees or the sky; he begged that a book might be granted him. 'Very well, if not on politics.' 'May I have an English Shakespeare, grammar, and dictionary?' These were given, and so he laboured and pored for a while, till light broke in and a new glory streamed into his captive life.

Penzance, August 27.—At the Land's End breathing in the beauty of the scene. I could not help rather wishing myself in the Longships Lighthouse, with Duty so clearly defined and so really important, yet so much time left for one's own meditations.

[To Elizabeth Carne] *Penjerrick, October 3.*—Thy most welcome letter would have been acknowledged much sooner, but I had such a mass and variety of everybody's business to attend to as quite bewildered my poor little mind. Now, however, the pressure from without has greatly abated, and poor little mind aforesaid is, I really hope, getting into a more tidy and manageable condition . . .

Jane has all her children in the North except little Gurney, who is my heart's delight, and a perfect mass of sunshine to us. I have never before had a child thrown so much on my

---

* Hungarian patriot who led the revolution of 1848 and fled his country on the surrender to Austria in 1849.
† Advocated the independence of Poland.

care, and most delicious I find the tender little dependence.
And then I have also the very new and very exalting
experience of my presence or absence being absolutely a
matter of importance to one dear human being. And oh how
much that dear mother and I do make of each other!
. . . Maurice's new book, 'Theological Essays,' is a great
event to me . . . It fills one with ponderings on large
subjects, and I trust he helps one to ponder them in a large
and trustful spirit, or, at least, to desire to do so. In his special
results there is plenty of matter for difference as well as
agreement, but for the spirit in which he seeks them—thank
God.

[To J. M. Backhouse] *Penjerrick, November 2.*—Pray thank
Aunt Charles for the sight of the enclosed portrait of the
Stevensons. How incalculable is the national importance of
one such genuine Christian family. Tell her that the King's
College Council has decided *against* F. D. Maurice, pro-
claiming him (as Socrates before him) a dangerous teacher for
youth! This may probably be but the beginning of ordeals for
the brave and faithful soul. He has expected it for months,
but it comes at last as a very painful blow. His beautiful
book, 'The Kings and Prophets of the Old Testament,'
dedicated to your friend Thomas Erskine in such a lovely
letter, seems to me an admirable preparation for his present
discipline. But I imagine him in deep anxiety lest party spirit
and revenge should be awakened in the hearts of those who
feel how much they owe him.

November 29.—The Enys's brought a very remarkable
woman over here for several hours—Courtney Boyle, for
twenty years Maid of Honour to Queen Adelaide, of whom
she speaks with most reverent affection. Though now in years
and most eccentric in dress, she is very beautiful and very
charming. Her grey hair all flows back at its own sweet will,
in utter ignorance of combs and hairpins, and on the top is
placed a broad-brimmed black beaver hat with a feather in it,
which she often takes off and carries in her hand. She warbles
and whistles like a bird, and was in thorough harmony with
Nature and Uncle Joshua. As she stood on our bridge and
looked at what is called the London road, she remarked, 'The
World is all very well in its place, but it has no business here.'
She often pays long visits to W. S. Landor, when he takes her

back into the old times, and they have Dante and Beatrice and such like at table with them.

December 10.—Amelia Opie is gone Home, after an illness borne with much gentle peace and trust, and ended with severe bodily conflict. I have had a series of leave-takings amongst my cottage friends, and a dog and a cat followed me so pertinaciously that it was some trouble to dispense with them. And sitting down under the hedge, old Pascoe and I read of Christian and Hopeful passing over the River, and we looked across to the cottage of one who had long been trembling on its banks, but had now been carried over, and welcomed by the Shining Ones.

1854

Torquay, January 30.—Charles Kingsley called, but we missed him.

February 3.—We paid him and his wife a very happy call; he fraternising at once, and stuttering pleasant and discriminating things concerning F. D. Maurice, Coleridge, and others. He looks sunburnt with dredging all the morning, has a piercing eye under an overhanging brow, and his voice is most melodious and his pronunciation exquisite. He is strangely attractive.

February 25.—The St. Petersburg Peace Deputation has greatly flourished. They had half-an-hour's colloquy with the Czar, who talked very freely over European politics and told them of his pacific desires and bellicose necessities. He ended by shaking hands and saying, 'You would like to see my wife.' So they saw her, and she had evidently been watching the previous interview, for she told them that there were tears in the Czar's eyes as they spoke to him. He means to send a reply to the Address from the Society of Friends: every King looks over the precipice of War, but happily with far more of shuddering than heretofore.

[To Elizabeth Carne] *Falmouth, March 18.*—As for C. Kingsley, I can't half answer thy questions: we saw much more of his wife than himself, and of her rather intimately. He has rather the look which thou suggests *a priori*, but his wife's stories of him are delightful: the solemn sense of duty under which he writes, the confirming letters he has received from far and near from ardent young spirits, who thank him for having rescued them from infidelity. Such things console him greatly for being ranked amongst his country's plagues. 'Yeast' was the book which was written with his heart's blood; it was the outcome of circumstances, and cost him an illness. Thou knows that Anthony Froude, the author of the burnt 'Nemesis,'* has become his brother-in-law.

Hast thou read William Conybeare's clever paper on Church Parties in the October *Edinburgh?* We had the Low, High, and Broad admirably illustrated at Torquay—the Stevensons, the Kingsleys, and a family of very charming people, one of whom gave me· a long discourse on the blessings of auricular confession. It is very delightful to get beneath all those crusty names and find the true human heart beating right humanly in each and all.

The British fleet has reached Copenhagen. Such is to-day's news. The staff does not start till next week for Constantinople. . . . So neither Cobden's Doves, nor the fanatical Quakers, nor the European Powers are likely to interfere with what thou considers the right way of settling a Vexed Question. Poor Czar! what strange dreams he must have, and what a strange awakening! . . .

March 27.—Judge Talfourd died suddenly on the Bench at Stafford after a striking charge, in which he dwelt on the lack of sympathy between the classes, and the fruitful source of crime which this proved—employers and employed holding a mechanical rather than a human relation to each other.

May 24.—Madame de Wette is staying with us, the widow of the well-known Professor.† She is lively, shrewd, warm-hearted, and with much knowledge of books and men. Professor Vinet was her dear friend, and of him she gives lovely scraps and sketches. She described an amusing evening she spent with the Emperor Alexander at her sister's house at Basle, where all etiquette was put aside and they were as happy as birds. She told him that they would hope to see him again at Basle, but with a smaller attendance (he was then on

---

* *Nemesis of Faith*, publicly burnt by William Sewell, professor of moral philosophy at Oxford.
† German philosopher and theologian who edited Luther's letters.

his way from Paris with 30,000 men).

July 23.—We had a visit from Sir Charles Lemon and Dr. Milman, the Dean of St. Paul's. He is bowed down more with study than age, for his eyes are bright and keen, and have a depth of geniality and poetic feeling lying in them, overshadowed as they are by black shaggy eyebrows; the features are all good, and the mouth very mobile in form and expression. He is most friendly in manner and free in conversation; greatly open to admiring the beautiful world around him, and expressing himself with a poet's choice of language, and sometimes with a Coleridgean intoned emphasis. They are going to explore our coast, winding up with Tintagel, whither as a boy he was poetically attracted, and wrote a poem called 'The City of Light,' made up of King Arthur, the Anglo-Saxons, and all sorts of things which he was utterly incompetent to put together. 'And when is Arthur coming again?' said I, with a laudable desire for information. 'He has come,' was the reply; 'we have had our second Arthur: can he be better represented than in the Duke of Wellington?'

The Dean used often to see and hear S. T. Coleridge, but his wonderful talk was far too unvaried from day to day; also, there were some absolute deficiencies in it, such as the total absence of wit; still it was very remarkable . . .

[To Elizabeth Carne] *Penjerrick, July 29.*—My dear E.,— Indeed I would have maintained a decent silence for some weeks, but then there is Mamma's gratitude about the fruit! and Papa's words concerning Madeira earths, which, lest I forget, I will here set down . . .

Uncle and Aunt Charles are just returned from their long and eventful absence. . . . She has brought home three little baby tortoises, most exquisite black demonettes an inch and a half long, with long tails, who, I have no doubt, often prove comforters. 'What am I doing—thinking—reading?' My dear E., very little of either. Taking Life far too easily, and enjoying it far too much—I mean the indolent part of it. The only book I shall chronicle is the 'Heir of Redclyffe,' which I read with the Tregedna cousins—an exquisite and inspiring vision of persevering and successful struggle with the evil part of human nature; and H. Martineau's history of thirty English years, really giving one a very interesting insight into the birth of many Ideas which have now got into jackets and trousers.

[To Elizabeth Carne] *Penjerrick, November 21.*—Now I have been a little long in writing, haven't I? But only listen to me, and grant that there has been little time for letter-writing. These daily peace-essays, published in a paper called the *Times,* are enough to account for any one's being kept in a breathless silence of attention, awe-stricken, shuddering, asking with round eyes, 'What next?'

But besides this, Robin and I have been with Barclay to Southampton, and seen him off for Alexandria in the good ship *Indus,* and then with heavy hearts went to London. Everything on board the *Indus* looked promising; the second officer magnificently gave up his luxurious cabin, and when the bell rang we left our Brother, feeling that we ought to be thankful for the present and trustful for the future. His brother-in-law, John Hodgkin, came down that morning from London to see him off; he was in every way a great comfort and strength, for we had a little time of solemn silence and as solemn prayer before going on board, which, though most touching, was essentially strengthening and helpful. The weather has been so fine since he left that we feel we have had no pretext for anxiety, and all we hear and all we know argues that he is doing the very wisest thing possible, and that there is every probability of its bringing him into a very different state of health from that in which we part from him. And how different from an embarkation for Sebastopol!

F. Maurice was much cheered by the good beginning of his People's College, and especially by the unexpectedly large attendance of his own Bible-class on Sunday evening . . .

1855

[To Elizabeth Carne] *Falmouth, January 10.*—My poor dear afflicted friend, who can't enlist!—I quite agree with thee, not one word about the War . . . Our notions get a little revolutionised in times like this. Pray, pray that whatever is Christian in us may be deepened, strengthened, vitalised in these times of strong temptation, when so many uncertificated angels of light are filling our atmosphere and bewildering the most earnest souls. My silence on the subject of War has like thine reached the third page, so I will *break* it by a winding-up remark of my dear friend F. D. Maurice after a chat we had had on this same topic. I—'Won't the World come to think with *us* some day?' (!) F. D. M.—'They will be brought to think *rightly* on the subject, though it may be very differently from either you or me.'

[To Elizabeth Carne] *Falmouth, January 31.*— . . . I am rather flattered to find that we are considered such an easy-going people, captious only on that one unmentionable topic, War! I had fancied we were the acknowledged nuisance of good society from our multiform and multifarious crotchets and 'testimonies.' Why! what a fuss we made about the Slave Trade and Slavery: then there was no peace with us because the prisons must needs be looked after; then the asylums for the insane must be differently managed; then we positively refused to swear on any consideration; a large majority of us equally decline drinking anything more stimulating than coffee, and strongly urge the same course on others; then how dogged we are in practical protest against a paid ministry: in fact, there is no end to our scrupulosities, and we surely are considered the most difficile and bizarre body in Christendom (if we are to be found there). But perhaps thy special allusion is to our not vigorously opposing the money-getting spirit of the age. Ah, my dear Elizabeth, there is a grievous amount of truth in this (supposed) charge, but I will say that it is *in spite of* the earnest advice and beseeching of our official superiors. I always try to account for the phenomenon by remembering that we are essentially a middle-class community; that amongst us industry, perseverance, and energy of character are habitually cultivated, and that as our crotchets keep us out of almost all the higher walks of professional life, this industry, perseverance, and energy is found in the money market, and is apt to succeed therein. All I can say in apology (for it *does* require an apology) is, that the wealth we gain is not generally spent on ourselves alone. But pray tell us candidly which of the other crying evils of our country thou wouldst urge on our attention, for there are many listening for 'calls' who would thankfully take a good hint. . . .

March 3.—From Barclay letters have come, ending cheer-

fully from a tomb under the shadow of the Pyramids, with
the mild-visaged Sphinx as next-door neighbour, and his
friend H. Taylor in the tent at his side, four Arabs watching
over their slumbers to warn away wolves and Bedouins. He is
feeling better for this beginning of desert life, and chose the
old tomb because it is warmer by night and cooler by day
than the tent; so he had it fresh sanded, and a carpet hung
before the door.

[To E. Lloyd] *Falmouth, April 7.*—I will not let the week
close without asking thy pity and thy prayers. Ah! and thy
thanksgivings too. For God in His Fatherly Love has been
pleased to send us a great sorrow; but consolations *far* beyond
the sorrow He has been pleased to grant also.

It was last Sunday that the tidings reached us that our
dearest Barclay had been called hence to be for ever with his
Lord. Twenty-four tranquil, peaceful, holy hours succeeded
the breaking of a blood-vessel, and then he fell asleep—
literally fell asleep—and awoke in his Saviour's arms. It was
all so painless, so quiet, so holy, that how can we but give
thanks, and pray that we may not envy him, but rather bear
our little burdens faithfully and meekly for a few short years,
and then—!

It was so beautiful that he had asked the Missionary Lieder
and his wife to come and visit him at his encampment by the
Pyramids, because they were in trouble; so they came, and
had some bright, most enjoyable days together; and thus,
when the last illness came they nursed him with parental
tenderness; and even after the spirit had fled, they cared for all
that was left,* and watched beside him in the desert. Mrs.
Lieder has kindly written most minute details of those days,
and *all* our thoughts of him are thoughts of peace. Even his
very last words it is granted us to know. In answer to some
remark of Mr. Lieder's, he said, 'What a mercy it is that
Christ not only frees us from the guilt of sin, but also delivers
us from its power.'

April 26.—I could fill volumes with remembrances and
personal historiettes of interesting people, but for whom
should I record them now? How strangely the heart falls back
on itself, exhausted and desolate, unless it gazes upward until

---

* A slab of Cornish granite was sent out to cover the grave, near Cairo.

the clouds open, and the—!

[To Clara Mill] *Penjerrick, May 7.*—And then thy poor brother, with his failing health* and depressed spirits, walking up Etna! Think of my boldness, I actually wrote to him! It came over me so strongly one morning that Barclay would like him to be told how mercifully he had been dealt with, and how true his God and Saviour had been to all His promises, that I took courage, and pen, and wrote a long history. Barclay had been the last of our family who had seen him, and he said he was very affectionate, but looked so grave, never smiling once; and he told him that he was about to winter in the South by Sir James Clark's order. I hope I have not done wrong or foolishly, but I do feel it rather a solemn trust to have such a story to tell of Death robbed of its sting and the Grave of its victory. It makes one long to join worthily in the eternal song of 'Thanks be to God, who giveth us the victory through our Lord Jesus Christ!' I can still report of our little party as fairly well, though perhaps feeling what an earthquake it has been, not less now than at first.

[To Elizabeth Carne] *Penjerrick, June 13.*—With all my heart I congratulate thee on being at home once more—that blessed, blessed, essentially English luxury. The Swiss have their mountains, the French their Paris, the English their Home. Happy English! . . .

Hast thou read Kingsley's 'Westward-ho!'? It is very magnanimous in me to name him for it is all in thy interest; a fine foe-exterminating book of Elizabeth's time, done and written in the religious spirit of Joshua and David. For Spaniards read Russians, and it is truly a tract for the times, *selon toi.*

[To Elizabeth Carne] *November 16.*—Papa has been busy making bottled compasses for Brunel's great ship [SS Great Eastern], who begged him to get at some magnetic results for him, but Papa must experiment in the neighbourhood of much larger masses of iron than he can scrape together here. One thing, however, he has made out, that a needle suspended in water becomes quiet in its true position wonderfully sooner than when, as usual, hung in air—hence bottled compasses. But if thou and Dr. Cumming say that the world

---

* John Stuart Mill was travelling in Italy and Greece in search of health. Both he and his wife wrote letters of sympathy to Caroline.

is at its last gasp, what is the use of inventing any worldly thing, when either destruction or intuition is so nigh at hand? The dear old world! one certainly fancied it in its very infancy blundering over BA *ba*, AB *ab;* but it may be dotage, for truly one sees people nowadays quite *blasés* at twenty. Which was its period of manhood? I suppose Kingsley would not hesitate in giving it to the reign of our Elizabeth. But Kingsley is no prophet of mine, however much he may sometimes rejoice and at others strike me with awe. Ah! and that would only apply to England; and, if I remember rightly, nothing short of the destruction of a world would satisfy Dr. Cumming. Oh! the comfort and blessing of knowing that our Future is in other hands than Dr. Cumming's; how restful it makes one, and so willing to have the veil still closely drawn which separates Now from Then. It often strikes me that one must look forward to some catastrophe for London, similar in spirit, however diverse in form, to what befell Babylon, Jerusalem, and Palmyra, but the   How   and   When?   .   .   .

Ah, yes! I admit sorrowfully enough that there has been a canker in our Peace, that we have not received it in a holy enough spirit or turned it to highest uses; and yet in reading, as I have just done, the history of the 'Thirty Years' Peace' (it is by H. Martineau, and I can't help it!), one cannot but feel that those thirty years were not wasted; that great strides were made in the right direction, towards education, mutual comprehension of nations, classes, and individuals, sympathy with the weak and suffering, and a few other things . . .

1856

Penjerrick, March 2.—Sir Charles Lemon and his sister paid us a visit: as an illustration of Macaulay's preternatural quickness, he mentioned a friend of his travelling with him and reading a new book which Macaulay had not seen. The friend grew weary and indulged in a ten minutes' sleep; on awakening, they resumed their talk, which fell on topics *apropos* of the book, when Macaulay was full of quotations, judgments, and criticisms. 'But I thought you had not seen it,' said his friend. 'Oh yes; when you were asleep I looked at it'; and it seemed as if no corner of it were unexplored.

March 29.—One of my poor friends, Mrs. Bastin, told me of having, whilst living in Liverpool, passed for dead after cholera for twenty-four hours; the authorities wanted her buried, but her brother-in-law, a pious man, declared, 'No, she don't look like death, she was not prepared to die, and no one shall go near her but me.' So he rubbed and prayed, and prayed and rubbed, and at last her life was restored to her thankful family. In the very next court lived a man who had to go away for a day or two, so he said to his wife, 'If you are taken ill, send for So-and-so.' In a few hours she was taken ill of that terrible cholera, and had the indicated doctor. A few hours later he said she was dead, and the next morning her funeral left the house. On its way to the cemetery it met her husband; he said, 'You may do what you like with me, but you shan't bury my wife till I've looked on her'; so the funeral party turned round and accompanied him home. Then he had the coffin-lid removed, and drew out his wife and laid her on the bed, reminding them of what had happened at the Bastins'. He too rubbed, and, I hope, prayed, and in time her life returned; and many times after that did the two women meet and exchange notes about their strange and awful experience . . .

[To Elizabeth Carne] *Penjerrick, June 27.*—What can I tell of our London interests? The Yearly Meeting? No, that thou wouldst be sure to treat profanely. The luminous fountain at the Pantechnicon?* Well, it was very beautiful, leaping up to the top of the dome, and being flooded from thence with colour. The Nineveh Marbles? We saw them, in a very edifying manner, under the convoy of Edward Oldfield, who made the old life live again for us with marvellous vividness and authenticity. And the Print Room, containing also the drawings of the old masters, Cellini's beautiful vase, and Albert Dürer's marvellous carving. Oh! and the Peace fireworks and illuminations [to mark the end of the Crimean War], which I saw so well from the top of our friend's house, and which were indeed excitingly beautiful. Or the blaze of azaleas and rhododendrons at Bury Hill? Or [Martin] Tup-

---

* Built in 1830 as a bazaar, with a façade of Doric pillars, in Motcomb Street, Belgravia; now a saleroom.

per, the Proverbial Philosopher? from whom I heard neither Philosophy nor Proverb; the Coleridges and Christabel's birthday fête? a picturesque garden party around her June-pole. Or Oxford? where we spent a few glorious hours, subdued, overawed by the sense of age and nationality which seems to fill the place . . .

They are building a wonderful Museum, with a glass Gothic dome or roof, and one or two hundred pillars of British marbles interspersed amongst the masonry. They have beautiful red serpentine, but not the green; would it be very difficult or expensive to supply them with one? I was delighted to hear of their successful experiment to unite Town and Gown by a Working Man's College; about two hundred Town students have now mustered, and a capital staff of collegians are delighted to teach them. They talk of one for the women too, but ladies are not numerous at Oxford . . . Fare-thee-well, good Queen Bess. With much love from Penjerrick to Penzance, thy ever affectionate,—

C. F.

[To Elizabeth Carne]   *Penjerrick, August 29.*—We have embarked on a beautiful book, Arthur Stanley's 'Palestine' thou wouldst be much interested in it, I think. He writes charmingly, seeing things so clearly, and seeing them in their bearings, geographical and otherwise, like a true pupil of Dr. Arnold's and there is such a high and thoughtful tone over it all . . .

September 7.—M. A. Schimmelpenninck is gone. She said, just before her death, 'Oh! I hear such beautiful voices, and the children's are the loudest.'

November 8.—Well, I have heard and seen Gavazzi [Italian preacher, reformer and patriot]: his subject was, 'The Inquisition, its Causes and Consequences'; his moral, 'Beware, Englishmen, of the tendencies to Hierarchy in your country when the thin end of the wedge is introduced; it will work its way on to all this.' He is most dramatic, has a brilliant power of comedy, and some terrible flashes of tragedy in him; it is all action and gesticulation, such as would be intolerable in an Englishman, but as an Italian characteristic it is all kindly welcome, and certainly most telling. But notes of his discourse would be very poor; it was the manner that made his words so desperately vivid. He died, dreadfully for us, under the torture of the wet linen on the face; it made every one breathe thick, and two ladies had to leave the room . . .

1857

Penjerrick, January 1.—A new book and a New Year! what will they contain? May God keep evil out of them, and all will be well.

January 10.—George Smith [Cornish antiquary and theologian] dined here, and gave a good easy, conversational lecture on the recent Assyrian and Egyptian discoveries, and their connection with Scripture History . . . I like his face, so full of honesty, sense, and kindliness.

January 12.—Reading [Charles Reade's] 'Never Too Late to Mend,' one of the weightiest events of late. Oh those prison scenes! how they haunt one! How they recall those despairing women's eyes I met in the model gaol at Belfast!

April 2.—Ernest de Bunsen is with us. I wish I could chronicle a great deal of his talk; it is marvellously vivid, and he seems equally at home in all religions of human thought: deep metaphysics, devout theology, downright boyish merry-making, the most tangled complexities of court intrigues, and then his singing! He is truly a man of infinite aptitudes. Took him to Carclew, where he was a perfect bottle of champagne to Sir Charles; and to Roscrow, where the boys were lost in admiration and delight. He has been translating William Penn's life into German, and sent a copy to Humboldt, from whom he has received two charming letters about it, in one saying that he has read every word, and that the contemplation of such a life has contributed to the peace of his old age . . . In the course of our talk he said, 'Forgive to the fullest extent and in the freest spirit, but never forget anything; it is all intended to be a lesson to profit our after-life, for there is no such thing as chance.'

April 5.—Heard Professor Nichol's lecture at Truro, when for two hours he held us poised in those high regions, until we felt quite at home . . .

June 12.—Warrington Smyth [mineralogist and lecturer at the School of Mines] talked with great delight of Florence

Nightingale. Long ago, before she went to Kaiserswerth, he and Sir Henry de la Beche dined at her father's, and Florence Nightingale sat between them. She began by drawing Sir Henry out on Geology, and charmed him by the boldness and breadth of her views, which were not common then. She accidentally proceeded into regions of Latin and Greek, and then our Geologist had to get out of it. She was fresh from Egypt, and began talking with W. Smyth about the inscriptions, &c., where he thought he could do pretty well; but when she began quoting Lepsius, which she had been studying in the original, he was in the same case as Sir Henry. When the ladies left the room, the latter said to him, 'A capital young lady that, if she hadn't so floored me with her Latin and Greek!'

July 9.—We are reading the Life of Charlotte Brontë, a most striking book . . . She is like her books . . .

Dublin, August 22.—Paying diligent attention to some sections of the British Association's Meeting . . . Father read his paper on the temperature in Mines in the Geological Section, though Section A cried out vehemently for it . . . When Dr. Forbes [Professor of Botany, London] disputed some of the facts . . . Papa answered very well and with no nervousness, and Lord Talbot de Malahide, the President, made him a very handsome speech of acknowledgment . . .

August 28.—An extremely interesting collection of African Explorers—Dr. Barth, De l'Abbadie, and Dr. Livingstone discussed the risings of African Rivers, and why the Niger got up so much later than the others . . . Dr. Barth . . . is a well-burnt, hard-featured, indomitable sort of man; De l'Abbadie very dark in complexion, hair, and eyes, with a singular pose in his head, as if, said some one, he were accustomed to wear a pig-tail. Dr. Livingstone tall, thin, earnest-looking, and business-like; far more given, I should say, to do his work than to talk about it. Finished the evening with supper and gossip with the wise men at the President's.

August 29.—A grand dinner and soirée to all the *savants* at the Vice-Regal Lodge. Papa enjoyed it greatly, as it gave him a two hours' *tête-à-tête* with Dr. [Thomas Romney] Robinson [astronomer in charge of Armagh Observatory].

[To Elizabeth Carne] *Penjerrick, September 5.*— . . . Papa and I returned yesterday from Dublin (so I'm not going to

talk about most wretched India [the Mutiny] and all my poor
young cousins there), where a most successful British Association Meeting hath been holden. We were with our dear
friends the Lloyds, which was not the least pleasant part of
the affair . . . Dr. Livingstone's lecture I should like everybody to have heard. People say it was signally lacking in
arrangement, but I have no nose for logic; I thought one just
mounted his ox and went on behind him amongst those
loving, trusting, honest, generous natives of his . . . Even
more [cheering] was his assurance that the Niger Expedition
had not been made in vain; that frequently in the interior,
and more and more as he approached the coasts, he found
there had been tidings of a white nation who loved black
people; and he reaped abundant benefit from this prestige.
Oh, if Sir Fowell Buxton might have known it! . . . Dr.
Livingstone, the Whatelys, &c., came to the Lloyds' after the
lecture, and the ladies agreed on sending a sugar-cane press to
his chief in remembrance of that evening. There is a great
deal of quiet fun about Dr. Livingstone . . .

Falmouth, October 16.—The Ernest de Bunsens are with us;
he read us last night Mendelssohn's 'Elijah' . . . The last
time he saw Mendelssohn, they had played and sung several
things together . . .

November 15.—Papa has had the great interest and satisfaction of seeing the theory of stratification being caused by
pressure well disproved, and his own conviction of its being
produced by an inherent crystallising power in rocks, call it
chemical galvanism or what you will, well confirmed, by
finding that a great lump of clay, thrown aside from Pennance Mine some five years ago, has arranged itself in thin
laminae, just like the ordinary clay slate. This seems to
determine a vexed question in geology.

1858

[To Elizabeth Carne] *Falmouth, January 5.*—I did dearly
love thy last letter; it was the most earnest, friendly New
Year's greeting that had reached me, and it called up a deep
Amen from my dull and sleepy heart. Thy facts, too, were so

very cheery and thankworthy. Yes, let us take all the
Christmas blessings along with us on our New Year's
road . . . Of [Henry Thomas] Buckle's book [History of
Civilisation in England, volume I, 1857], I have only heard
through Lady Trelawny, who thinks it a most remarkable
work, full of genius, power, and insight . . . But I shall hear
more about it soon, as we go to Carclew, to be with her for a
day or two, to-morrow.

January 10.—George Cook[e]* had much to tell of the
Carlyles. He has just finished two volumes of 'Frederick the
Great,' which has been a weary work. He seems to grow
drearier and drearier; his wife still full of life and power and
sympathy, spite of the heavy weight of domestic dyspepsia.
Kingsley pays him long visits, and comes away talking just
like him . . .

[To Elizabeth Carne] *January 25.*—Thy peep into Buckle is
very interesting, and quite confirms Lady Trelawny's
view . . . When I read thy remarks on him to Papa, he
thought thee most right in the abstract, but that the Facts of
general history supported Buckle's view . . .

November 12.—Heard Thomas Cooper† lecture on his own
vagaries, practical and speculative, and their solution. He
began by an autobiographical sketch, dwelling on the mischief done by inconsistent professors, who seemed to have
badgered him out of Methodism into scepticism; then, seeing
the cruel wrongs of the stocking-weavers of Leicester, drove
him into Chartism; he was in the thick of a bad riot, much of
which he encouraged, but he did not intend the incendiary
part of it. However, he was taken up and convicted of
sedition, and imprisoned for two years. Then and there he
sank the lowest, in loveless, hopeless unbelief. His study of
Robert Owen, and discovery of the fallacy of his reasonings,
seemed to do much to bring him round again; and then going
about England with Wyld's Model of Sebastopol seemed to
have had some mysterious influence for good; and here he is—
Convert, Confessor, and Reasoner. He is a square-built man,
with a powerful, massive face; he walks up and down the platform and talks on as if he were in a room, with extreme

---

* A regular caller at 5 Cheyne Row.
† Edited the *Midland Counties Illuminator*, a Chartist newspaper; published a political
  epic, *The Purgatory of Suicides.*

clearness, excellent choice of language, and good pronunciation, considering that he was formerly a poor shoemaker, and
had to teach himself the much he has learnt.

1859

[To Elizabeth Carne] *Penjerrick, January 24.*—So thou canst
see nothing fitting for Italy but slavery to some foreign power
or other, and this spite of all that Sardinia has done for herself
and her neighbours in the last few years. Read [Edmond]
About's desperately keen book, 'La Question Romaine,' and
admit that against frightful odds there is a national spirit still,
and that there are genuine men in that nation. Doubtless
their history through the Middle Ages tells of anything but
Unity, but there is a great thirst for it now in many
quarters . . .

September 4.—A full week has driven by. We spent two days
at Carclew with Dr. Whewell and his wife, Lady Affleck. He
was as urbane and friendly as needs be, and seemed determined to live down Sydney Smith's quiz about Science being
his forte, and Omniscience his foible . . . There is a capital
element of fun in that vast head of his; witness his caricatures
of Sedgewick in his Cornish Sketchbook. He made me notice
the darkness of sky between two rainbows, a fact only lately
secured, and a part, he says, of the whole theory of the
rainbow . . . Of the Working Men's College at Cambridge,
he is quite sure it is doing the teachers great good, whatever it
does to the learners . . . He told of a talk he had had with
Martin amongst his pictures, which he assured him were the
result of the most studied calculation in perspective; he had
been puzzled how to give size enough to an angel's hand, and
at last hit on the expedient of throwing a fold of his garment
behind the sun.

September 24.—The little *Fox* has gained her quest and
brought distinct tidings of Franklin's death in 1847; the vessel
crushing in the ice in 1848; multitudes of relics found in
various cairns, which were their posts of observation around
that dreary coast: Bibles with marked passages and notes,
clothes, instruments, all sorts of things of most touching

interest, so preserved by the climate; many skeletons they
found, and some they could identify by things they had about
them. It is a comfort to believe that they were not starved, as
thirty or forty pounds of chocolate was found with them, and
Sir John Franklin may have died a quite natural death a year
before the catastrophe.

[To Elizabeth Carne] *Penjerrick, November 25.*—Thanks,
Eccellentissima, for thy last letter, written under evident
difficulties . . . I am reading that terrible book of John
Mill's on Liberty, so clear, and calm, and cold . . . He looks
you through like a basilisk, relentless as Fate. We knew him
well at one time, and owe him very much; I fear his
remorseless logic has led him far since then. This book is
dedicated to his wife's memory in a few most touching
words. He is in many senses isolated, and must sometimes
shiver with the cold.

[To Elizabeth Carne] *Falmouth, December 23.*—No, my
dear, I don't agree with Mill, though I too should be very glad to
have some of my 'ugly opinions' corrected, however painful the
process; but Mill makes me shiver, his blade is so keen and so
unhesitating . . .

December 31.—The old year is fled, never to come back
again through all Eternity. All its opportunities for love and
service gone, past recall. What a terrible thought . . .

1860

Paris, May 25.—Madame Salis Schwabe took us to Ary
Scheffer's studio, and introduced us to his daughter and to
Dr. Antonio Ruffini. What deep, and beautiful, and helpful
things we saw there! The Marys; the Angel announcing the
Resurrection to the Woman, the paint of which was even wet
when he died. Earthly sorrow rising into celestial joy—a
wonderful picture of his dying mother blessing her two
grandchildren, and his own keen-eyed portrait. His daughter
had gathered around her an infinity of personal recollections,
and it felt very sacred ground.

Falmouth, September 22.—Alfred Tennyson and his friend,

Francis Palgrave, at Falmouth, and made inquiries about the Grove Hill Leonardo, so of course we asked them to come and see it; and thus we had a visit of two glorious hours both here and in the other garden. As Tennyson has a perfect horror of being lionised, we left him very much to himself for a while, till he took the initiative and came forth. *Apropos* of the Leonardo, he said the Head of Christ in the Raising of Lazarus was to his mind the worthiest representation of the subject which he had ever seen. His bright, thoughtful friend, Francis Palgrave, was the more fond of pictures of the two: they both delighted in the little Cuyp and the great Correggio; thought the Guido a pleasant thing to have, though feeble enough; believed in the Leonardo, and Palgrave gloated over the big vase. On the leads we were all very happy and talked apace. 'The great T.' groaned a little over the lionising to which he is subject, and wondered how it came out at Falmouth that he was here—this was *apropos* of my speaking of Henry Hallam's story of a miner hiding behind a wall to look at him, which he did not remember; but when he heard the name of Hallam, how his great grey eyes opened, and gave one a moment's glimpse into the depths in which 'In Memoriam' learnt its infinite wail. He talked a good deal of his former visit to Cornwall, and his accident at Bude, all owing to a stupid servant-maid. In the garden he was greatly interested, for he too is trying to acclimatise plants, but finds us far ahead, because he is at the western extremity of the Isle of Wight, where the keen winds cut up their trees and scare away the nightingales in consequence. But he is proud and happy in a great magnolia in his garden. He talked of the Cornish, and rather liked the conceit of their countryism; was amused to hear of the refractory Truro clergyman being buried by the Cornish miners, whom he forbade to sing at their own funeral; but he thought it rather an unfortunate instance of the civilising power of Wesley. By degrees we got to Guinevere, and he spoke kindly of S. Hodges' picture of her at the Polytechnic, though he doubted if it told the story very distinctly. This led to real talk of Arthur and the 'Idylls,' and his firm belief in him as an historical personage, though old Speed's narrative has much that can be only traditional. He found great difficulty in reconstructing the character, in connecting modern with ancient feeling in representing the

Ideal King. I asked whether Vivien might not be the old
Brittany fairy who wiled Merlin into her net, and not an
actual woman. 'But no,' he said; 'it is full of distinct personality, though I never expect women to like it.' The river Camel
he well believes in, particularly as he slipped his foot and fell
in the other day, but found no Excalibur. Camel means
simply winding, crooked, like the Cam at Cambridge. The
Welsh claim Arthur as their own, but Tennyson gives all his
votes to us. Some have urged him to continue the 'Idylls,' but
he does not feel it expedient to take people's advice as an
absolute law, but to wait for the vision. He reads the Reviews
of his Poems, and is amused to find how often he is
misunderstood. Poets often misinterpret Poets, and he has
never seen an Artist truly illustrate a Poet. Talked of
Garibaldi, whose life was one out of Plutarch, he said, so
grand and simple; and of Ruskin as one who has said many
foolish things; and of John Sterling, whom he met twice, and
whose conversational powers he well remembers.

Tennyson is a grand specimen of a man, with a magnificent head set on his shoulders like the capital of a mighty
pillar. His hair is long and wavy, and covers a massive head.
He wears a beard and moustache, which one begrudges as
hiding so much of that firm, powerful, but finely chiselled
mouth. His eyes are large and grey, and open wide when a
subject interests him; they are well shaded by the noble brow,
with its strong lines of thought and suffering. I can quite
understand Samuel Laurence calling it the best balance of
head he had ever seen. He is very brown after all the
pedestrianising along our south coast.

Mr. Palgrave is charmingly enthusiastic about his friend; if
he had never written a line of Poetry, he should have felt him
none the less a Poet; he had an ambition to make him and
Anna Gurney known to each other as kindred spirits and of
similar calibre. We grieved not to take them to Penjerrick,
but they were engaged to the Truro river; so, with a farewell
grasp of the great brown hand, they left us.

September 28.—Holman Hunt and his big artist friend, Val
Prinsep, arrived, and we were presently on the most friendly
footing. The former is a very genial, young-looking creature,
with a large, square, yellow beard, clear blue laughing eyes, a
nose with a merry little upward turn in it, dimples in the

cheek, and the whole expression sunny and full of simple boyish happiness. His voice is most musical, and there is nothing in his look or bearing, spite of the strongly-marked forehead, to suggest the High Priest of Pre-Raphaelitism, the Ponderer over such themes as the Scape-goat, the Light of the World, or Christ among the Doctors, which is his last six years' work. We went to Grove Hill, and he entirely believes in the Leonardo being an original sketch, especially as the head of our Lord is something like that of one of Leonardo's extant studies; he is known to have tried many, and worked up one strongly Jewish one, but not of a high type, which at last he rejected. Holman Hunt entirely agrees with F. D. Maurice about the usual mistaken treatment of St. John's face, which was probably more scarred with thought and inward conflict than any of the other Apostles, and why he should have ever been represented with a womanish expression is a puzzle to him. At the early period of Art they dared not step beyond conventional treatment. He spoke of Tennyson and his surprise at the spirited, suggestive little paintings of strange beasts which he had painted on the windows of his summer-house to shut out an ugly view. Holman Hunt is so frank and open, and so unspoiled by the admiration he has excited; he does not talk 'shop,' but is perfectly willing to tell you anything you really wish to know of his painting, &c. He laughed over the wicked libel that he had starved a goat for his picture, though certainly four died in his service, probably feeling dull when separated from the flock. The one which was with them by the Dead Sea was better off for food than they were, as it could get at the little patches of grass in the clefts; still it became ill, and they carried it so carefully on the picture-case! but it died, and he was in despair about getting another white one. He aimed at giving it nothing beyond a goat's expression of countenance, but one in such utter desolation and solitude could not but be tragic. Speaking of lionising, he considers it a special sin of the age, and specially a sin because people seem to care so much more for the person doing than for the thing done.

October 5.—We have had Miss Macaulay here, Lord Macaulay's sister: a capital clear-headed woman, with large liberal thoughts and great ease in expounding them . . .

Penjerrick, December 15.—Baron Bunsen is gone; illness had brought him so low that his friends could only long that he

might be delivered from his weary pain—but how much has
gone with him? . . .

1861-71

[To Lucy Hodgkin] *Leyton, May 1861.*—The Brights are
staying here, so we consider ourselves a very pleasant party.
John Bright is great fun, always ready for a chat and a fulmina-
tion, and filling up the intervals of business with 'Paradise
Regained.'

. . . One likes to have his opinion on men and things, as it is
strong, clear, and honest, however one-sided. But he flies off
provokingly into pounds, shillings, and pence when one wants
him to abide for a little amongst deeper and less tangible
motives, powers and arguments.

[To M. E. Tregelles] *Grove Hill, December 23.*—After parting
with thee the other evening, I found myself continually cooing
over those comfortable words:

> 'Yet why be sad? for Thou wilt keep
> Watch o'er them day by day:
> Since Thou wilt soothe them when they weep
> And hear us when we pray.'

And this is just the prose Fact of the case, full of real substantial
comfort, in all the chances and changes of this mortal life. And
another prose Fact which is often voted poetical, seems to me
that we are really nearer together in spirit when separated in
body, as the thoughts and sympathies are perfectly independent
of geography, and they naturally fly off on their own errands
when a little anxiety is added to our love.

This has been a sad day with its tolling bells [for the funeral of
the Prince Consort], its minute-guns, the band parading the
streets playing the 'Dead March in Saul'; but also a day on
which many and fervent prayers have arisen from loving hearts,
which we will hope have been felt as a sort of warm atmosphere
round the poor stricken heart, which we hear is firmly resolved
not to forget its high duties in the midst of its great desolation.
The union prayer-meeting was held to-day that there might be a

concentration of spiritual force in this direction, and very true I thought the prayers were for the Queen, and for her son, and for all the mourners. It made one almost feel as if fresh blessings would be granted her, deeper perhaps than she has ever yet known. Is not this experience of many a bereaved heart?

This wretched American business! To-day it seems all terribly real to us, as a large Confederate merchantman has broken the blockade, and has come into our harbour with a cargo for England—no, there is only rumour of its approach. The Northern States privateer is reported in the offing on the watch for her, and a British ship of war and certain gunboats are come to keep the peace in our seas.

[To Elizabeth Carne] *Penjerrick, July 15, 1862.*—I rise from the reading of thy paper on Buckle, to thank thee warmly. Having now read the book it dealt with, all bonds were broken, and I have eagerly devoured it at a sitting, and again and again cried 'Bravo!' in my heart. My dear, it is in such a fine gentlemanly tone, no theological or other contempt, but full of Christian boldness and Christian love: a sort of utterance one need not be ashamed of at the Day of Judgment—a use of the Light which has been accumulating for some six thousand years (or more?), which He who gives it will deign to bless. Oh, if our controversies for at least eighteen hundred years had been conducted in this same spirit, instead of the rancour and arrogance, unfairness and self-conceit, which have unhappily characterised all parties, surely we should be in different regions now, and jesting Pilate would have no excuse for asking 'What is Truth?' . . .

[To J. M. Sterling] *November 28.*—Thou shalt rejoice with me over my poor Scotchman at the Sailors' Home. (My romances are so apt to centre there!) Well, he was brought in several weeks ago, frightfully ill and suffering; a very perilous operation might possibly have relieved him, but they dared not attempt it here, and wanted to send him to a London hospital. He earnestly desired to be left here to die quietly, and I own I was very glad when at last they let him have his way, as it seemed very probable that the operation would be fatal. Well, somehow, we formed a very close friendship. He had frightened away the good people (the clergyman, &c.) by his stormy language, when really he was half delirious from agony; but we were nearer the same level, and so, as I said, we formed a romantic friendship. He poured out the

story of his life, which had separated him from all his friends
for more than twenty years. 'Oh! I was a bad, bad, bad boy!
My life has been one course of sin!' and he was utterly
hopeless of forgiveness. Oh! the fixed despair of those poor
eyes. I urged him to allow me to write to his family to tell of
his contrition and ask forgiveness; but he said it was impossible that they could forgive him; the prodigal had wasted *his
own* share of his father's heritage, but he had wasted theirs,
and then ran away from them to America, and broke their
hearts. What he would give to fall down before his father and
beseech his forgiveness! but it was all too late. He cried
bitterly, but for a week or two he would not let me make the
attempt, which he was certain was utterly useless. He was
evidently sinking, and I felt so strongly that if it were possible
to win the forgiveness of his family, he would then be able to
believe in a higher forgiveness; so last Sunday I wheedled his
father's address out of him, and got his tacit consent to my
letter going, though he was certain there would be no one
there to receive it. The thought of my Scotchman haunted me
to-day, so in I went and found a most loving letter from his
brother hailing him as alive from the dead; I ran down to the
Sailors' Home and found another from his sister in ecstasy of
joy, and telling of his father's complete forgiveness and tender
love. 'He would have spent his last shilling to come to you,
but he is gone!' Oh, I have never seen anything more
exquisitely touching than the floods of wonder and ecstasy
when I took in my treasures. It was still an almost incredible
joy; he poured forth his thankfulness and his tears before God,
to think that he had still brothers and sisters who forgave
him, and loved him, and received him as alive from the dead.
His father he had felt certain was dead, so that was no shock,
but to think how his love had clung to him to the last! Now I
believe he will find no difficulty in believing in that Higher
Love which has already done such great things for him! He
covered his sister's letter with kisses, saying, 'It's my sister's
heart, her heart.' She had telegraphed to a soldier brother
near Chatham to come to him at once, so two or three may
possibly be with him in a few days! I hope that all this joy
will not have killed him before they come, but I should think
it must hasten the end. I did not leave him till he was much
quieter, and I have since been writing most happy letters to

them both. There, my dear, is a long story for thee, but I could not help telling thee what has made me quite tipsy. Excuse my happiness, and believe me, thy C. F.

Falmouth, January 20, 1863.—We had a great treat in hearing Charles Kean read Richard III., Alexander's Feast, the Prisoner of Chillon, &c., very fine and very dramatic; we saw something of him and his wife afterwards, and liked our theatrical friends greatly.

[To Elizabeth Carne] *Blois, June 6.*—This Spanish frisk* has been most memorable; the great object of the journey accomplished far beyond their hopes, though in a way to save the Queen's pride and their vanity. Many think that it is a first and very important step in the direction of religious liberty, from which they will not dare to recede with all Europe looking on, and speaking its mind very distinctly.

We saw a good deal of some very thoughtful and liberal-minded Spaniards, but it is sad to see in what a state of timidity and unmanliness some of the really superior ones are kept by the narrow laws of their country. I wonder what has become of all the *ci-devant* prisoners? Have you got them in England? I hope not. They would be in worse peril there than in the prisons of Granada. Anna Maria and I contrived to get a great deal of common-place enjoyment out of the excursion, whilst our betters were engaged in conference with their brother deputies. They were a gallant set of men, representing ten different nations, and we felt very proud of them.

Penjerrick, March 9, 1864.—Mrs. Welsh [aunt of Mrs. Carlyle] has settled amongst us very cordially. Her accounts of Mrs. Carlyle are piteous—it is such a weary, suffering sickroom, the nerves all on edge, so that she can see scarcely any one; poor Carlyle is miserable.

April 17.—Garibaldi came to Par to see his Englishman, and we, armed with a friendly introduction and a kind invitation from the Colonel† and Mrs. Peard, went to meet him. Amongst the flags erecting to welcome him was a grim Austrian banner, which was soon lugged down. It was moonlight before he arrived; there was a pause as the train

---

* Caroline, with her father and sister, had gone to Spain with representatives of other countries to intercede for the release of Matamoros, who had been imprisoned as a Protestant.

† 'Garibaldi's Englishman' who distinguished himself at the battle of Melazzo, 1860.

drew up at the platform, and then the General was almost
lifted out of the carriage, and stood with the lamps lighting
up his face. It was full of deep lines of pain and care and
weariness, but over and through it all such a spiritual beauty
and moral dignity. His dress was picturesque in form and
colour—the red shirt, the grey cloak lined with red, the
corner flung gracefully over one shoulder. Colonel Peard was
there, his duty being to protect his chief from the enthusiasm
of the crowd. The next morning he gave us a cordial
reception; a good night had done wonders for him, and had
taken off twenty years from his apparent age. We talked of his
last night's reception, and I asked if he had ever been at
Falmouth as was reported. 'Never,' he said; 'but I was at
Portsmouth in '55:' he hopes to come and visit us some day.

July 2.—Have just returned from a visit to Professor Adams
at Cambridge. He is so delightful in the intervals of business,
enjoying all things, large or small, with a boyish zest. He
showed and explained the calculating machine (French, not
Babbage), which saves him much in time and brain, as it can
multiply or divide ten figures accurately. We came upon an
admirable portrait of him at St. John's College before he
accepted a Pembroke Fellowship and migrated thither. Next
day we met Professor Sedgwick, looking so aged; and whilst at
Trinity we had a pleasant talk with Dean Stanley and Lady
Augusta.

[To J. M. Sterling] *Penjerrick, November 25, 1865.*—I fear I
shall not get to the Crag to-day to report on the casualties of the
last few days, as it is still blowing great guns; and it is piteous to
watch the great trees rocking and shuddering under the weight
of the gale, the tall cypress sometimes bending to an angle of 45°.
It is wonderful that more mischief is not done before our eyes. At
Grove Hill, several large trees were torn up by their roots, and
did as much mischief—like Samson, in dying—as they
conveniently could. What we see makes one think tragically of
what we do not see. Another vessel is ashore in our harbour—twelve or fourteen are reported ashore in Plymouth
Harbour; but what of those of whom we hear nothing, and
perhaps shall never hear? Oh, it is a doubtful luxury to live on
the coast and watch those grand creatures struggling across the
Bay, partly dismasted—almost beaten—but not quite! God
help them, and those who love them . . .

Having got out, how could I resist the temptation of giving my betters the slip, and creeping away to the Crag to see what might be left of it? And I rejoice to say that it has stood all gallantly; a few old trees gone, but nothing to signify . . . Hast thou ever seen the earth breathing and throbbing? It looks very uncanny—caused by the heaving of the great roots. Four wrecks are reported between here and the Lizard, but no lives lost in the harbour! Yours, C. F.

Penjerrick, March 18, 1866.—I have just been brought through a sharp little attack of bronchitis, and feel bound to record my sense of the tender mercy that has encompassed me night and day. Though it may have been in part my own wilfulness and recklessness that brought it on, that and all else was pardoned, all fear of suffering or death was swallowed up in the childlike joy of trust: a perfect rest in the limitless love and wisdom of a most tender Friend, whose Will was far dearer to me than my own . . . I had before been craving for a little more spiritual life on any terms, and how mercifully this has been granted! and I can utterly trust that in any extremity that may be before me the same wonderful mercy will encompass me, and of mere love and forgiving compassion carry me safely into Port.

Mentone, March 5, 1867.—Called by appointment on Carlyle at Lady Ashburton's. He has a sort of pavilion separate yet attached to her villa, where he may feel independent. Found him alone reading Shakespeare, in a long dressing-gown, a drab comforter wrapped round and round his neck, and a dark-blue cap on, for he had a cold. He received us very kindly, but would untwist his comforter, and take off his cap, and comb his shaggy mane in honour of the occasion. He looks thin, and aged, and sad as Jeremiah, though the red is still bright in his cheek and the blue in his eye, which seems to be set more deeply than ever; there is a grim expression in his face, which looks solemn enough.

First he launched out, I think, on the horrors of the journey, 'I should never have come but for [Professor John] Tyndall, who dragged me off by the hair of my head, so to speak, and flung me down here, and then went his way. He had better have left me alone with my misery. Pleasures of travelling! In that accursed train, with its devilish howls and yells driving one distracted!' 'But cannot you read in trav-

elling?' 'Read! No it is enough for me to reflect on my own
misery; they ought to give you chloroform as you are a living
creature.' Then of the state of England and the Reform Bill:
'Oh! this cry for Liberty! Liberty! which is just liberty to do
the Devil's work, instead of binding him with ten thousand
bands, just going the way of France and America, and those
sort of places; why, it is all going downhill as fast as it can go,
and of no significance to me; I have done with it. I can take no
interest in it at all, nor feel any sort of hope for the country. It
is not the Liberty to keep the Ten Commandments that they
are crying out for—that used to be enough for the genuine
Man—but Liberty to carry on their own prosperity, as they
call it, and so there is no longer anything genuine to be found;
it is all shoddy. Go into any shop you will and ask for any
article, and ye'll find it all one enormous lie. The country is
going to perdition at a frightful pace. I give it about fifty
years yet to accomplish its fall.'

Spoke of Gladstone: 'Is not he a man of principle?' 'Oh,
Gladstone! I did hope well of him once, and so did John
Sterling, though I heard he was a Puseyite and so forth; still it
seemed the right thing for a State to feel itself bound to God,
and to lean on Him, and so I hoped something might come of
him; but now he has been declaiming that England is in such
a wonderfully prosperous state, meaning that it has plenty of
money in its breeches' pockets and plenty of beef in its great
ugly belly. But that's not the prosperity we want. And so I say
to him, "You are not the Life-giver to England; I go my way,
you go yours, good morning" (with a most dramatic and final
bow). Which times were the most genuine in England? Cromwell's? Henry VIII.'s? Why, in each time it seems to me there
was something genuine, some endeavour to keep God's commandments. Cromwell's time was only a revival of it. But now
things have been going down further and further since George
III.'

A little knock at the door, and a lady in black appeared
and vanished, which was a signal that Lady Ashburton was
going presently, but he said she wished to see us first, as she
was going to see the Bunsens at Florence. He liked to hear of
the Sterlings, and of our being all near together in Cornwall.
'I have always,' he said, 'a sort of pious feeling about
Falmouth and about you all, and so had she who is gone

away from me, for all your kindness to John Welsh [cousin of Mrs. Carlyle]; you couldn't do a greater kindness than all you did for him and his mother. He was a true, genuine man; give him anything to do, and you may be sure it was well done, whether it was to be seen of human eye or no. He worked hard, for the one unquestionable foremost duty he felt was to raise his mother out of her troubles; he could see no other till that was done, and well done, and he did it and died. I was once in Falmouth harbour for two hours in an Irish steamer, and I gave my card to a respectable-looking, seafaring sort of man, who promised to take it to your late brother. I remember taking a leaf out of my pocket-book and writing on it my regrets at not being able to land.' . . .

Lady Ashburton's is a winning and powerful face, with much intellectual energy and womanly sweetness. She encouraged our coming again to see Carlyle, thinking it quite a kindness to stir him up. She was glad he had spoken of anything with pleasure, 'for,' she added, 'I'm very fond of the old man, and I did what I thought was for the best, and I really hope he is the better for it in spite of himself, though sometimes it seems as if it was altogether a failure.' Lady Ashburton goes to Rome and will return here. She leaves 'her one treasure,' an only little girl, and Carlyle under the care of two good, kindly, wise-hearted ladies.

[To J. M. Sterling] *Mentone, March 17, 1867.—* . . . Mr. Carlyle is gone; we only saw him once more, and then I thought his 'Good-bye' so impressive that it felt like parting, and when we called again he was gone. I was so interested to see how the true man came out when he talked of you . . .

[To Charlotte O'Brien] *Penjerrick, October 14, 1868.—*We have just had the John Brights staying with us, and enjoyed it very much; his conversation is so varied, he is so simple and unreserved in telling one all manner of things one wishes to hear about, and then there is such downright manliness in the whole nature of the man, which is refreshing in this rather feeble age. How did you like him in your part of Ireland? Here he had nothing for the public, though they wanted to present an address, but would talk and read poetry until ten o'clock to us.

The Polytechnic took place the week before, and proved quite a pleasant occasion. We had various scientific people staying with us:—the Glaishers,* who had much to tell, both about balloons and meteors; Dr. Balfour Stewart, of the Kew Observatory, who has gone on to look after the branch observatories at Valentia and Dublin; then Frank Buckland was staying at my Uncle Charles's, and you might have seen him in his glory, lying on the pavement outside the drawing-room door, with the three monkeys sprawling about him. He gave a very amusing lecture one evening on oysters and salmon. Since all these people left we have had Mr. Opie (great nephew of a great uncle!) painting a very successful portrait of my dear Father, and now we are alone.

It must have been delightful to get an experienced sister to assist in the parish work, but don't let them talk thee into joining a sisterhood. Woman's work may be well done without all that ceremony . . .   I trust with thee that Parliament may be greatly enlightened as to the remedy for Ireland, in the wisest way, of all the questions which would have to be considered, if Gladstone's *auto-da-fĕ* should be accomplished.

[To Elizabeth Carne, seven days before her death] *Penjerrick, January 5, 1871.*—And now, dear, thank thee so much for that earnest pamphlet. Thank thee for so bravely speaking out the conviction, which was doubtless given thee for the good of others as well as thy own, that nothing short of communion with our present Lord can satisfy the immense need of man. How true that we are so often fed with phrases, and even try sometimes to satisfy ourselves with phrases whilst our patient Master is still knocking at the door. I trust that the seed thou hast been faithfully sowing may lodge in fitting soil, and bring forth flowers and fruit, to the praise of the Lord of the garden, and to the joy of some poor little human creature with whom He deigns to converse.

In hopes of a happy meeting whenever the fitting time may come, and with very loving wishes for the new-born year,—

Ever thine very lovingly

Caroline Fox.

---

* James Glaisher, meteorologist and astronomer, helped to establish daily weather reports for the *Daily News* in 1849.

INDEX